The Colleges, Their Constituencies and the Courts

SECOND EDITION

Robert M. Hendrickson

EDUCATION LAW ASSOCIATION

NO. 64 In the Monograph Series

Disclaimer

The Education Law Association (ELA) is a private, nonadvocacy, and nonprofit association of educators and attorneys. The opinions expressed in this publication are those of the author and do not represent official views of the Association.

Published by
Education Law Association
300 College Park, Dayton, Ohio 45469-2280
(937) 229-3589
ela@udayton.edu
www.educationlaw.org

Acknowledgements

A number of individuals contributed to the preparation of this book: Trudi T. Haupt, the staff assistant to the Higher Education Program at Penn State, contributed substantial time and effort to the preparation of this manuscript. Judy Leonard, staff assistant to the Department of Education Policy Studies, assisted in the preparation and editing of the document. Graduate research assistant Kris Otto contributed to the research and writing on this book. Ms. Otto was significantly involved in the revisions to Chapter III "State Relations," and Chapter IX "Liability Issues." Professors Annette Gibbs, The University of Virginia, and Jonathan D. Fife, former Executive Director of the Eric Clearinghouse on Higher Education and now at the Virginia Polytechnic Institute, read, commented, and edited the manuscript. The patience and guidance of Bob Wagner, the Executive Director of the Education Law Association were most appreciated. Credit for the layout and production of the publication go to Sheila Sandapen, the Publications Editor of ELA. It was a pleasure to work with Sheila. All these efforts helped this book reach completion.

Special thanks is also extended to my wife Linda J. Hendrickson, my son Lieutenant Michael J. Hendrickson and his wife Jennifer Tressler Hendrickson, and my son Mark S. Hendrickson whose patience and encouragement made this project bearable.

About the Author

ROBERT M. HENDRICKSON is Head of the Department of Education Policy Studies and Professor of Education at The Pennsylvania State University. From 1985 to 1993 he served as Professor-in-Charge of Penn State's Higher Education Program. He received his bachelor's degree from North Dakota State University, and an M.S. in Education and an Ed.D. in Higher Education, with a minor in law, from Indiana University. His areas of expertise in teaching and research include legal aspects of higher education and organizational theory and administration in higher education. He authored the first edition of *The Colleges, Their Constituencies and the Courts* in 1991. He has published articles on legal issues in a number of journals and coauthored three monographs for AAHE-ERIC and ASHE/ERIC entitled *Governing Board and Administrator Liability, Academic Employment and Retrenchment: Judicial Review and Administrative Action,* and *The College, the Constitution, and the Consumer Student.* Dr. Hendrickson has written the "Higher Education" chapter in the *Yearbook of Education Law* from 1983 through 1998 and wrote a Case Citations contribution on "Admission in Higher Education." He has chaired the Education Law Association Membership Committee and Dissertation Awards Committee, was a member of the Education Law Board of Directors and served as program chair for the 1991 annual conference. He recently served as an expert witness in a faculty promotion and tenure case.

Foreward

Few higher education professionals would disagree that the day-to-day work and activities of those who lead the nation's colleges and universities have changed dramatically during recent years. The knowledge and abilities required are more complex, more business-organization oriented, and more consumer driven. This is true for those serving academe whether they be instructors, full-time faculty, academic support staff, deans, student affairs directors, or financial affairs personnel from entry-level positions to the chief financial officer. These new knowledge requirements and complexities likewise apply to provosts, vice-presidents, and presidents. Perhaps no area has changed so significantly as that of the law and its influence on colleges and universities, whether they are chartered as private institutions or supported directly with public funds.

For many administrators in academe, including academic department chairs, their training and educational preparation programs did not provide the knowledge or understanding of the applicable law that is necessary for contemporary professional practice. While the law is continuously evolving and varies from state to state, broad legal concepts do exist as they apply to colleges and universities. This volume addresses the key cases, state and federal statutes, and administrative rules and regulations that provide an understanding of the concepts necessary to design institutional policies which, in turn, guide professional practice.

Robert M. Hendrickson, Head of the Department of Education Policy Studies and Professor of Education at Pennsylvania State University, has provided comprehensive and insightful research into these legal issues that face today's leaders in academe. Chapter I sets the stage and describes the legal parameters of the nation's court system and the historical heritage of both public and private higher education institutions, including their legal relationships with their constituencies. Hendrickson explains federal authority versus state authority over higher education and the legal mandates of various state agencies and local government relative to colleges and universities in Chapters II and III. He addresses the scope of legal control of institutional boards of trustees and describes the imperatives of sunshine laws that require states' governmental organizations and agencies to operate openly and publicly.

Chapter IV is devoted to faculty employment issues. The courts, during recent years, have dealt with legal actions brought against higher education institutions involving the nonrenewal of tenure track faculty contracts, denial of tenure, termination of tenured faculty for cause, and issues involving academic freedom and faculty speech. Hendrickson's research and report of these cases provide valuable information for those concerned with faculty employment. Since courts typically rely on institutional policies to define the legal parameters surrounding faculty employment, Hendrickson correctly concludes that institutions not only must have clearly defined policies, they must follow them, and likewise be able also to show that they follow their policies without discrimination and without arbitrary or capricious action. Finally, the intent of these institutional policies should be designed to uphold concepts of fundamental fairness and to uphold institutional academic integrity.

The quest for equity and diversity in employment in higher education is the focus of Chapter V. Diversity in this context, of course, refers to attempts to insure that the employees of an institution come from a multiplicity of ethnic, racial, gender, and sometimes religious backgrounds, mirroring society at large. The quest for equity and diversity have often resulted in clashes between legal mandates of equal protection under the law and institutional plans to achieve diversity. Hendrickson's resourceful balancing of these institutional prerogatives with the case law provides a valuable legal context in understanding policy implications for those institutional administrators responsible for both policy formulation and policy implementation.

Hendrickson addresses the thorny employment issues concerning sexual harassment in Chapter VI. Since claims of sexual harassment can be brought under both hostile work environment and quid pro quo theories, faculty and administrators should be knowledgeable of these legal concepts and understand the applicable case law. This chapter considers the issues not only from the pure legal perspective but concludes with appropriate guidelines for effective governance and management.

Chapter VII is devoted to collective bargaining in higher education. Since the labor relation's statutes were designed for business organizations, their application to higher education institutions has been problematic. Courts, for example, have had to determine which employees of college and universities are "employees," allowed to bargain collectively, as opposed to "managers," not allowed to bargain collectively. Hendrickson provides the case law that sets the legal parameters for determining which collective bargaining issues are grievable and those that are not.

Student-institutional relationships is the focus of Chapter VIII. The author begins by acknowledging that this legal relationship is central to the mission of colleges and universities and proceeds to define and describe the approaches that courts use in determining which obligations and responsibilities colleges hold for accommodating their students. Admission access, affirmative action in admissions, gender discrimination, discrimination surrounding disabilities, and the issues of standardized tests in college admissions are examined. Finally, the constitutional rights of students are depicted using applicable case law to show college administrators how to deal with student issues of speech, whether religious or hate speech, commercial speech, and freedom of association. Due process rights are covered, and the latest case law surrounding the use of mandatory student activity fees is presented.

The final chapter considers institutional liability issues where students are concerned. While an entire book could be devoted to this area, Hendrickson describes and summarizes the key elements for determining when institutions may be found liable in student legal claims. He shows how institutions can take reasonable care to foresee potential dangers and remove them.

Anyone employed by a college or university deals with these issues on a day-to-day basis, and this volume provides valuable information and equally worthwhile guidelines for effectively designing and implementing institutional policy.

Annette Gibbs
Bunker Professor of Higher Education and
Director of the Center for the Study of Higher Education
University of Virginia Curry School
Charlottesville, Virginia

Table of Contents

CHAPTER I

Higher Education Law

The law and higher education, comparable to the diversity of higher education institutional types in the United States, has evolved over time. There was a time when the courts were reluctant to review the actions of institutions and their relationships with students, the public, or employees. However, over time the courts have brought institutions of higher education under closer scrutiny in a variety of matters. In the eyes of a number of experts, the watershed case is *Dixon v. Alabama*.[1] It brought the court through the college gates and began the process of constitutional challenges to institutional relationships with constituencies. This spotlight on institutional relationships was accentuated by the legislative regulatory phase of the 1970s.[2]

This book will review litigation in a number of these areas in detail. In order, however, to understand judicial action in higher education, one needs a basic understanding of the concepts of: judicial review and justiciability; federalism and the application of the Bill of Rights to citizens of the states; the legal development of two sectors of higher education (public and private); and the application of the state action doctrine to private higher education. Based on this background information, subsequent chapters will define the relationship between higher education corporations and various constituencies.

Judicial Review and The Supreme Court

The concept of judicial review is alive today and the Supreme Court's power still rests on the premises established in *Marbury v. Madison*.[3] The case involved a clash between the Jeffersonian Democrats and the Marshall Court. John Marshall, as a federalist Secretary of State under President John Adams, had appointed a number of judges to several courts, but in the press of last minute details of leaving office, failed to deliver the letters of appoint-

---

[1] 294 F.2d 150 (5th Cir. 1961), *cert. denied*, 286 U.S. 930 (1961).
[2] D. Bok, BEYOND THE IVORY TOWER 243, (1982), and GOVERNMENT REGULATION OF HIGHER EDUCATION (W. Hobbs ed., 1978).
[3] 1 Cranch 137 (1803).

ment to the judges. The new secretary of state refused to deliver the appointment letters and Marbury and other disgruntled former appointees sued, requesting a court-ordered appointment. John Marshall, as the new chief justice of the Supreme Court, needed to walk a political tight rope between his outgoing Federalist Party and the newly elected Jeffersonian Democrats. Marshall's well-crafted decision established the concept of judicial review but also developed a definition for nonjusticiable issues. The case is credited with establishing four basic principles. First, the opinion established the United States Constitution as the supreme law of the land. Second, it ruled that any law repugnant to the Constitution was null and void. Third, the Supreme Court was vested with the authority to review laws in light of the constitution; i.e., judicial review. Fourth, some questions are political questions, or nonjusticible questions, which are outside the purview of the courts. On this last principle, Marshall ruled that the appointment of judges is outside the purview of the courts and is a matter of executive decision making. Thus, in what some call a master stroke, Justice Marshall established the concept of judicial review while ruling that the appointment of judges is a political or nonjusticiable issue.[4] The concept of justiciability[5] has been applied to higher education litigation in the area of academic issues such as the assignment of grades, the award of degrees, and the assignment to faculty of rank and tenure.

The Supreme Court uses a doctrine called "standing to litigate"[6] as a sifting mechanism for determining what to review. Standing deals with the relationship of the person bringing the action to the wrong. This relationship is described as a nexus between the litigant and the wrong. The aggrieved party, for example, would have standing to litigate the issue; however, others may have standing because of a relationship to the wrong. For example, a nexus would exist between private church related schools and the denial of first amendment rights of citizens forced by law to attend public schools. More recently, the courts have allowed an individual to sue on behalf of a class of individuals who, as a group, were aggrieved (a class action suit). This individual claiming representation of the class may be a bona fide member of the particular class of people, a group or organization. The individual may seek to represent the class, who, for specific

---

[4] G. Gunther & N.T. Dowling, Cases and Materials on Constitutional Law 14 (1970).
[5] *Id.* at 174.
[6] *Id.* at 106.

reasons, cannot represent itself. The specific reasons for a claim to represent a class may include educational or economic disadvantage or ignorance of the deprivation enforced against the class. Class action suits in higher education have typically surrounded issues of discrimination against female employees.

The Court System

The federal court system deals with treaties, violations under federal law and constitutional questions of citizen's rights and governmental authority. The Supreme Court of the United States is the ultimate arbitrator and their rulings set precedent. Federal Circuit Court of Appeals opinions are significant where there are not opposing opinions issued by other circuit courts, there has been no appeal of the opinion or where the Supreme Court either affirmed or refused to hear the case on appeal. Federal District Court cases that are consistent with other court rulings, and have not been overturned on appeal can be given considerable weight. When two district courts or circuit courts have reached different conclusions in similar situations, an issue in law exists that must be resolved by a higher court.

State court decisions set precedent only within the borders of that state. However, decisions in one state's case law can be used to speculate on how another state's court might rule in a similar situation. States are typically organized in a court system similar to the federal court system with a court of original jurisdiction, an appeals court, and a high court. However, the nomenclature for these courts varies from state to state. Issues of the importance of cases are similar to that on the federal level. Cases decided by the highest court have the most significance. The cases cited here should be read with these notions of precedence in mind.

Public and Private Higher Education

The original colonial colleges established in the New World were not thought of as either public or private.[7] There was a struggle to establish the nature of the relationship between the colonial government and these colleges. While these institutions remained primarily in the control of denominations, the colonies,

---

[7] J. Brubacher & W. Rudy, HIGHER EDUCATION IN TRANSITION 32 (3rd. ed. 1976).

and later the states, supported their existence by awarding revenues from bridge and ferry tolls and other public sources.[8] The struggle for control of these institutions would culminate in the *Dartmouth College Case*.[9] The case raised the issue of who owned Dartmouth College—the state or the board of trustees who chartered the institution. The Supreme Court ruled that Dartmouth College had a contract in the form of its charter in effect at the time of the State's ratification of the Constitution. New Hampshire was compelled to uphold the contract under the provisions in the Constitution. This case, which served to define the nature of corporate law in the new nation, set aside two sectors of higher education and allowed for the establishment of public corporations. Thus, we have a diversity of institutions in higher education, some controlled by private entities, and some controlled by the state. Based on control, the law is applied differently to public institutions and private institutions. For example, the Fourteenth Amendment applies constitutional guarantees to public institutions but not to private institutions. Private institution constitutional guarantees will be mandated where a finding of state action or an interdependent relationship exists between the state and the private institution. Some liability issues may also be differentially applied to the two sectors, as are some aspects of contract law. These differences will be discussed under specific topics in subsequent chapters of this book.

The Concept of Federalism and Public Institutions

The Bill of Rights or the first ten amendments to the United States Constitution define the relationship between a citizen and the federal government. The Constitution itself defines the powers of the three branches of government. Those powers not enumerated in the Constitution as belonging to one of the three branches of government were reserved to the states respectively.[10] The Fourteenth Amendment applies the Bill of Rights to citizens in their relationship with state government[11] and requires the state guarantee to citizens those rights. Thus, the Fourteenth Amendment becomes the vehicle for the application of those rights enumerated in the Bill of Rights to students or employees at state

---

[8] *Id.* at 35.
[9] Trustees of Dartmouth College v. Woodward, 4 Wheat 518 (1819).
[10] Gunther & Dowling 199 (1970).
[11] *Id.* at 447.

controlled (public) colleges and universities. Significant litigation is based on this constitutional relationship.

The Private Sector and State Action

The relationships between private colleges and universities and various constituencies, such as students or faculty, are primarily governed by the contracts in existence between the two parties. These contracts may be written or implied, and the provisions are typically found not only in the contractual documents but also in other school policy documents and past institutional practices. While private institutions are not technically obligated to honor constitutional guarantees, many private institutions on moral grounds have incorporated constitutional guarantees into their contractual documents. Thus, we find private institutions honoring due process requirements or privacy requirements similar to those mandated by the constitution to the public sector.

There is a legal doctrine called "state action" which applies when a private entity becomes an agent of state government, mandating the guarantee of constitutional rights.[12] State action is found when a private corporation is performing a state function in the place of the state,[13] operating under color of state law,[14] or when an interdependent relationship exists between the state and the private entity.[15] The United State Supreme Court has ruled that to reach a finding of state action, one needs to "sift facts and weigh circumstances."[16] Facts and circumstances could be the degree that a private entity is relied on to provide a service the state normally would provide or the degree that the state controls the policies and daily management of the institution, either by law or through an interdependent relationship. Case law indicates that this is an area of difficulty, which is why some have termed it the "murky waters" of state action.[17]

The act of licensing private entities to operate within a state might arguably be sufficient to invoke the state action doctrine. The Supreme Court in *Moose Lodge # 107 v. Irvis*,[18] ruled that the

---

[12] W. Lockhart, Y. Kasimar, & J. Choper, CONSTITUTIONAL LAW: CASES-COMMENTS-QUESTIONS 1229 (1970).

[13] *Id.* at 1237; *see* Evans v. Newton, 382 U.S. 296 (1966).

[14] *Id.* at 1254; where state law or state courts enforce a violation of constitutional rights by private entities: i.e. state laws requiring all licensed private schools in the state to be segregated. *See* Shelley v. Kramer, 334 U.S. 1 (1948).

[15] Cooper v. Aaron, 358 U.S. 1 (1968).

[16] Rietman v. Mulleky, 387 U.S. 369 (1967).

[17] R. Hendrickson, *State Action And Private Higher Education*, 2 J. L. & EDUC. 53, (1973).

[18] 407 U.S. 163 (1972).

licensing of an organization was not of itself enough to implicate the state action doctrine. The licensing procedure was an attempt to control the consumption of alcohol and, as a regulatory scheme, did not make the operation of the lodge a joint venture between the state and the private entity. The implications for higher education were significant since most states license private colleges and universities operating within their state borders. Failure to find "state action" means that private institutions are placed under different standards as far as Constitutional guarantees than their public counterparts.

College and University Relationships

When colleges open their doors, they establish certain relationships with the government, the public, and various constituencies. For example, the federal government has established a research relationship with institutions of higher education, a regulatory relationship to promote public policies, and a financial relationship in the form of grants and loans to the institution and students.

Federal, state and city governments have both financial and regulatory relationships with colleges and universities. Public colleges have been subjected to state coordination and accountability. City governments have conflicts in the enforcement of ordinances involving land use, city taxes, and health and safety regulations. These controversies are outlined in the two chapters on intergovernmental relationships. Addressed are issues surrounding the relationship between the federal government and higher education institutions as well as the states and their relationship with institutions operating within their borders.

Federal regulations involving the prohibitions of discrimination in employment and constitutional rights have served to define the parameters of the relationship between colleges and universities and their employees. A specific chapter addresses academic freedom and faculty employment rights. One of the themes of these relationships is the quest for equity and diversity; a specific chapter addresses litigation in this area. The specific relationship between faculty and institutions is defined by the terms of the employment contract, concepts of academic freedom, free speech rights, and constitutional rights to property and liberty. Sexual harassment as an emerging faculty employment issue is treated in a separate chapter. Another involves employee rights to bargain collectively, and a chapter is devoted to higher education litigation under collective bargaining.

Student-institutional relationships involve a number of legal duties defined by the relationships. These range from supervisory duties embodied in the old concept of *in loco parentis* to the emerging constitutional guarantees applied to public institutions. A chapter of the book addresses those rights granted to students within the constitutional relationship. Fiduciary relationships also exist between students and institutions requiring a duty to meet student's safety and educational needs. These relationships give rise to controversies surrounding the doctrine of educational malpractice, consumer rights, and protections defined by the concepts of tort liability. A specific chapter is devoted to these relationships.

Conclusion

This book will discuss and analyze the evolving legal relationships between students, their constituencies, and institutions of higher education as defined by the courts. The relationships between institutions and federal and state government will be explored to determine how these laws and legal opinions define the organization and operation of higher education institutions. The rights of faculty, students, and the public will be illuminated. These discussions will enhance understanding of higher education in the United States.

CHAPTER II

Federal Authority Versus State Authority

States' rights versus federal power is an issue that has been addressed since the adoption of the Constitution. The Constitution reserves education as a responsibility of state government.[19] Under what circumstances would federal powers supersede the rights of the state? Several concepts serve to answer this question. One is sovereign immunity that prohibits a private citizen from suing the state in federal court.[20] Another is the state's right to exist as a sovereign entity.[21] The competing concept under the Supremacy Clause of the Constitution allows federal law to preempt state law under certain circumstances.[22] The courts have attempted to define the scope and reach of each of these competing Constitutional provisions and case law will be reviewed to better understand the relationship between the states and the federal government.

Federal laws and regulations where Congress intended or implied a desire to preempt state law have resulted in a series of clashes between states and the federal government. One of those clashes is the federal government's implementation of title VI of the Civil Rights Act of 1964. Another example discussed is where the federal government has extended its control over higher education by linking compliance with various regulations to the receipt of federal financial assistance.

State Sovereignty and Sovereign Immunity

The Tenth Amendment to the United States Constitution limits federal regulation of states to the extent that those regulations preempt state sovereignty. Sovereignty is defined as the supreme, absolute and uncontrollable power by which any independent state is governed.[23] The Eleventh Amendment to the United States

---

[19] U.S. Const. Amend. X.
[20] U.S. Const. Amend. XI.
[21] U.S. Const. Amend. X.
[22] U.S. Const. art. VI, cl. 2.
[23] BLACK'S LAW DICTIONARY 1396 (6th ed. 1990).

Constitution prevents private citizens from suing the state in federal court under the concept of sovereign immunity. However, courts have traditionally found two exceptions to state sovereign immunity and state sovereignty under the Commerce Clause, and the Fourteenth Amendment of the United States Constitution. The Commerce Clause gives Congress the power to regulate interstate commerce, while the Fourteenth Amendment gives Congress the power to develop regulatory schemes to enforce and protect those rights such as due process and equal protection. The question is whether these congressional powers abrogate the bar of private citizens to bring suit against the state in federal court (sovereign immunity[24]) or inhibit the state's powers as a sovereign.

An example of this issue involved the authority of the Congress of the United States to extend the authority of the Age Discrimination in Employment Act of 1978 (ADEA) to state employees. In *Equal Employment Opportunities Commission v. Wyoming*,[25] the United States Supreme Court reviewed congressional power to extend ADEA to cover the retirement age of state game wardens. The lower court,[26] citing *National League of Cities v. Usery*,[27] had ruled that the federal government's regulations under the Commerce Clause must prevail when balanced against the state's interest to discriminate on the basis of age. However, as in *National League of Cities*, the lower court in the *Wyoming* case determined that the reach of ADEA through the Commerce Clause exempted law enforcement officials, such as state game wardens, because of the privileges and immunities defined by the Tenth Amendment to the Constitution.[28]

The *National League of Cities, supra* involved an attempt to extend the Fair Labor Standards Act's wage and hours provisions to state employees. The United States Court found that the Tenth Amendment barred the federal government from extending the wage regulations to state employees. The Court reasoned that while the Commerce Clause allows the federal government to regu-

---

[24] Sovereign immunity protects the state from suit by private citizens in federal court. BLACK'S LAW DICTIONARY 1396 (6th ed. 1990).

[25] 406 U.S. 226 (1983).

[26] EEOC v. Wyoming, 514 F. Supp. 595 (D. Wyo. 1981).

[27] 426 U.S. 833 (1976).

[28] EEOC v. Wyoming, 514 F. Supp. 595, 596 (D. Wyo. 1981). The concept of sovereign immunity under the Eleventh Amendment is related to the concept of the privileges and immunities provisions of the Tenth Amendment. For a detailed discussion of sovereign immunity; *see* K. Brickley, M. Ryan, *Millers v. Rutgers and Kovats v. Rutgers: Application of the Eleventh Amendment in Suits Against State Colleges and Universities*, 13 J. C. & UNIV. L. 407 (1987); P. Swan, *The Eleventh Amendment Revisited: Suits Against State Government Entities and Their Employees in Federal Courts*, 14 J. C. & UNIV. L. 1 (1987).

late labor, the Tenth Amendment is designed to limit federal regulatory power to the extent that it would "allow the national government [to preempt] the essentials of state sovereignty."[29] In another case, the Court further clarified what a state must prove in order to uphold immunity from federal regulation. *Hodel v. Virginia Surface Mining & Reclamation Association*[30] articulated a three-part test to establish immunity.

> [...]First, there must be a showing that the challenge statute regulates the 'states as states.' ...Second, the federal regulation must address matters that are indisputably 'attribute[s] of state sovereignty.' ...And third, it must be apparent that the States' compliance with the federal law would directly impair their [states'] ability 'to structure integral operations in areas of traditional government functions.'[31]

In *Wyoming*, the United States Supreme Court used the three-part test in *Hodel* to determine whether the state should be immune from an otherwise legitimate exercise of congressional authority under the Commerce Clause by extending ADEA to state employees. As a result of using this test, the Court found that the state is not impaired in its interest to regulate the preparedness of game wardens. ADEA has provisions that allow an employer (such as the state) to prove that age is a bona fide criterion of the job. Therefore, if the state could prove that age was an essential factor in the performance of game wardens, it could use age as a valid employment criterion. The regulation does not prevent the state from performing essential governmental duties. This ruling has implications for a variety of federal regulations governing the employment practices of the state, which will be discussed in other chapters of this monograph.

Sovereign immunity under the Eleventh Amendment is another way to protect states against encroachment by the federal government. Sovereign immunity appears to have been strengthened by a more recent Supreme Court ruling: *Seminole Tribe of Florida v. Florida*.[32] The case again raised the issue of whether Congress has the power to abrogate state sovereign immunity under either the Commerce Clause or the Fourteenth Amendment. The facts of the case centered on whether the Indian Gaming Regulatory Act (IGRA) could be used to force Florida to negotiate with

---

[29]*Id*. at 855.
[30]452 U.S. 264 (1981).
[31]*Id*. at 287-288 (citations omitted).
[32]517 U.S. 44 (1996).

the Seminole Tribe to establish a gambling casino on the reservation. The IGRA allowed a tribe to conduct gaming activities on
the reservation as long as they established a valid compact with
the state within which the reservation is located. When the Governor of Florida refused to negotiate a compact with the Tribe, the
Tribe sued in federal court to order the Governor to negotiate in
good faith. Rejecting the state's claim to Eleventh Amendment
sovereign immunity, the Federal District Court refused to grant
the state's motion to dismiss.[33] However, the Eleventh Circuit
Court of Appeals reversed and dismissed the suit, finding that
Congress did not have the power under the Indian Commerce
Clause to abrogate state sovereign immunity protections.[34] The
Supreme Court, upon review, ruled that historically the Court has
found only two circumstances where state sovereign immunity is
abrogated: the Commerce Clause and the Fourteenth Amendment.
While the Court found that the Indian Commerce Clause and the
Commerce Clause were indistinguishable, the Court abandoned
its Commerce Clause ruling in *Pennsylvania v. Union Gas Company*,[35]
finding the case to be of questionable precedential value. By finding that Articles I and III of the Constitution cannot be used to
circumvent a state's sovereign immunity, the court said that states'
Eleventh Amendment protection from prosecution is not abrogated
by the Commerce Clause. The implication for a number of congressional acts governing public higher education would be further
tested in the courts under the concept of state sovereign immunity.

In light of the *Seminole* case, the issue of state sovereign immunity protection from prosecution again centered on the Age
Discrimination in Employment Act. Several courts in Minnesota[36]
and Alabama[37] held that Congress had not abrogated Eleventh
Amendment immunity in the passage of ADEA. However, using
the Fourteenth Amendment, federal district courts in Kansas[38] and
Texas[39] found that state sovereign immunity had been abrogated
by the ADEA. Further, the Tenth Circuit found that ADEA claims
brought by a private individual against a public university were
not barred by Eleventh Amendment immunity.[40]

---

[33] 801 F. Supp. 655 (S.D. Fla. 1992).
[34] Florida v. Seminole Tribe of Fla., 11 F.3d 1016 (11th Cir. 1994).
[35] 491 U.S. 1 (1991).
[36] Humenasky v. Regents of the Univ. of Minn. 958 F. Supp. 439 (D. Minn. 1997).
[37] MacPherson v. University of Montevallo, 938 F. Supp. 785 (N.D. Ala. 1997).
[38] Teichgreaber v. Memorial Union Corp. of the Emporia State Univ., 946 F. Supp. 900 (D. Kan. 1996).
[39] Hodgson v. University of Tex. Med. Branch at Galveston, 953 F. Supp. 168 (S.D. Tex. 1997).
[40] Hurd v. Pittsburg State Univ., 109 F.3d 1540 (10th Cir. 1997).

It would appear from the above cases that state sovereign immunity is not preempted by federal regulations applied to the state emanating from congressional powers under the Commerce Clause. This will significantly impact those federal laws authorized through the Commerce Clause which regulate public higher education. However, neither the state nor its public higher education institutions are protected from suit in federal court (sovereign immunity) with respect to those congressional laws designed to enforce Fourteenth Amendment rights.

Federal Preemption Through the Supremacy Clause

The Supremacy clause of the Constitution[41] is another means by which federal law can take precedent over state law by preemption. There are basically three ways in which federal laws would preempt state laws: expressed preemption, inferred intent to preempt, and conflict preemption.[42] Expressed preemption is the clearest form of preemption in that Congress, acting within its scope and powers, clearly preempts in its legislation state laws that may conflict with the act. One example is the Employee Retirement Income Security Act of 1974 (ERISA) which preempted state laws affecting employee benefit plans.[43]

Inferred intent to preempt exists where there is no clearly stated preemption, but intent to preempt can be inferred under two circumstances. The first circumstance, "occupation of the field" is where the federal law is "so pervasive as to make reasonable the inference that Congress left no room for the States to supplement it."[44] But, "the Supreme Court has expressed reluctance to infer preemption by occupation of the field where lawmakers might have been expected to approach their subject in a comprehensive manner."[45] The second circumstance of inferred congressional intent is a field marked by a "dominant federal interest," that is, *"...a field in which the federal interest is so dominant that the federal*

---

[41] U.S. Const. art. VI, cl. 2. "This Constitution, and the Laws of the United States which shall be made in Pursuance thereof ...shall be the supreme law of the land...."

[42] L. J. Falik, *Exclusion of Military Recruiters From Public School Campuses: The Case Against Federal Preemption*, 39 UCLA L. Rev. 941, at 950, 951, 955 (1992).

[43] *Id*. at 950.

[44] *Id*. at 951; citing Rice v. Santa Fe Elevator Corp., 331 U. S. 218 (1947).

[45] *Id*. at 952; citing Hillsbrough County v. Automated Lab., 471 U.S. 707 (1985); New York Dep't of Social Servs. v. Dublino, 413 U.S. 405 (1973).

system will be assumed to preclude enforcement of state laws on the same subject."[46] Examples of such fields are international relations and laws governing aliens. The most frequently cited Supreme Court case is *Hines v. Davidowitz,*[47] which is also used in the third category—conflict preemption.

Conflict preemption is implicated when there are conflicting state and federal regulatory schemes. There are two types of conflict. The first type is where it is impossible to enforce both the state and federal regulatory scheme at the same time.[48] The second type of conflict exists when state law blocks the achievement of the purposes and objectives of the federal law. The standard used by the Supreme Court to determine whether this type of conflict implicates preemption of federal law is *Hines.*[49] This type of conflict preemption was also at issue in *United States v. City of Philadelphia,*[50] a recent case in higher education.

City of Philadelphia involved whether the Judge Advocate General Corps of the United States Military should be allowed to recruit at Temple University Law School, a public institution. The U.S. Military's (The Corps) recruitment policy, prohibiting the selection of homosexuals, is in violation of Philadelphia's Human Rights Ordinance and a Commission on Human Relations order. Students at Temple and other area institutions brought action before the Philadelphia Commission on Human Relations. The Commission found the University violated the city's Human Relations Ordinance when it allowed the United States Military, which discriminates on the basis of lifestyle orientation, to recruit at the Law School. Temple University and the United States sued the city, claiming federal laws, which removed federal defense funds from institutions that refuse to allow military recruitment preempted the local ordinance. In regard to Congressional legislation the court stated:

> "We believe that only one reasonable conclusion can be drawn from this legislation: Congress considers access to college and university employment facilities by military recruiters to be a matter of paramount importance. In other words, we think that Congress views such access an integral part of the military's effort to conduct "intensive recruiting campaigns to obtain enlistments."[51]

---

[46] *Id.* at 953; citing Rice, 331 U.S. at 230.

[47] 312 U.S. 52 (1941).

[48] Falik at 955; citing Florida Lime and Avocado Growers, Inc. v. Paul, 373 U.S. 132 (1963).

[49] *Id.* at 955.

[50] 798 F.2d 81 (3d Cir. 1986).

[51] *Id.* at 86.

In arguing its case, the government presented evidence that there has been significant recruitment of military officers from the Philadelphia area. The court stated:

Even viewing this evidence in the light most favorable to the Commission, we believe that the government has demonstrated, in the words of the Supreme Court, that the Order has "potential to frustrate" effective recruiting of skilled personnel in the Philadelphia area.[52]

The court rejected the city's argument that recruitment evidence should be restricted to the law school data rather than evidence reflecting recruitment data for all schools in the area. The court found that the Commission's Order significantly impaired the military's ability to recruit skilled personnel it requires as designated by Congress. This case is an example of conflict preemption of state law because a conflict with a city ordinance makes impossible the implementation of a congressional mandate.

The Clash Between Federal and State Authority

Title VI of the Civil Rights Act of 1964 as a regulatory scheme has origins in the Fourteenth Amendment Equal Protection Clause, and its scope depends on whether the institution receives federal financial assistance. It was designed to achieve integration, and it has been used to break up the dual systems of historically black higher education institutions, and predominately white institutions in the southern and border states. Title VI is an excellent example of the influence that these types of federal regulations can have on state systems of higher education. This over thirty-year conflict between certain states and the federal government is yet to be resolved. The government is still defining the desired goals used to determine if a state system of higher education is in compliance with title VI.

Title VI of the Civil Rights Act of 1964 states: "No person in the United States shall, on ground of race, color, or national origin, be excluded from participating in, or be denied the benefits of, or be subjected to discrimination under any program or activity receiving federal financial assistance."[53] Title VI was passed to reinforce the Fourteenth Amendment Equal Protection Clause and also to give more teeth to integration emanating from the Court's ruling in *Brown v. Board of Education*.[54] The enforcement of this

---

[52] *Id*. at 87.
[53] Pub. L. No.88-352, 78 Stat. 241 (1964).
[54] 347 U.S. 483 (1954).

new law fell to the Department of Health, Education, and Welfare's (HEW) Office of Civil Rights (OCR). In the 1980's, when the Supreme Court ruled in *Grove City College v. Bell*,[55] the scope of title IX and other similar legislation such as title VI was narrowed to cover only a specific program receiving federal funds. Three years later, however, Congress passed the Civil Rights Restoration Act of 1987[56] that broadened the definition of a "program" to include the whole institution or state system of higher education where only one program of the organization receives federal funds.[57] While it became clear that compliance with title VI in K-12 education could be achieved through the redrawing of school district boundaries and busing, compliance in higher education was much more elusive. In state systems of higher education there is no geographic determination as to school attendance; indeed, students are free to chose among the public institutions that admit them. Certainly, a state system can open up admissions and access and remove color barriers. After those changes, however, what if students continue to select institutions based on their own race, thereby perpetuating a dual system of higher education as appeared to be the case in Louisiana and Mississippi? This dilemma continues to haunt title VI compliance through the 1990s. Reviewing the case law gives a better understanding of this enforcement dilemma and how it perpetuates the clash between federal and state authority over higher education. This case law is forked, one tine is the *Adams* litigation, an attempt to achieve compliance by monitoring a federal agency, and the other is enforced state compliance through active litigation in a number of states, specifically Alabama, Louisiana, and Mississippi.

The *Adams* Litigation[58]

In the late 1960s, the Office of Civil Rights (OCR) of HEW reviewed higher education title VI compliance in nineteen southern and border states, and notified ten that they were operating racially dual systems of higher education in violation of title VI.[59] Five states (Florida, Louisiana, Mississippi, North Carolina, and

---

[55] 465 U.S. 555 (1984). A case discussed in more detail under title IX of the Education Amendments of 1972.

[56] P.L. 100-259 (1987), 102 Stat. 28.

[57] R. Hendrickson, B. Lee, F. Loomis, Jr. & S. Olswang, *The Impact of the Civil Rights Restoration Act on Higher Education*, 60 WEST'S EDUC. L. RPT. 671 (1990).

[58] Adams v. Richardson, 351 F. Supp. 363 (1972).

[59] F. Loomis, Jr., STATE POLICY AND PLANNING SYSTEMS: RESPONSES TO THE LEGAL MANDATE TO DESEGREGATE HIGHER EDUCATION IN VIRGINIA AND SOUTH CAROLINA, Unpublished doctoral dissertation, The Pennsylvania State University, University Park (1994).

Oklahoma) refused to submit reorganization plans, and the plans that Arkansas, Georgia, Maryland, Pennsylvania, and Virginia submitted were viewed as inadequate; however, HEW failed to initiate enforcement proceedings against any of the states.[60] Kenneth Adams, an African American Mississippi college student, brought a class action suit in the United States District Court for the District of Columbia claiming HEW was refusing to enforce title VI. Judge John H. Pratt agreed with the plaintiff and ordered the ten states to eliminate the vestiges of their dual systems of higher education.[61] The court order was later expanded to seventeen state systems of higher education.[62] The District Court acknowledged HEW's right under the statute to solicit compliance plans from the states, but noted that the agency had failed to act in a timely way. HEW was ordered to require the states to meet the 120-day limit as defined in title VI regulations. On appeal, the United States Court of Appeals for the District of Columbia affirmed the lower court decision as it pertained to elementary and secondary education, but modified the order for state higher education systems.[63] Acknowledging the complex problems surrounding the desegregation of dual state systems of higher education,[64] the court upheld the 120-day compliance time frame for plan submission, and further ordered that after 180 days of noncompliance, the agency would be required to commence sanction procedures (loss of federal funding).[65] A 1977 consent decree expanded the court order's reach to all fifty states.[66] With the continuing expansion of the scope of the court order, the issue of agency responsibility and court authority under the Constitution began to emerge.

This new issue fully emerged when a motion filed by the *Adams* litigants, joined by the Women's Equity Action League (WEAL), challenged the ending of the 1977 consent decree.[67] The defendants, the states involved, appealed to the Circuit Court alleging violations of the separation of powers doctrine of the Constitution where the court had intervened in the day-to-day

---

[60] M. C. Brown, II, Defining Collegiate Desegregation: The Quest for A Legal Standard of Compliance After Adams, Unpublished doctoral dissertation, The Pennsylvania State University (1997).

[61] Adams v. Richardson, 351 F. Supp. 636 (D.D.C. 1972).

[62] Adams v. Richardson, 356 F. Supp. 96 (D.D.C. 1973).

[63] Adams v. Richardson, 480 F.2d 1159 (D.C. Cir.1973).

[64] *Id.* at 1164.

[65] *Id.* at 1165.

[66] Adams v. Califano, 430 F. Supp. 118 (D.D.C. 1977).

[67] Adams v. Bell, No. 3095-70 (D.D.C., March 24, 1977). *See* Adams v. Bennett, 675 F. Supp. 668 (D.D.C. 1987); Adams v. Bell, 711 F.2d 161 (D.C. Cir. 1983). This case affirmed the District Court's refusal to issue an injunction requested by *Adams* plaintiffs to end settlement negotiations between HEW and North Carolina.

administrative affairs of an executive branch agency.[68] The case was remanded to the District Court to determine whether the plaintiffs had standing to litigate and whether the court order violated the separation of powers doctrine. On remand, Judge Pratt reversed his own previous decisions and vacated what had been seventeen years of court-ordered monitoring of OCR compliance enforcement.[69] The judge ruled that the plaintiffs lacked standing because of the lack of a nexus between the receipt of federal financial assistance and "a palpable personal injury"[70] discrimination by the state higher education system.[71] He also found that the court-ordered perpetual supervision of an agency of the executive branch of government was a violation of the separation of powers provision in Article III of the Constitution.[72]

On appeal, the District of Columbia Circuit Court of Appeals ruled on the standing issue and found that the plaintiffs had standing to litigate emanating from their direct injury—discrimination.[73] The court then asked the parties to return and reargue the separation of powers issue. A year later, the Court of Appeals dodged the separation of powers issue and ruled that Congress, when passing title VI, had not authorized a private action against the executive branch of government. The court acknowledged, however, Congress's authority to provide for such an action.[74] With this decision, eighteen years of court-ordered compliance monitoring of HEW's OCR ended. Future compliance efforts would have to focus on state-by-state litigation.

Litigation Against the States

A number of states were involved in litigation concerning title VI and dual systems of higher education. In many cases private individuals initially brought the action against the state, and the United States later joined as a plaintiff.[75] Three states—Mississippi, Louisiana, and Alabama—set the tone for the direction this litigation would take. A standard for compliance review established by the Supreme Court in the Mississippi case, *United States v. Fordice,*[76] evolved from litigation begun in a number of states.

---

[68] Women's Equity Action League v. Bell, 743 F.2d 42 (D.C. Cir. 1984).

[69] Adams v. Bennett, 675 F. Supp. 668 (D.C. Cir. 1987).

[70] *Id.* at 676.

[71] *Id.* at 677.

[72] *Id.* at 680.

[73] Women's Equity Action League v. Carvazos, 879 F.2d 880 (D.C. Cir. 1989).

[74] Women's Equity Action League v. Carvazos, 906 F.2d 743 (D.C. Cir. 1990).

[75] Ayers v. Allain, 674 F. Supp. 1523 (N.D. Miss. 1987); Geier v. Dunn, 337 F. Supp. 573 (M.D. Tenn. 1972); Knight v. James, 514 F. Supp. 567 (M.D. Ala.1981).

[76] 505 U.S. 717 (1992).

The Stage is Set for a Supreme Court Decision

In *Ayers v. Allain*,[77] Mississippi, African Americans citizens were later joined by the United States in claiming that institutions designed to serve predominantly African American students were inferior to predominantly white institutions. They also claimed that admissions standards, program approval mechanisms, and resource allocations had been designed to maintain the status quo of a discriminatory dual system of higher education. The state, on the other hand, asserted that it had acted affirmatively to recruit members of the other race to both white and black institutions, and that actual enrollment alone was not the sole determinant of title VI compliance. The District Court, relying on *Bazemore v. Friday*,[78] ruled that attendance was voluntary at public institutions of higher education, and the state's compliance would be determined by whether state policies were designed to disestablish the dual system of higher education.[79] The court noted that, consistent with *Bazemore*,[80] policies, not current enrollment patterns, would be used to measure title VI compliance. The court found that the less selective admissions policies of the public black institutions did not perpetuate a dual system,[81] and funding schemes were based on differences in institutional mission, not racial discrimination.[82] The court also noted the state's efforts to eliminate duplication of programs in Jackson, Vicksburg, and Natchez were other examples of how Mississippi, with a coordinated system of higher education, had met its title VI compliance responsibilities to eliminate a dual system of higher education.[83] On appeal, the United States Court of Appeals for the Fifth Circuit reversed, rejecting the application of the *Bazemore* standard because *Ayers* involved *de jure* segregation.[84] The Appeals Court relied on *Geier v. Alexander*[85] and

---

[77] *Supra* note 56.
[78] 478 U.S. 385 (1986).
[79] Ayers v. Allain, 674 F. Supp. 1523 (N.D. Miss. 1987).
[80] Bazemore at 3013. The case established that with membership in voluntary 4H clubs, title VI compliance would be determined by racially neutral policies, not the racial composition of the clubs.
[81] Ayers at 1557.
[82] *Id.* at 1546, 1562.
[83] *Id.* at 1542, 1543, 1563, 1564.
[84] Ayers v. Allain, 893 F.2d 732 (5th Cir. 1990).
[85] 801 F.2d 799 (6th Cir. 1986).

Green v. School Board of New Kent County[86] where both required the removal of all *de jure* segregation and stated:

> The badge of inferiority that marks black institutions has not been removed. As such there remains in Mississippi's higher education system vestiges of discrimination that distorts the perceptions of African American students. The racial composition of the student body is not simply the result of student choice.[87]

The court found that the lower admissions standards of the black institutions and underfunding of those institutions by the state perpetuated their inferior image.[88] The court also cited the failure of white institutions to publicize the exceptions to admissions standards for recruitment of African American students, the absence of African American faculty at white institutions, predominance of faculty without doctorates at black institutions, and program duplication as factors perpetuating *de jure* segregation. On appeal, however, the Fifth Circuit *en banc,* vacated this opinion and reinstated the District Court opinion.[89] The invitation to grant *certiorari* by the Supreme Court[90] would be fueled by the litigation in Louisiana.

Prior to the publication of the above Fifth Circuit *en banc* decision, a District Court in Louisiana rejected the District Court decision in Mississippi.[91] While not rejecting *Bazemore,* the court found that participation in voluntary clubs required a lower standard than desegregation of education, a necessity for good citizenship.[92] The court found that a racially distinguishable dual system of higher education continued in Louisiana and that little had been done to implement policies to disestablish that system. The court believed that Louisiana's twenty-two institutions, governed by four governing boards, served to perpetuate the dual system. The court criticized the state for locating historically black and predominantly white institutions in close proximity, resulting in duplication of programs and unnecessary competition for students.[93] Finding that the state had failed to implement the 1977 consent decree, the court ordered a special master to develop a plan to dismantle the dual system of higher education. In 1989, the court heard objections to the special master's report, but or-

---

[86] 391 U.S. 430 (1968).
[87] Ayers at 735.
[88] *Id.* at 755.
[89] Ayers v. Allain, 914 F.2d 676 (5th Cir. 1990).
[90] *Cert. granted,* Ayers v. Mabus, 499 U.S. 958 (1991).
[91] United States v. Louisiana, 692 F. Supp. 642 (E.D. La. 1988).
[92] *Id.* at 656.
[93] *Id.* at 657.

dered the restructuring of the Louisiana system of higher education as proposed by the special master.[94] The capstone of the reorganization was the elimination of the four governing boards, substituting a single board of higher education to govern all state institutions. The order included specifications regarding the makeup of the board, the selection process, and board duties. Further, it included orders to merge certain programs, eliminate other programs, end Louisiana's opened admissions policy,[95] and impose higher admissions standards and monetary recruitment incentives. These orders where challenged by both Grambling University and Southern University, the two most prominent historically black institutions in the state, slated to lose key programs as a result of the order.[96] Some even charged that the court usurped the legislative powers of the state through the court order. But this issue of state sovereignty was never raised by any of the parties on appeal. This saga of litigation in both Louisiana and Mississippi made it ripe for the Supreme Court to render a decision on title VI compliance in state higher education systems.

The Fordice Decision[97]

The United States Supreme Court reviewed the Court of Appeals decision in the Mississippi case, vacating and remanding based on the following instructions. The Court noted that *Bazemore* did not excuse the state from the required elimination of policies that perpetuated a *de jure* dual system of higher education. The Court then identified three key factors used to determine whether an institution's policies perpetuate a continuing violation of title VI. The first factor is whether the policy is traceable to the previous system and perpetuates segregation. Second is whether the policy is without sound educational justification, and third is whether the policy can be practicably eliminated.[98] Based on the issues already litigated in Mississippi, the Court identified four policy areas that the lower court should review on remand, and said that the lower court should apply the above three factors to each of these policy areas. The Court wanted the lower court to review the four policies of the present system in Mississippi: "ad-

---

[94] United States v. Louisiana, 718 F. Supp. 499 (E.D. La. 1989).

[95] Any citizen of the state who graduated from a Louisiana high school was eligible to attend any of the state's public institutions.

[96] United States v. Louisiana, 718 F. Supp. 521 (E.D. La. 1989); United States v. Louisiana, 718 F. Supp. 525 (E.D. La. 1989); *appeal dismissed sub nom.*, Board of Supervisors of So. Univ. and Agricultural and Mechanical College v. United States, U.S. (1990); United States v. State of La., 692 F. Supp. 642 (E.D. La. 1988), *appeal dismissed*, U.S. (1990).

[97] 505 U.S. 717 (1992).

[98] *Id.* at 731.

missions standards, program duplication, institutional mission assignment, and the continued operation of all eight public universities."[99] The Court cautioned that it did not intend to limit the lower court to these four policies, but made clear that the court was free to add other policies in its review. The Court stated:

> Because the former *de jure* segregated system of public universities in Mississippi impeded the free choice of prospective students, the state in dismantling that system must take the necessary steps to ensure that this choice now is truly free. The full range of policies and practices must be examined with this duty in mind. *That an institution is predominantly white or black does not in itself make out a constitutional violation* [emphasis added]. But surely the State may not leave in place policies rooted in its prior officially-segregated system that serves to maintain the racially identifiability of its universities if those policies can practicably be eliminated without eroding sound educational policies.[100]

This decision became the standard against which each state's litigation is adjudicated.

Mississippi

On remand, the Federal District Court for the Northern District of Mississippi, following the guidelines set out in the Supreme Court, found that the state's policies perpetuated *de jure* segregation of higher education and ordered remedies.[101] The court found that the admissions policies in question were vestiges of *de jure* segregation and ordered the establishment of uniform admissions standards for all institutions and the development of new remedial and scholarship programs. The court determined that institutional missions also perpetuated the dual system, as did program duplication. The court ordered the merger of a historically black institution and a predominantly white institution. The maintenance of a racially identifiable athletic conference was another *de jure* segregation policy. The court also found that current funding, while more equitable than it had been in the past, maintained the status quo of resource disparity between the historically black institutions and the white institutions. A committee was established by the court to monitor the state's compliance effort.

---

[99] *Id.* at 732.
[100] *Id.* at 743 (emphasis added).
[101] Ayers v. Fordice, 879 F. Supp. 1419 (N.D. Miss. 1995).

The plaintiffs, African American citizens, appealed this decision primarily on the issue of the closure and/or merger of an historically black institution. The Fifth Circuit (*en banc*) affirmed in part, reversed in part, and remanded.[102] The court affirmed the establishment of a uniform admissions standard and new remedial programs, but reversed the elimination of existing remedial programs. The court also found that using entrance examination scores to award scholarships was a practice traceable to *de jure* segregation policies. The development of new academic programs at historically black institutions was appropriate, but the proposed merger needed more clarification, particularly as it related to duplication of programs. The Fifth Circuit affirmed the district court findings that library allocations were justifiable, and that funding allocation, hiring and salary practices, and the composition of the governing board were not traceable to *de jure* segregation.

Louisiana

In light of the Fifth Circuit's *en banc* decision involving Mississippi[103] and *Fordice*, the Federal District Court in Louisiana asked the parties to appear and show cause why the court order should not be vacated. The court reinstated the order, finding it complied with the guidelines outlined in *Fordice*.[104] The state appealed to the Fifth Circuit, who vacated in part, reversed in part, and remanded for further action.[105] The Fifth Circuit affirmed the district court's finding that program duplication was traceable to prior *de jure* segregation and perpetuated the dual system of higher education. The Fifth Circuit found, however, that the four-board governance system, adopted as part of the state constitutional revisions of 1974, was not traceable to the *de jure* dual system of higher education. Further, the district court failed to show how this four-board system had a "disproportionate impact that can be traced to a discriminatory purpose."[106] The court also found that in terms of opened admission, the district court had shown how opened admission would perpetuate the dual system, but failed to establish its traceability to *de jure* segregation policies. It is interesting to note that because of Louisiana's opened admissions policy, it has higher percentages of African American students enrolled at predominantly white institutions. Opened admissions

---

[102] Ayers v. Fordice, 111 F.3d 1183 (5th Cir. 1997).
[103] Ayers v. Allain, 914 F.2d 676 (5th Cir. 1990).
[104] United States v. State of La., 811 F. Supp. 1151 (E.D. La. 1992).
[105] United States v. State of La., 9 F.3d 1159 (5th Cir. 1993).
[106]*Id.* at 1167.

had been adopted as part of the consent decree of the 1970s, which is why it is not traceable to policies designed to perpetuate the dual system of higher education. Although the case was remanded to the district court, an out-of-court settlement was reached between Louisiana and the United States in 1994.

This settlement agreement provided for the continuation of the four-board governing system, composed of a coordinating board and three system governing boards. The agreement also included an outlay of $57 million for the development of new programs at the historically black institutions and other-race doctoral scholarships at the predominantly white institutions, and a capital outlay of $65 million to complete those projects that were outstanding under the old consent decree and to develop new projects to improve facilities. In addition, the agreement stated that the Law Centers of LSU and Southern University would develop joint programs to encourage the enrollment of other-race students in each law program. It also called for the establishment of a community college in Baton Rouge. The total cost to the state over the next ten years to implement the settlement agreement is $122 million.

Alabama

In a case in litigation since 1983,[107] the District Court for the Northern District of Alabama, in a 1991 opinion, wrote a comprehensive history of the development of the dual system of higher education in Alabama and ordered the disestablishment of this segregated system.[108] The Eleventh Circuit affirmed in part, reversed in part, and remanded this case in light of the Supreme Court decision in *Fordice*.[109] The District Court issued a subsequent finding and a court order that included orders already affirmed. They specifically found that admissions standards, determination of mission, program duplication, hiring practices, curriculum, and the State's land-grant mission of extension ser-

---

[107] Knight v. Alabama, 628 F. Supp. 1137 (N.D. Ala 1983), *rev'd and remanded*, 828 F.2d 1532 (11th Cir. 1987), *rehearing en banc, aff'd in part, rev'd in part, remanded*, 791 F.2d 1450 (11th Cir. 1986), 796 F.2d 1487 (11th Cir. 1986) *cert. denied* 479 U.S. 1085 (1987).

[108] Knight v. Alabama, 787 F. Supp. 1030 (N.D. Ala. 1991). This case is a must read for those interested in the historical development of Historically Black Institutions or dual systems of higher education; approved new admissions policy, 801 F. Supp. 577 (N.D. Ala. 1992), appointment of monitor approved, 829 F. Supp. 1286 (N.D. Ala. 1993).

[109] Knight v. Alabama, 14 F.3d 1534 (11th Cir. 1994).

vices perpetuated a dual system of higher education and ordered appropriate remedies.[110] The court also set up a special master and a compliance committee to monitor the court order. The most recent litigation saw the court finding that the Eleventh Amendment barred the court from applying interest to a post-judgment award of capital improvement funds to two historically black institutions.[111]

In summary, this litigation clearly demonstrates the clash between a state's authority to provide education under the constitution with the federal government's authority to enforce equality under the Equal Protection Clause of the Fourteenth Amendment. Through title VI, the United States reclaimed the right to withhold federal funds if states refused to comply with its regulations. These cases serve to show how states' powers are not as broad and as sweeping as we might think. Underlying much of this litigation and the compromises reached was the scope of both the courts and the federal government's power to usurp states' sovereignty. Federal regulations emanating from the Fourteenth Amendment have particularly strong clout over state sovereignty claims.

Federal Regulatory Authority

Constitutional authority is not the only means by which the federal government has acquired some control over state systems of higher education. The notion that institutions must comply with certain federal regulations in order to receive federal financial assistance has become a dominant way to award federal funds to states, local governments, and private entities. For example, there are a number of federal regulations discussed later in the faculty employment and students' rights sections of this monograph that are based on the receipt of federal financial assistance. Regulations such as title IX of the Education Amendments of 1972, the Rehabilitation Act of 1973, and the Age Discrimination in Employment Act of 1967 (ADEA) were all based on receipt of federal financial assistance. Other regulations tied to receipt of federal financial assistance which have had a significant impact and been litigated in higher education include such topics as Medicare reimbursement for medical education, and the human subjects and animal welfare regulations attached to the award of federal re-

---

[110] Knight v. Alabama, 900 F. Supp. 27 (N.D. Ala.1995).

[111] Knight v. Alabama, 962 F. Supp. 1442 (N.D. Ala. 1996).

search grants. All of these are complex topics involving certain types of institutions, particularly research universities and institutions with teaching hospitals and highlight the kinds of issues faced by both state and federal parties.

Medicare Reimbursement for Medical Education

Providers of medical education, such as teaching hospitals, can be reimbursed for the costs of graduate medical education (GME) under the revised Medicare statute.[112] Under this statute, the hospital can bill direct costs of Medicare qualified treatments if students, as interns or residents, are involved, for educational purposes, in the treatment and medical testing required for patients. Further, indirect costs of medical education involved in the provision of Medicare service will be reimbursed; however, the law forbids the *redistribution of costs from educational institutions* to patient care or teaching hospitals affiliated with those institutions. Thus, institutions are prohibited from increasing patient care costs by redistributing medical education costs not billed the previous years to patient care. In 1985, Thomas Jefferson University attempted to redistribute what would have been nonsalary GME allowable patient care costs, for which reimbursement had not been previously sought, to the Thomas Jefferson University Hospital for reimbursement under Medicare. The fiscal intermediary, as per the Medicare statutes, disallowed the reimbursement for GME. The Reimbursement Review Board reversed on the issue of GME reimbursement, allowing reimbursement, but the Secretary of Health and Human Services, agreeing with the fiscal intermediary, found that reimbursement was an impermissible redistribution of GME costs. Both the district court and the Third Circuits affirmed.[113] This ruling, however, was in direct conflict with a Sixth Circuit ruling.[114] On appeal, in *Thomas Jefferson University v. Shalala*,[115] the United States Supreme Court upheld the Secretary's interpretation of the regulations on the *redistribution of costs* for GME as reasonable and consistently applied. The Court also deferred to the experts' reasoned opinions regarding regula-

---

[112] 42 CFR § 413.85(c) 1993.
[113] Thomas Jefferson Univ. v. Sullivan, 993 F.2d 879 (1993), *cert. granted*, 510 U.S. 1039 (1994).
[114] Ohio State Univ. v. Secretary, Dept. Health and Human Services, 996 F.2d 122 (6th Cir. 1993).
[115] 512 U.S. 504 (1994).

tory interpretations in complex and highly technical programs such as Medicare. Because reimbursement for allowable GME under Medicare involves amounts of several million dollars per teaching hospital, the litigation continues, but the Secretary's interpretation continues to hold.[116]

Research Grant Regulation

Several federal regulations have been passed that hinge on the receipt of federal research dollars for institutional compliance with these regulations. Federal regulations regarding human subjects[117] require institutions to set up a review board to review all research proposals to ensure the protection of human subjects. Although there is little litigation surrounding this regulation, the regulation has had a profound effect on the way dissertations and other research projects or surveys are conducted on college campuses. The regulation's requirements of a consent form and the review process are particularly illustrative of the reach of the federal government into institutional academic affairs. Another federal regulation has had a profound effect on the way institutions conduct research involving animals. Under the regulations adopted by authority of the Animal Welfare Act,[118] institutions must establish an Institutional Animal Care and Use Committee (IACUC) to review all projects which use animals for experimentation.[119] The only litigation filed under this regulation has been states' sunshine laws where animal rights groups attempted to gain access to IACUC deliberations.[120] This law also has altered procedures for conducting animal research at institutions of higher education. Institutional compliance with both of these regulations is linked to the receipt of federal funds.

---

[116]*See* Shalala v. Guernsey Memorial Hosp., 514 U.S. 87 (1995); University of Ky. v. Shalala, 639 F. Supp. 639 (1994); Board of Regents of Univ. of Minn. v. Shalala, 53 F.3d 940 (8th Cir. 1995); Regents of Univ. of Cal. v. Shalala, 82 F.3d 291 (9th Cir. 1996); Good Samaritan Hosp. Regional Medical Ctr. v. Shalala, 85 F.3d 1057 (2d Cir. 1996); St. Paul-Ramsey Med. Ctr., Inc. v. Shalala, 91 F.3d 57 (8th Cir. 1996). For a more detailed treatise on this issue, *see* K. Horger, *Medicare Reimbursement To Provider University Hospitals For Graduate Medical Education Expenses in Light Of Thomas Jefferson University v. Shalala*, 23 J.C. & U.L. 133 (1996).
[117]45 CFR § 46 (1997).
[118]7 U.S.C. §§ 2131 *et seq.*
[119]9 CFR § 2.31(a) (1997).
[120] *See* Robinson v. Indiana Univ., 659 N.E.2d 151 (Ind. Ct. App. 1995); Board of Trustees of the State Univ. of N.Y. v. Fox, 658 N.Y.S.2d 653 (N.Y. App. Div. 1997).

Conclusion

Certain provisions in the United States Constitution mark the boundaries of state versus federal authority over higher education. The Constitution reserves authority over education generally to the states and the Eleventh Amendment supports the state's authority to be free from prosecution in federal court under the concept of sovereign immunity. However, states' claims to sovereign immunity will be abrogated where federal laws emanate from the Fourteenth Amendment or where Congress specifically provides or intends that the law supersedes state law. Further, the Supremacy Clause of the Constitution allows Congress the power to enact laws that supersede state regulations. By linking certain federal regulations to the receipt of federal financial assistance the federal government has been able to extend its reach further into the control and regulation of public higher education. This clash between the state's authority over its higher education institutions and attempts by the federal government to gain some control over public higher education will continue to manifest itself in litigation, with the courts becoming the arbitrator of these conflicts.

CHAPTER III

State Relations

Case law defines the relationships, spheres of influence, and authority of various state agencies and local government over institutions of higher education. Litigation probes both the limits and reach of these governmental units. This chapter is divided into four topics that address issues regarding the nature of the relationships between higher education, both public and private, and levels of state government: State legislative authority, states' agency authority, which includes the areas of licensing and accreditation, the authority of boards of trustees, and sunshine laws that require states' governmental units to operate openly and publicly.

State Legislative Authority

State legislative authority is bounded by federal constitutional limits, individual rights as defined in federal constitutional amendments, powers defined in individual state constitutions, and other contractual obligations. The focus here is primarily on state legislative authority operating through state statutes, state constitutions and their amendments, and other legislative action. All interact to yield ways in which legislation is restricted to a certain scope along with ways in which actions of a state legislature may be limited. These limitations vary from state to state, except where limitations involve the powers and rights spelled out in the federal Constitution. The chapter on federal-state relationships discusses the ways that federal and state laws sometimes interact.

The establishment of legislative authority was challenged in a series of cases regarding the South Dakota legislature's decision to close the University of South Dakota at Springfield. Control of the property and buildings would be transferred to the Board of Charities and Corrections for conversion of the facility into a prison. In *Kanaly*,[121] state taxpayers sued, challenging this decision. The state supreme court found that a federal law, the 1889 Enabling Act,[122] designated that federal land be deeded over to the state, and the land, or the proceeds from the sale of the land, be used to

---

[121] 368 N.W.2d 819 (S.D. 1985).
[122] Enabling Act Ch. 180, 25 Statutes at Large 676 (1889).

support public schools in the state. Plus, acreage was specifically designated for use by the normal school at Springfield under the Enabling Act of the state constitution.[123] The court found this property to be trust property dedicated to education, and also found that the legislative transfer of this property to the Board of Corrections required that the trust be appropriately compensated.[124] The court stated: "The existence at the City of Springfield of an institution of higher education is not required by the Enabling Act or the constitution of the state. A perpetual trust fund for school purposes is one thing, a perpetual school is quite another ...."[125] The court found that the state could transfer the school property into trust assets, provided that the trust fund was not impaired in any way. Shortly before this decision was handed down, the state legislature transferred the trust fund and lands of the Springfield school to the other normal schools in the state.

In a companion case, taxpayers challenged the realignment of the proportion of mineral lease money given to the university at Springfield to the other three existing normal schools. The court found that the realignment of the mineral lease money violated neither the Enabling Act nor the state constitution.[126] The legislature, therefore, had authority to transfer the property as long as compensation for the transfer was placed in a perpetual trust to be used for the promotion of public schools—in this case, the other three normal schools in the state.

Several years later, taxpayers again sued, alleging that the property that had been deeded to the normal school at Springfield required the maintenance of a public normal school in Springfield. The court acknowledged the state's obligation to use property that had been deeded it by private citizens in accordance with reservations placed in the deed, but also acknowledged that no such reservations were placed in the deed of property to the Springfield institution.[127] In a related case, students brought action alleging that their contractual and constitutional rights were violated when the school was closed because they were denied continued access to academic degree programs. The court ruled that existing contracts with students terminated at the end of the academic year. No subsequent contract existed with the students; therefore, no constitutional or contract rights existed.[128] The legis-

[123] Enabling Act, Art. VIII, § 21, S.D. Const.
[124] Kanaly v. State, 401 N.W.2d 551, 553 (S.D. 1987).
[125] Id.
[126] Merkwan v. State, 375 N.W.2d 624 (S.D. 1985).
[127] Kanaly v. State, 403 N.W.2d 33 (S.D. 1987); see also Kanaly v. State, 401 N.W.2d 551 (S.D. 1987); plaintiff's attempt to recover attorneys fees resulting from the litigation was denied by the court.
[128] AASE v. State, 400 N.W.2d 269 (S.D. 1987).

lation closing the institution allowed for the students' matriculation at another South Dakota institution for completion of degree requirements.

The question of the scope and limits of legislative authority came to light in a Pennsylvania case that raised a question of a violation of constitutional rights.[129] In this case, the plaintiffs, several private hospitals, claimed that legislative action to establish a medical education center and health care facility of the Pennsylvania State University bypassed the certificate of need requirements for establishing health care facilities. Therefore, this action violated the Supremacy Clause and the plaintiffs' due process and equal protection rights, they argued. The National Health Planning and Resources Development Act[130] provided that the groups proposing additional and new health care facilities show a certificate of need before commencing construction. A state law required by the federal act had a similar requirement.[131] The state exempted the university from any certificate of need provisions. The court found that congressional action establishing the certificate of need requirements was within a line of cases setting regulations on federal spending. This type of legislation does not come under the Supremacy Clause.[132] The court found that the plaintiffs failed to establish a property right under an act designed to regulate health care facilities as opposed to an act designed to benefit health care facilities.[133] Finally, the equal protection claim failed where it was evident that the exempting legislation had a legitimate state interest, here, the education and training of medical personnel.[134]

More recently, the application of a state human rights act was tested in the courts. Two African Amerian students at a state university in Illinois alleged racial discrimination, one as motivation for his academic dismissal and the other as the reason for the denial of her request to retake final examinations. The Illinois Supreme Court ruled that the alleged racial discrimination in this case could not be challenged under the state's Human Rights Act because the university was not a "public place of accommodation" defined as the type of institution covered by the act, and, therefore, found for the university.[135]

---

[129] Harrisburg Hosp. v. Thornburgh, 616 F. Supp. 699 (M.D. Pa. 1985).

[130] 42 U.S.C. § 300k et seq. (1974).

[131] Pennsylvania Health Care Facilities Act, Pa. Cons. Stat. Ann. 448.101 (Purdon Supp. 1985).

[132] Harrisburg Hosp. v. Thornburgh, 616 F. Supp. 699, 705 (M.D. Pa. 1985). The Supremacy Clause of the United States Constitution [U.S. Const. art. 6, cl. 2] declares that federal law is the supreme law of the land.

[133] *Id.* at 710.

[134] *Id.* at 713.

[135] Board of Trustees of S. Ill. Univ. v. Department of Human Rights, 636 N.E.2d 528 (Ill. 1994).

Kentucky saw a challenge to its legislative authority when its Law Enforcement Foundation Program was contested by a state university's campus police officers who unsuccessfully sought to receive funds under the program. An appellate court, denying the officers' right to funds, found that the state university was not a "local government unit" under this legislation nor were the campus police officers "police officers" under the meaning of the program.[136]

The third angle from which to consider a state's legislative authority, through the interaction of state and federal law, was tested in Kentucky. There, a state statute, operating through the federal Randolph-Sheppard Vending Stand Act, required all state agencies, including universities, to hire blind vendors. At one state university, negotiations with a blind vendor broke down. The vendor then sought declaratory and injunctive relief to prevent the university from contracting with a private vendor. An appellate court ruled that although the Department for the Blind did not have the right of first refusal, the university must negotiate a fair agreement with the blind vendor, which would not subject him to unreasonable competition.[137]

In another case, an amendment to the state constitution was challenged in Arkansas. This amendment prohibits the use of public funds to perform abortions unless the abortion is necessary to save a mother's life. An activist unsuccessfully sued a university medical school and its genetics program under this amendment, seeking to enjoin the program from providing genetic counseling and asking the court to define "mother's life." The Supreme Court of Arkansas found that although genetic counseling might be a factor in deciding whether to have an abortion, the counseling did not amount to performing abortions under the amendment. Plus, the court declined to define "mother's life" because the plaintiff had raised no controversy surrounding its definition.[138]

In sum, then, these cases explore the limits and scope of states' legislative authority. This authority not only varies from state to state but also sometimes interacts with federal law, which must also be considered, if applicable, in resolving these legal questions.

---

[136] Wellman v. Blanton, 927 S.W.2d 347 (Ky. Ct. App. 1996).
[137] Kentucky State Univ. v. Kentucky Dep't for the Blind, 923 S.W.2d 296 (Ky. Ct. App. 1996).
[138] Knowlton v. Ward, 899 S.W.2d 721 (Ark. 1994).

State Agency Authority

State agency authority over certain aspects of higher education has resulted in opposition to this agency action in the form of litigation. A number of questions surround the authority of state agencies to establish relationships with or regulate institutions of higher education. State agency authority also includes the areas of licensing and accreditation, which some states oversee directly and which other states have delegated to private voluntary accrediting agencies.

One case, in South Dakota, involved the jurisdiction of two state agencies over employment qualifications and removal at institutions of higher education within the state.[139] At issue was the State Department of Labor's claim of jurisdiction over public employees' labor disputes, particularly professional employees, at the state's postsecondary institutions. The state supreme court ruled that even though the state constitution gave the Board of Regents control over employment qualifications, salaries, and discharge of professional employees by non-conflicting statute, the Labor Relations Act[140] gave the Secretary of Labor jurisdiction over labor disputes of public employees through a grievance procedure.

In Kentucky, a court said that a county board of health could enforce state laws and regulations at a state university, but it did not have the authority to enforce local laws or enact local regulations against the university or any other state agency.[141]

In California, an appeals court ruled that a corporation, which held nursing review courses for state certification exams, must pay fees annually at each instructional site. Regulations requiring this fee stemmed from California's Council for Private Post Secondary and Vocational Education.[142]

Agency authority, then, is governed by state statutes and constitutional provisions. A determination of whether agency action is consistent with the law will include a review by the court of the intent of the law and past precedent. However, the court will not review decisions, that are within the agency's authority unless the decision ignored considerations mandated by statute or was an arbitrary or capricious decision.

---

[139] South Dakota Bd. of Regents v. Meierhenry, 351 N.W.2d 450 (S.D. 1984).

[140] S.D. Codified Laws Ann. Ch. § 3-18 et seq. (1969).

[141] Lexington-Fayette Urban County Bd. of Health v. Board of Trustees of Univ. of Ky., 879 S.W.2d 485 (Ky. 1994).

[142] RN Review for Nurses v. State, 28 Cal. Rptr. 2d 354 (Cal. Ct. App. 1994).

As mentioned earlier, state agency authority also includes the areas of licensing and accreditation. Most states have certain procedures in place in order to certify institutions to operate within their boundaries and to award degrees. Some states, however, have deferred this responsibility to private accrediting associations, other states license only non-accredited institutions, while some states maintain specific licensing procedures for all institutions operating within their boarders.

Occasionally, states develop procedures to regulate private educational institutions from other states or jurisdictions that attempt to establish a branch in a new jurisdiction. For example, one case involved the denial of a license to a Florida institution to award degrees in the District of Columbia because it failed to meet the District's licensing requirements.[143] The Educational Institution Licensure Commission, established by law, had been formed to certify that institutions meet certain statutory requirements, including those of "reasonable number and properly qualified faculty" and "suitable classroom, laboratory and library equipment."[144] The court affirmed the Commission's decision to deny a license to the Florida university in question because the university failed to show that it would provide adequate faculty and library resources in the District of Columbia.

In Massachusetts, a flurry of litigation has surrounded the accreditation of the Massachusetts School of Law at Andover, a private law school. This litigation includes an antitrust challenge to the American Bar Association's (ABA's) denial of accreditation to the school.[145] The ABA found, among other accreditation standards violations, that faculty salaries were too low and the student-faculty ratio was too high, probably due to the law school's large reliance on adjunct professors.[146] The law school, however, was unsuccessful in alleging that the ABA's accreditation standards were in violation of antitrust laws, namely section 1 of the Sherman Act,[147] because the court dismissed the suit for lack of personal jurisdiction over certain personally named defendants.[148]

A later case filed by the same law school in a different jurisdiction, again naming the ABA as a defendant, alleged unfair competition, fraud, deceit, tortious misrepresentation, and breach

---

[143] Nova Univ. v. Educational Inst. Licensure Comm'n, 483 A.2d 1172 (D.C. 1984).

[144] D.C. Code Ann. § 29-815 et seq. (1981), at 815.

[145] A. Portinga, *ABA Accreditation of Law Schools: An Antitrust Analysis*, UNIV. OF MICHIGAN J. OF L. REFORM, 29 (Fall 1995-Winter 1996): 635-70.

[146] P.J. Kolovos, *Antitrust Law and Nonprofit Organizations: The Law School Accreditation Case*, N.Y.U. L. REV., 71 (June 1996): 689-731.

[147] 15 U.S.C. § 1 (1994).

[148] Massachusetts Sch. of Law at Andover, Inc. v. American Bar Ass'n, 846 F. Supp. 374 (E.D. Pa. 1994).

of contract.[149] Here, the court said that it could assert jurisdiction under the Higher Education Act even though the law school neither sought nor received federal funds.

More recently, a federal district court granted summary judgment to the ABA, which the Third Circuit affirmed in this continuing litigation.[150] The court said that the ABA's accreditation standards were not a cause of state bar examination application requirements, that these bar examination requirements could not be the basis for antitrust liability, and that the school had not been injured by the ABA's faculty salary standards. The law school then sought to intervene in the government's antitrust suit against the ABA for purposes of appeal and for access to records.[151] Ultimately, the District of Columbia Circuit affirmed the portion of the lower court decision that denied the law school's intervention for appeals purposes but reversed the portion of the decision that had denied the law school access to certain information. The law school could then have access to information about the ABA that had been acquired in the course of the government's investigation. Litigation surrounding this law school and the ABA appears to continue to be unfolding.

In Nevada, a graduate of a non-accredited (proprietary) law school was denied a license to practice law. The reason for the denial was based on state rules which required attorneys licensed in Nevada to have graduated from law schools accredited by the American Bar Association (ABA). An exception would be granted, however, if the attorney could demonstrate a functional equivalence based on years of practice in another state. Although waivers had been granted to others in the state who had graduated from the same non-accredited law school, this particular graduate had no experience as an attorney and was, therefore, properly denied a license, the Supreme Court of Nevada said.[152]

In another case, an accrediting agency's relationship to a school was questioned. Certain Native American students sued an accrediting agency for monetary damages related to federally guaranteed student loans. The students argued that the accrediting agency was negligent in accrediting and failing to monitor the proprietary institute in which they were enrolled. The court, however, dismissed the suit because the plaintiffs failed to state a claim

---

[149] Massachusetts Sch. of Law at Andover, Inc. v. American Bar Ass'n, 914 F. Supp. 688 (D. Mass. 1996).

[150] Massachusetts Sch. of Law at Andover, Inc. v. American Bar Ass'n, 107 F.3d 1026 (3d. Cir. 1997).

[151] Massachusetts Sch. of Law at Andover, Inc. v. United States, 118 F.3d 776 (D.C. Cir. 1997).

[152] *In re* Amendola, 895 P.2d 1298 (Nev. 1995).

upon which relief could be granted. The appellate court affirmed, adding that the accrediting agency had no duty to students enrolled in an institute it had accredited.[153]

In the area of licensing, graduates of an Ohio college of massotherapy failed to demonstrate "minimally adequate performance" on the massage therapy licensing examination, and consequently the state medical board put the college on probation. The college sued, but the court found that the phrase "minimally adequate performance" was not vague and the board had reliable evidence to act in accordance with this language.[154]

Also in the area of licensing, after graduation from a four-year architecture program in New York, the graduate in question was denied a license to practice in Florida, where architects were required to graduate from five-year programs. The court said that even though the graduate held a license in a different jurisdiction, he was not qualified to be licensed in Florida.[155]

The above cases are examples of states' interest in protecting the public from fraudulent degrees through ensuring that institutions of higher education are accredited or licensed. The appropriate criteria set out by a state or by a private voluntary accrediting association used to evaluate higher education institutions has been upheld in the courts as long as licensing or accreditation decisions are not conducted in an arbitrary and capricious manner.

Boards of Trustees

Powers and duties possessed by boards of trustees or boards of regents will be determined, in the case of public institutions, by a state's constitution or its statutes. In the case of private institutions, it is determined by statutes regulating the charter of nonprofit, private corporations or educational institutions. A review of some of the cases involving board authority will enhance understanding of how limits are drawn on these organizations. In recent years litigation seems to gravitate toward one of two areas: membership of boards and the scope of boards' authority. Membership issues include the election and selection of board members; authority issues tend to focus on boards' decisions with respect to both academic and funding matters.

---

[153] Keams v. Tempe Technical Inst., Inc., 110 F.3d 44 (9th Cir. 1997.)

[154] Midwestern College of Massotherapy v. State Med. Bd. of Ohio, 670 N.E.2d 1074 (Ohio Ct. App. 1996).

[155] Cases v. Department of Business and Prof'l Regulation, Bd. of Architecture and Interior Design, 651 So.2d 772 (Fla. Dist. Ct. App. 1995).

Board Membership

As mentioned above, issues surrounding board membership can call into question concerns regarding members' election. For example, in Illinois, state legislation operated to terminate elected members of boards of trustees before the expiration of their term of office. The state supreme court found this legislation invalid under the state constitution because it did not allow the trustees to finish their term, thereby violating the right to vote guarantees present in the state constitution.[156]

Board members' selection, as opposed to their election, is a slightly different matter that has surfaced in the courts. In one case, the governor of Alabama appointed two trustees to a state university's board of trustees after they had been rejected by the state senate's confirmation committee. The Alabama Supreme Court held that because the state senate's statuary right of advice and consent resulted in senate rejection, the appointees had no authority to move into these trustee positions.[157]

In Mississippi, a court found that the Board of Trustees of State Institutions was an administrative part of the executive branch of state government and its members could be appointed, as they had been under state law. The plaintiff in this action, a private citizen, had argued that the trustees were a fourth branch of government and therefore voting was necessary to ensure adequate representation, as in the legislature. This argument, as noted above, failed.[158]

In Florida, a board appointed the state commissioner of education to the presidency of a public university. The state supreme court confirmed that this action was appropriate because no common law rule prohibited appointing a board member to a position within the system.[159]

Scope of Board Authority

Aside from questions of membership, the decisions of boards of trustees also are challenged. These decisions tend to deal with academic or funding matters. In the academic realm, a challenge to a decision made by a board of trustees in Illinois arose. A com-

---

[156] Tully v. Edgar, 664 N.E.2d 43 (Ill. 1996).
[157] Dunn v. Alabama State Univ. Bd. of Trustees, 628 So.2d 519 (Ala. 1993).
[158] Van Slyke v. Board of Trustees of State Insts. of Higher Learning, 613 So.2d 872 (Miss. 1993).
[159] State *ex rel.* Clayton v. Board of Regents, 635 So.2d 937 (Fla. 1994).

munity college board decided, for financial reasons, to discontinue over 500 academic courses of the college. Taxpayers were unsuccessful in their suit, which challenged the board's authority on this matter. An Illinois court confirmed that the board had the power to take this action for the financial reasons given.[160]

In another academic matter, the Board of Trustees of the City University of New York made certain retrenchment decisions, which included a reduction in the number of credits required to earn associate and baccalaureate degrees. Citizens challenged these retrenchment decisions, and the court ruled that the credit reduction was arbitrary and capricious. The court went on to say that other retrenchment decisions the board made, however, were within its power.[161]

In California, academic matters and board jurisdiction came together. A public community college and the state community college board planned to offer adult education programs without negotiating with the local school district. The school district challenged, but was not successful. The court found that the community college was not required to obtain agreement with the local school district before offering adult education programs.[162] Funding decisions is another area where the board is frequently challenged. For example, in California certain employees and a labor union questioned the decision of a community college's board of trustees to turn over the management of the school bookstore to a private company. The court, finding nothing in the state's Education Code prohibiting this special services contract with a private company, granted summary judgment in favor of the board of trustees.[163]

Another funding decision arose in Connecticut when the University of Bridgeport found itself in financial difficulty. As a result, its Board of Trustees decided that the institution would merge with the Professors' World Peace Academy to alleviate these difficulties. Many individuals challenged this decision, including one of the University's "life trustees." The Supreme Court of Connecticut, however, ruled that this "life trustee" did not have standing to challenge the decision because her position was honorary. There-

---

[160] Espinosa v. Board of Trustees of Community College Dist. No. 508, 632 N.E.2d 279 (Ill. App. Ct. 1994).

[161] Polishook v. City Univ. of N.Y., 651 N.Y.S.2d 459 (N.Y. App. Div. 1996).

[162] Orange Unified Sch. Dist. v. Rancho Santiago Community College Dist., 62 Cal. Rptr. 2d 778 (Cal. Ct. App. 1997).

[163] Service Employees Int'l Union, Local 715 v. Board of Trustees of the W. Valley/Mission Comm., 55 Cal. Rptr. 2d 44 (Cal. Ct. App. 1996).

fore, she did not enjoy the full management responsibilities and privileges of a regular trustee.[164]

In Texas, regents and other public officials adopted certain policies with respect to funding higher education. Mexican-American citizens who lived near the Mexican border unsuccessfully challenged these policies in a class action suit. The Supreme Court of Texas found that the funding formula used neither disadvantaged state citizens living in the border area, nor did it violate the U.S. Constitution.[165]

In a decision regarding funding in Colorado, a court affirmed that a publication of a state university's board of regents violated state law against using public funds for political activities because certain paragraphs advocated voting on two referenda. The holding was limited to these paragraphs, however, and did not apply to the publication as a whole.[166]

In Indiana, a public university's board of trustees paid a private foundation to perform fundraising activities. The State Board of Accounts sought access to this private foundation's corporate records under the state's Public Records Act. An appeals court denied access, ruling that the private foundation was not under the Board of Accounts jurisdiction. The court went on to say that private donations, although received for the benefit of the state university, were not public funds, and that the foundation's receipt of fees from the board of trustees was not a "grant or subsidy" from a public agency.[167] This case introduces the concept of sunshine laws, which will be discussed more fully in the next section.

Sunshine Laws

Sunshine laws are "laws which require that meetings of governmental agencies and departments be open to the public with reasonable access to the records of such proceedings."[168] These laws sometimes apply to public institutions of higher education. One author has dubbed the application of sunshine laws to higher education institutions a "trilemma" because the laws force a balance between three competing interests: those of the state institution, the public, and the individual.[169] That is, the institu-

---

[164] Steeneck v. University of Bridgeport, 668 A.2d 688 (Conn. 1995).

[165] Richards v. League of United Latin Am. Citizens, 868 S.W.2d 306 (Tex. 1993).

[166] Regents of the Univ. of Colo. v. Meyer, 899 P.2d 316 (Colo. Ct. App. 1995).

[167] State Bd. of Accounts v. Indiana Univ. Found., 647 N.E.2d 342 (Ind. Ct. App. 1995).

[168] BLACK'S LAW DICTIONARY (6th ed., 1990).

[169] H. Cleveland, *The Costs and Benefits of Openess: Sunshine Laws and Higher Education*, 12 J. C. & UNIV. L. 2 (1985).

tion needs to operate efficiently and effectively; the public has a right to know what is occurring in the institution as a governmental entity, a fundamental component of our democratic system; and individuals within the institution have rights to privacy. The outcomes of sunshine law litigation, then, attempt to strike a balance between institutional efficiency and effectiveness, public information, and individual privacy. Therefore, although the concept of openness, on which sunshine laws are based, is a noble one that has evolved through common law, it competes with the structure of higher education institutions and their operation.

These laws vary by state; the generic term "sunshine laws" more specifically refers to laws dedicated to freedom of information, public records, or open meetings. Their reach can extend deep into the institution's hierarchy. For example, "at one extreme, such as in the relatively closed state of Pennsylvania, only business meetings of the Board of Trustees or Regents must be open; at the other extreme, as in Florida, institutional committees, subcommittee, and/or advisory board committee meetings must be open as well. Thus, the Regents in Pennsylvania may meet in closed executive session, while, in Florida, any business transacted by Board Members within the Board's committee structure must be opened to the public. Nevada goes so far as to require the Board of Regents to establish and monitor open meeting laws for university student groups."[170]

Litigation attempts to define the boundaries of sunshine laws by determining the laws' reach into higher education institutions, the scope of what is covered under the law, and the exemptions to sunshine laws. Recently, sunshine law litigation, in addition to the more traditional disputes surrounding presidential selection and board activities, has come to include litigation on topics such as student records and disciplinary matters, campus safety and security issues, the intersection of public and private entities, and animal care, use, and experimentation. Although plaintiffs vary, newspapers and reporters often file suits.

Presidential and Board Activity

In Nebraska, the board of regents of a state university was found to not have violated open meeting laws. The board held a closed emergency meeting to discuss a personnel matter, the continuation of the university president. An appellate court found this meeting to be in compliance with the law.[171]

---

[170] H. Cleveland at 133.
[171] Meyer v. Board of Regents of Univ. of Neb., 510 N.W.2d 450 (Neb. Ct. App. 1993).

In Michigan, the board of regents served as the search committee for a new president. The committee chairman, after informal consultation with other board members, reduced the candidate list to a single finalist. Then, board members traveled to visit the finalist to interview him. This process was challenged under Michigan's freedom of information and open meeting laws, and was found to be in violation of both. The Supreme Court of Michigan ruled, with respect to the freedom of information claim, that the travel records had to be released, and with respect to the open meeting claim, that the informal consultation was equivalent to a vote and, therefore, violated the open meeting statute.[172]

Also in Michigan, a public university's board of trustees appointed a "Presidential Selection Committee" (PSC) that conducted private interviews with presidential candidates and gradually narrowed the list of candidates. A newspaper sued under the state's Opened Meeting Act (OMA) in order to gain access to information on these candidates. The appellate court agreed with the newspaper, ruling that the OMA applied to the PSC because the PSC's activities constituted "decisions" under the OMA. If the committee's activities had been found to be merely "ministerial," however, the OMA may not have applied.[173]

In New Jersey, a college board of trustees, meeting in closed session, granted a housing allowance to two vice presidents. Upon suit by a union, an appellate court ruled that the board had violated the state's Open Meeting Act. The court, however, entered judgment for the board because it had subsequently provided notice of an open meeting at which it ratified the vote, thereby correcting its error.[174]

Student Records and Disciplinary Matters

Litigation surrounding sunshine laws with respect to students surrounds the need to maintain student privacy. The privacy interests tested in court run the gamut from personal information to educational and disciplinary records. For example, in Illinois, a court ruled that release of names, addresses, and telephone numbers of a public university's incoming first-year students to an

---

[172] Booth Newspapers v. University of Mich. Bd. of Regents, 507 N.W.2d 422 (Mich. 1993).

[173] Federated Publications, Inc. v. Trustees of Mich. St. Univ., 561 N.W.2d 433 (Mich. Ct. App. 1997).

[174] Council of N.J. State College Locals v. Trenton State College Bd. of Trustees, 663 A.2d 664 (N.J. Super. Ct. Law Div. 1995).

off-campus housing provider was not an invasion of privacy under the state's Freedom of Information Act.[175]

Students and Discipline

Certain students in Illinois were awarded state legislator's scholarships. Newspapers and reporters were unsuccessful in their attempts to gain access to information about these students by suing under the state's Freedom of Information Act. The court said that not only was this information exempt from the Freedom of Information Act, it also was prohibited from disclosure under the federal Family Educational Rights and Privacy Act (FERPA).[176]

Student records not deemed to be "educational," however, were not protected in Ohio as a result of a suit brought by the editor of a student newspaper. The Supreme Court of Ohio ruled that records detailing student disciplinary proceedings, especially as they related to locations of incidents, types of offenses, the age and sex of students involved, and resulting disciplinary penalties, were required to be disclosed under the Ohio Public Records Act. Further, the court ruled that these records did not come under the protection of FERPA.[177]

Campus Safety and Security

Sunshine laws regarding safety tend to protect individual identities while communicating information surrounding the incidents in question. For example, in Ohio, an applicant to a state university threatened the university's admissions officer. A newspaper successfully sued to obtain access to letters and a police report regarding this matter. An appellate court ruled that the identities of uncharged suspects and confidential informants must be protected before release, however.[178]

In Georgia, the editor of a student newspaper requested a copy of a security report regarding an alleged rape of a university employee. An appellate court ruled that the editor was entitled to the report, but only after the institution removed the alleged victim's name and any other identifying information from the re-

---

[175] Lieber v. Southern Ill. Univ., 664 N.E.2d 1155 (Ill. Ct. App. 1996).
[176] Gibson v. Illinois St. Bd. of Educ., 683 N.E.2d 894 (Ill. App. Ct. 1997).
[177] State *ex rel.* The Miami Student v. Miami Univ., 680 N.E.2d 956 (Ohio 1997).
[178] State *ex rel.* Beacon Journal Publ'g Co. v. Kent State Univ., 623 N.E.2d 51 (Ohio 1993).

port in order to comply with the state's rape victim confidentiality statute.[179]

In Pennyslvania, a student newspaper sued to obtain the public safety records of a community college, but was unsuccessful because the Supreme Court of Pennsylvania ruled that the college was not a public agency under the state's Right to Know Act.[180]

Intersection of Public and Private Entities

Although at first blush it seems clear that sunshine laws apply only to public entities, the application of the law becomes more murky when public entities are merged with or subsumed by private entities.

Cornell University is a case in point. Although many people consider it strictly a private university, some colleges within the university exist by virtue of state statute. Suit was brought to determine Cornell's nature (public or private) and ultimately to determine whether sunshine laws would or would not apply to Cornell. Administrators, faculty, and students had filed complaints regarding Cornell's University Conduct Code. A professor sued under New York's freedom of information law to gain access to these complaints, but was not successful. The court found that this private university was not subject to New York's freedom of information law, even though state statutory colleges existed within it.[181]

Sometimes the debate arises with regard to an entity that exists outside of a university. In Illinois, a city and a private university formed a downtown development corporation. Taxpayers unsuccessfully sued to gain access to the new entity's documents. The court found that the corporation was subject to neither Illinois' Open Meeting Act nor its Freedom of Information Act.[182]

Disclosure of donor information was debated in two states, with different results reached in each. In Ohio, donors' names were considered public records when they had donated to a private corporation formed to benefit a public university.[183] In Florida, however, the names of donors who supported a public college via

---

[179] Doe v. Board of Regents of the Univ. of Ga., 452 S.E.2d 776 (Ga. Ct. App. 1994).
[180] Community College of Phila. v. Brown, 674 A.2d 670 (Pa. 1996).
[181] Stoll v. New York State College of Veterinary Med. at Cornell Univ., 652 N.Y.S.2d 478 (N.Y. Sup. Ct. 1996).
[182] Hopf v. Topcorp, 628 N.E.2d 311 (Ill. App. Ct. 1993).
[183] State *ex rel.* Toledo Blade Co. v. University of Toledo Found., 602 N.E.2d 1159 (Ohio 1992).

their contributions to a private foundation were not considered public records.[184] These two situations illustrate quite well the need to explore the scope of sunshine laws specific to the state in question when confronting a legal issue on these matters. As seen, similar scenarios in different states can yield opposite results based on varying state laws.

Animal Care, Use and Experimentation

Animal care, use, and experimentation is emerging as a litigious area and will most likely be tested further in the courts in coming years. Courts in Vermont and Indiana reached different results when ruling whether citizens could gain access to universities' animal care and use committees. Vermont, based on state sunshine laws, ruled in favor of citizens allowing access to committee proceedings.[185] Indiana ruled against access based on state laws.[186] In an Ohio case, the state supreme court ruled that, under a state public records act, a state university was required to disclose the names and addresses of its animal researchers, but was not required to release correspondence between its legal counsel and its employees.[187] In Washington, an animal rights group successfully gained access to unfunded research proposals under the State Public Records Act. In its decision, the Supreme Court of Washington also ruled that funded proposals must be made public as well; however, confidential financial information and information pertaining to rights, such as patents, may be deleted. The university was unsuccessful in its argument that academic freedom exempted the release of unfunded proposals.[188]

In New York, federal law required a state university to collect and submit information to the federal government. An animal rights group sued under the state's freedom of information law to obtain access to these records, but was not successful. The court said that the university's maintenance of records for federal pur-

---

[184] Palm Beach Community College Found. v. WFTV, 611 So.2d 588 (Fla. Dist. Ct. App. 1993).

[185] Animal Legal Defense Fund v. Institutional Animal Care & Use Comm. of the Univ. of Vt., 616 A.2d 224 (Vt. 1992).

[186] Robinson v. Indiana Univ., 638 N.E.2d 435 (Ind. Ct. App. 1994).

[187] State ex rel. Thomas v. Ohio State Univ., 643 N.E.2d 126 (Ohio 1994).

[188] Progressive Animal Welfare Society v. University of Wash., 884 P.2d 592 (Wash. 1994).

poses did not come within the scope of the state freedom of information law because the maintenance was not "performance of a governmental or proprietary function for the state."[189]

Citizens in Louisiana and Indiana also were unsuccessful in their attempts to obtain access to animal records. In Louisiana, like the New York case above, the court said that because federal law governed the Animal Care and Use committee's records, neither the state's Public Records nor Open Meeting Acts applied.[190] In Indiana, an appellate court ruled against the citizens who sued to obtain access to a university's animal research records, reasoning that the Public Records Act of that state exempted research protocols and applications from disclosure.[191]

Conclusion

Sunshine laws, then, can vary from state to state in their application to similar matters. It is important, with respect to higher education, to research the law for each state, especially in the areas of presidential selection and board activities, student records and disciplinary matters, campus safety and security issues, the intersection of public and private entities, and animal care, use and experimentation.

As described in this chapter, the actions of higher education institutions intersect with state law in the areas of state legislative and agency authority, including licensing and accreditation matters, boards of trustees, and sunshine laws. Although some general legal guidelines can be provided in these areas, no blanket rules should be assumed and the specific language of the laws of each state should be investigated before taking actions that could result in legal challenge. Higher education administrators should exercise due care to ensure that, to the best of their knowledge, they act within the boundaries of state law.

---

[189] Citizens for Alternatives to Animal Labs v. Board of Trustees of the State Univ. of N.Y., 658 N.Y.S.2d 653 (N.Y. App. Div. 1997).

[190] Dorson v. Louisiana, 657 So.2d 755 (La. Ct. App. 1995).

[191] Robinson v. Indiana Univ., 659 N.E.2d 153 (Ind. Ct. App. 1995).

CHAPTER IV

Faculty Employment Issues

Every year the courts rule on issues involving the nonrenewal of tenure track faculty contracts, denial of tenure, termination of tenured faculty for cause, and questions involving faculty speech and academic freedom. These faculty members were hired as probationary faculty under one- or multi-year contracts and are evaluated for the award of tenure at the end of a specific period, usually six years. If awarded tenure, the faculty member would be employed by the institution under a contract without term. However, many nontenured tenure track faculty (hereinafter referred to as "probationary faculty") are not successful in their quest for tenure. Some are denied tenure after a review by their peers under provisions defined in the faculty handbook. Others never get to the review process because their one-year contract is not renewed during the probationary period. Those granted tenure, although holding a contract without term, could be terminated for cause—i.e. for violations of institutional policies or failure to adequately perform their jobs. These employer actions of nonrenewal of contract, denial of tenure, and termination of tenured faculty for cause will sometimes involve allegations of violations of academic freedom or free speech. This chapter reviews the case law and legal issues for each of these employer actions and issues surrounding employee speech rights.

Faculty Property Rights or Liberty Interests

In questions of employee rights, the contract terms establish a property right. A property right is based on the concept of ownership or the reasonable expectation of receiving something of value. Therefore, the existence of a contract or the reasonable expectation of renewal of a contract is a property right mandating due process. Where the terms of the contract have been violated or where the relationship was terminated during the contract period, the faculty member may have been denied property. Denial of property by a public institution implicates constitutional provisions requiring due process.

Another right guaranteed by the Constitution is one's good name and reputation, referred to as a liberty interest. Allegations or institutional actions that impugn one's good name at a public institution implicate this liberty interest. Actions that implicate this liberty interest require a public entity to provide due process.

While private institutions do not specifically guarantee these constitutional provisions, contractual arrangements and current practices require private institutions to conform to similar requirements. Also, concepts of fundamental fairness have resulted in some private institutions gravitating toward those constitutional guarantees required by the public sector.

Faculty employment rights were addressed by the United States Supreme Court in two decisions. *Perry v. Sindermann*,[192] covered the issue of a tenured faculty member's property rights and established the applicability of institutional documents and policies in faculty employment cases. Perry had been on the faculty of Odessa Community College for ten years. While Odessa Community College claimed they did not have tenure, a statement in the faculty handbook guaranteed continued employment based on good performance. Thus, it appeared that the college may have granted tenure from the time the individual was first employed. Given this confusing situation, the Court looked to practices at other state institutions, past institutional practice and industry standards to determine Perry's contractual rights. All employment documents and past practices were applied to the definition of contractual obligations, but the Court speculated that, absent a clear definition of tenure policies, the "common law of a particular industry,"[193] in this case standards established by the Amerian Assoication of University Professors (AAUP), might be used as a guide in determining contractual arrangements. The court said that a property right existed because contractual obligations required due process before termination. From this contractual obligation it can be inferred that Perry had tenure.

In a companion case, *Board of Regents of State Colleges v. Roth*,[194] the Court found no obligations to probationary faculty extending beyond the period of the probationary contract. Roth was hired under a one-year-contract. He would have been evaluated to determine whether he should be awarded a contract without term or tenure during his fifth one-year contract at the state college. During his second one-year-contract and within the time frame

---

[192] 408 U.S. 593 (1972).
[193] *Id.* at 602.
[194] 408 U.S. 564 (1972).

required for notification of nonrenewal, he was notified without reasons that his contract would not be renewed. Absent a contract, no property right existed requiring due process. Further, the act of nonrenewal without publicly stating reasons for the employment decision did not stigmatize the employee from seeking other employment. Thus, there was no basis for a liberty interest claim. It is against this backdrop that recent litigation has further defined the rights and limitations of those rights held by probationary or tenured faculty.

The Nonrenewal of Probationary Faculty

The relationship between probationary faculty and the institution involves balancing the employee's rights against the organization's rights. On the one hand, an employer, by virtue of employing an individual, has acquired obligations to that employee, which are either expressly stipulated or implied in this employment relationship. However, an institution has an interest in achieving organizational success and integrity and must be given certain latitudes to accomplish these goals. A review of the legal issues surrounding the nonrenewal of probationary faculty will illuminate the courts' efforts to balance these sometimes competing interests. This section of the chapter reviews the binding nature of the contract and its sole governance of the rights of the employee with primary focus on the nonrenewal of a tenure track or probationary contract. Constitutional questions regarding nonrenewal of probationary faculty will lead off the discussion.

Constitutional Issues

Constitutional questions implicated in the nonrenewal of a probationary faculty member involve the existence of a property right or a liberty interest, the attempted revocation of which would mandate due process. Property rights emanate from the existence of a contract or contract provisions that obligate the institution to certain employment actions. Liberty interests involve statements that impugn one's reputation, also requiring due process.

The Ninth Circuit Court of Appeals issued a ruling in *Goodisman v. Lytle*,[195] which articulates the legal principles used to determine the rights of probationary faculty. Citing *Roth*,[196] the

---

[195] 724 F.2d 818 (9th Cir. 1984).
[196] 408 U.S. 564 (1972).

court found that a property right existed if there was a "legitimate claim of entitlement" to a contract or the job.[197] Citing *Sindermann*,[198] the court noted that a mere "subjective expectation" of contract renewal does not create a constitutionally protected interest.[199] The court also noted that procedural requirements do not transform an employee's unilateral expectation into a constitutionally protected interest unless the requirements were designed to limit decision-making discretion. The policies in this case, however, did not limit decision-making discretion, but rather outlined relevant criteria for consideration of the award of tenure such as teaching, research, service, and fit with departmental, disciplinary, and collegial interests. These guidelines did not go so far as to establish a property right to tenure; therefore, nonrenewal did not require the due process procedures of notice and a hearing.

The Fifth Circuit decided a case involving claims of both liberty and property interests in *Wells v. Doland*,[200] and affirmed the lower court's holding. The existence of a formal policy for the award of tenure did not substantiate the plaintiff's claim of *de facto* tenure or a claim to a property right. Further, the court ruled that the reasons for nonrenewal—the lack of a terminal degree, complaints about teaching, and lack of leadership—did not impose a stigma on the plaintiff, establishing a liberty interest that would preclude future employment. More recently, the court affirmed that position in *Spuler v. Pickar*.[201] The Fifth Circuit Court found that the faculty handbook enumeration of the procedures to achieve tenure did not create a property right to continued employment. Similarly, the First Circuit Court of Appeals in Massachusetts found that the illumination of the procedures for promotion and tenure gave a probationary faculty member no more than a unilateral subjective expectation of tenure, which does not implicate a property right requiring a hearing in a nonrenewal decision.[202] The same arguments were raised in several other cases, with the result that a probationary faculty member has no property right claim when the institution elected not to renew the contract.[203]

---

[197] Goodisman, 724 F.2d at 820.
[198] 408 U.S. 593 (1972).
[199] Goodisman, 724 F.2d at 821.
[200] 711 F.2d 670 (5th Cir. 1983).
[201] 958 F.2d 103 (5th Cir. 1992).
[202] Beitzell v. Jeffrey, 643 F.2d 870 (1st Cir. 1981).
[203] E.g.: Batra v. Board of Regents of Univ. of Neb., 79 F.3d 717 (8th Cir. 1996); Staheli v. University of Miss., 621 F. Supp. 449 (D.C. Miss. 1985), *aff'd*, 854 F.2d 121 (5th Cir. 1988); *see* LaVerne v. University of Tex. Sys., 611 F. Supp. 66 (S.D. Tex. 1985); Dominguez v. Babcock, 696 P.2d 338 (Colo. Ct. App. 1985); Montgomery v. Boshears, 698 F.2d 739 (5th Cir. 1983); Harrison v. A.B. Ayers, 673 F.2d 724 (4th Cir. 1982).

A number of courts also ruled that the nonrenewal decision did not produce a stigma resulting in the deprivation of a liberty interest.[204] *Bunger v. the University of Oklahoma Board of Regents*[205] is a case in point. In *Bunger*, two untenured faculty members claimed both property right and liberty interest violations in the institution's decision not to renew their probationary contracts. The court found that the procedural policies regarding faculty did not establish a property right to renewal of their contracts. In addition, the nonrenewal decision did not create a deprivation of liberty preventing the faculty members from pursuing their chosen careers. In Nebraska, a court found that the due process rights of a probationary faculty member were not violated.[206] He was notified of the nonrenewal decision within the appropriate time period, was given reasons for the nonrenewal upon his request, and was granted a hearing in front of an administrator to refute the reasons. The procedures followed not only encompassed due process requirements of notice and a hearing, but also conformed to the institution's policy for nonrenewal. A Utah court found that the change in the nonrenewal policy requiring a hearing did not apply retroactively to contracts executed prior to the enactment of the new policy.[207] However, a Delaware case points out that institutions must be consistent and conform to stated hiring goals.[208] While the institution provided a valid reason for the nonrenewal decision (upgrading of the academic credentials of the faculty), the terminated faculty member was able to prove the reason was pretextual because the institution's subsequent advertisement for the open position listed as qualifications those that had been held by the terminated employee.

The Appeals Process

Some institutions allow the probationary faculty member to appeal the nonrenewal decision. Authority to appeal a nonrenewal decision originates from the policies as outlined in the faculty handbook or other institutional policies or state statutes. There is no universal due process right requiring an appeal of the nonrenewal

---

[204] Staheli v. University of Miss., 621 F. Supp. 449 (D.C. Miss. 1985), *aff'd*, 854 F.2d 121 (5th Cir. 1988); House v. University of Cent. Ark. *ex ref.* Bd. of Trustees of Univ. of Cent. Ark., 684 F. Supp. 222 (E.D. Ark. 1988); Dominguez v. Babcock, 696 P.2d 338 (Colo. Ct. App. 1985); LaVerne v. University of Tex. Sys., 611 F. Supp. 66 (S.D. Tex. 1985).

[205] 95 F.3d 987 (10th Cir. 1996).

[206] O'Connor v. Peru State College, 605 F. Supp. 753 (D. Neb. 1985), *aff'd*, 781 F.2d 632 (8th Cir. 1986).

[207] Moore v. Utah Technical College, 727 P.2d 634 (Utah 1986).

[208] Ohemeng v. Delaware State College, 676 F. Supp. 65 (D. Del. 1988), *aff'd*, 862 F.2d 309 (3d Cir. 1988).

decision. The structure of this appeals process varies from institution to institution—some might form a separate appeals committee, while others might use the grievance process existing at the institution. In *Simonel v. North Carolina School of the Arts*,[209] a faculty member appealed the nonrenewal decision using the college's grievance procedures. The college's policies provided that the grievance committee would decide whether the decision not to renew was based on impermissible grounds. The grievance committee found that the chancellor's decision not to renew the faculty member was based on personal malice. The court found that the chancellor who reviewed the grievance committee report and rejected it exceeded his authority under institutional policies. The policy did not provide for a review of the grievance committee finding by the Chancellor; therefore, the grievance committee report simply should have been accepted by the institution.

Discrimination Claims

The nonrenewal decision has resulted in claims of discrimination based on race, gender, and national origin under title VII of the Civil Rights Act of 1964.[210] In these cases, the courts have looked at the rights of a probationary faculty member from a different perspective. While reasons need not be given in the nonrenewal decision, in these cases the court will analyze the reasons to determine whether discrimination was in fact the basis for the negative decision.

Under a collective bargaining agreement, a Pennsylvania public college had established a renewal procedure for probationary faculty's contracts. A female probationary faculty member, plagued with low student evaluations of her teaching, failed to sign faculty evaluation committee evaluation reports. She was notified during the third contract year that her contract would not be renewed. In her unsuccessful claim brought in federal court under title VII, the court found[211] she failed to: establish a prima facie case of race discrimination; to establish that the proffered reasons for the employment decision were either a pretext for discrimination, or that discrimination was the motivating factor in the decision; and failed to establish a prima facie case for disparate impact.[212]

---

[209] 460 S.E.2d 194 (N.C. Ct. App. 1995).

[210] This section will deal only with examples of the nonrenewal of probationary faculty. A more extensive coverage of title VII as it impacts other employment decisions will be discussed in Chapter V.

[211] Elmore v. Clarion Univ. of Pa., 933 F. Supp. 1237 (M.D. Pa. 1996).

[212] For a discussion of Disparate Impact and Disparate Treatment under title VII see Chapter V.

In *Jiminez v. Mary Washington College*,[213] a black West Indies probationary faculty member sued when he was offered a terminal contract just short of review for tenure. He claimed both race and national origin discrimination under title VII. The plaintiff failed to establish that student evaluations of his teaching were tainted with discriminatory intent by white students, nor had the institution knowingly or improperly used tainted evaluations of teaching. His failure to obtain a Ph.D. degree was not a pretext for discrimination in the terminal contract decision, the court said. Similarly, an Asian professor failed to establish a prima facie case of race and ethnic discrimination in a Puerto Rico institution's decision not to renew his probationary contract.[214] When institutions decide not to renew the contract of probationary faculty who are eligible to bring a title VII claim because of the individual's race, ethnic background, or gender, the institution can prevail as long as the decision was not a pretext for discrimination. Decisions based on valid reasons that go to the probationary faculty member's performance of the job have been viewed by courts as free of discrimination.

Contract Terms

The terms of a contract between a probationary faculty member and an institution form the basis upon which courts have decided whether the rights of the tenure track employee have been violated.[215] The contract includes not only the letter of appointment, but also the faculty handbook, policy documents governing employment, and employment practices. The courts have consistently looked to these documents and institutional employment practices to determine the rights of the employee in nonrenewal or denial of tenure cases. The question of whether probationary faculty members are entitled to renewal of their one-year contracts during the stipulated probationary period were litigated in the federal courts. In Michigan, a faculty member was offered several successive one-year contracts that stated at the fifth year of employment, the faculty member would be evaluated for tenure.[216] After two years, he was notified that his third-year contract would not be renewed. He sued the institution, alleging that the letter's language specifying when a tenure review would take place guar-

---

[213] 57 F.3d 369 (4th Cir. 1995).

[214] Ombe v. Fernandez, 914 F. Supp. 782 (D. P.R. 1996).

[215] R. Hendrickson & B. Lee, ACADEMIC EMPLOYMENT AND RETRENCHMENT: JUDICIAL REVIEW AND ADMINISTRATIVE ACTION (1983).

[216] Upadhya v. Langenberg, 834 F.2d 661 (7th Cir. 1987).

anteed him five one-year contracts. The Seventh Circuit Court of Appeals found that each contract was issued for a one-year period and that the institution was not obligated to renew the contract for five years because it stipulated when a review for the award of tenure would take place.

A case involving a private university illustrates another example.[217] The probationary faculty member was offered a one-year contract with the understanding that after four probationary contracts he would be eligible for tenure. During his second year, before the date required in the institution's policies, he was notified that his contract would not be renewed. The notice was provided both verbally and by a certified letter that he refused to accept. The court rejected both his breach of contract and failure to notify claims. The court reasoned that his contract was clearly a one-year contract and nonrenewal did not breach it. The promise of four probationary contracts, the contract letter, and the faculty handbook, in the court's opinion, clearly spelled out the institution's intent to offer a one-year contract with no guarantee of renewal because the employee was a probationary faculty member. These written documents take precedence over any oral promises or statements.

Written language in letters and contracts will supersede any alleged oral promise of the award of tenure.[218] In Pennsylvania, a probationary faculty member was unsuccessful in his claim of guaranteed renewal of a two-year contract. The court found that the faculty handbook defined the contract period as "terminal" and guaranteed "consideration" for reappointment, not reappointment.[219] Oral statements about the possibility of reappointment were insufficient to obligate the institution beyond the terms spelled out in the contract. A similar situation arose in the Maryland case *Johns Hopkins University v. Ritter*.[220] A husband and wife, both full professors, were recruited to join the medical school at Johns Hopkins. The head of the department assured them that even though they were hired as visiting faculty, their positions as full professors with tenure were assured after the promotion and tenure process was completed. However, at the beginning of their one-year contract, problems developed between the couple and other department and college faculty. Before the tenure decision was finalized, a decision was made not to renew their contract.

---

[217] Dorsey v. Clark Atlantic Univ., 481 S.E.2d 848 (Ga. Ct. App. 1997).

[218] *See* Ozerol v. Howard Univ., 545 A.2d 638 (D.C. 1988); Gottlieb v. Tulane Univ. of La., 529 So.2d 128 (La. Ct. App. 1988), on remand from the Fifth Circuit, 809 F.2d 278 (5th Cir. 1987).

[219] Baker v. Lafayette College, 504 A.2d 247 (Pa. Super. Ct. 1986) at 254, *aff'd*, 532 A.2d 399 (Pa. 1987).

[220] 689 A.2d 91 (Md. Ct. Spec. App. 1997).

They sued, claiming they had a binding contract with the department head to receive a professorship with tenure. The trial court ruled for the plaintiffs, and The Special Court of Appeals of Maryland reversed. The appellate court found the department head could not bind the institution to an award of tenure, nor could he render the procedures under which tenure is awarded as a mere formality. The written provisions of the contract clearly superseded any oral promise.

An institution's obligation to review a faculty member during the probationary period has also been litigated. A case at the University of Louisville involved a pending decision of a grievance committee on the final disposition of a faculty member's tenure status, where a grievance was filed for failure to evaluate the faculty member's performance.[221] The court found that absent a final decision on the part of the grievance committee, this suit for injunctive relief was premature. It would appear from this case, however, that stipulations in institutional documents to evaluate performance during the probationary period obligate the institution to conduct such evaluations. A probationary faculty member's right to renewal is not implicated simply because a review process exists; institutional obligations do not go beyond what is stipulated in the contract.

The courts have typically relied on institutional policies and contract obligations to define the nature of the nonrenewal decision and the decision not to renew. The Tenth Circuit Court found that a probationary faculty member's due process rights were violated when a contract was withdrawn after the date for notification of renewal had passed.[222] The institutional policies defined a date that notification of the renewal decision for a one-year probationary contract must occur. After the institution offered to renew the contract by the prescribed date, final execution of the contract became embroiled in controversy. Based on the controversy, the vice president withdrew the offer and the probationary faculty member sued. The court said that institutions must operate within their policies governing the nonrenewal decision.

The nature of who makes the employment decision has also been litigated. In a college where a statute grants sole authority to the board for the hiring and firing of faculty, the board must take specific action not to renew a probationary faculty member's con-

---

[221] Ashley v. University of Louisville, 723 S.W.2d 866 (Ky. Ct. App. 1986).
[222] Calhoun v. Gaines, 982 F.2d 1470 (10th Cir. 1992).

tract.[223] Further, board hiring and firing powers cannot be superseded by a collective bargaining agreement.[224]

Several other nonrenewal cases involved the timely notice of nonrenewal of a probationary contract as required in faculty employment policy manuals. With timely notice, the institution's actions were upheld by state courts.[225] Failure to give timely notice raises the issue of *de facto* tenure.[226]

De facto Tenure

The renewal of a number of one-year contracts which exceeded the years in service required to achieve tenure by the institution, may yield arguments that the institution has awarded tenure by default. In one instance, a probationary faculty member received a terminal contract after being recommended twice for tenure by the Dean of Humanities.[227] The Fifth Circuit Court of Appeals found that recommendations to award tenure did not result in the acquisition of *de facto* tenure. In Maryland, a faculty member held the rank of instructor without tenure from 1972 through 1990 when she became a probationary assistant professor. In 1987 the institution changed its tenure policy, removing the option that an instructor could be tenured, but grandfathered in all those instructors who held tenure at that time. When the probationary faculty member was denied tenure, she claimed that she had acquired *de facto* tenure under the pre-1987 policies.[228] The Court of Special Appeals of Maryland found that theories of *de facto* tenure were not available where the institution had formal written policies governing the award of tenure. Further, the court found that there was no evidence that the policy the faculty member relied on for her claim was incorporated into her one contract as an instructor. In a Virginia case, a probationary faculty member claimed entitlement to tenure because the institution had renewed the faculty member's contracts uniformly for nine years.[229] The court found that renewing contracts over a nine-year period did not yield a finding of *de facto* tenure. This institution had a

---

[223] Blanchard v. Lansing Community College, 370 N.W.2d 23 (Mich. Ct. App. 1985).

[224] Board of Trustees of Community College Dist. 508 v. Cook County College Teachers Union, Local 1600 AFT, AFL-CIO, 522 N.E.2d 93 (Ill. App. Ct. 1987); Williams v. Weaver, 495 N.E.2d 1147 (Ill. App. Ct. 1986).

[225] Brown v. North Dakota State Univ., 372 N.W.2d 879 (N.D. 1985); Smith v. State, 389 N.W.2d 808 (N.D. 1986); Dominguez v. Babcock, 696 P.2d 338 (Colo. Ct. App. 1985); Dorsey v. Clark Atlantic Univ., 481 S.E.2d 848 (Ga. Ct. App. 1997).

[226] *See* Howard Univ. v. Best, 547 A.2d 144 (D.C. 1988).

[227] Wells v. Doland, 711 F.2d 670 (5th Cir. 1983).

[228] Marriot v. Cole, 694 A.2d 123 (Md. Ct. Spec. App. 1997).

[229] Sabet v. Eastern Va. Medical Auth., 775 F.2d 1266 (4th Cir. 1985).

clearly defined tenure policy which awarded tenure for a stipulated contract period (five years for full professors, three years for
associate professors, and two years for assistant professors). Therefore, nonrenewal at the end of the contract period yielded no
institutional obligations to the former employee.

The clarity of tenure policies in the cases above removed the
threat of a finding of *de facto* tenure. Clarity of policies also was
evident in a private college case.[230] The court found that a faculty
member had not achieved *de facto* tenure after receiving ten one-
year contracts while holding probationary faculty status. The court
found that the college, while endorsing the AAUP policies on promotion and tenure, added two important caveats to the faculty
handbook. First, the handbook stated that only the board had the
authority to grant tenure, and second, tenure or promotion could
not be acquired automatically at the institution. Clarity of policy
was also present in a Louisiana case when a faculty member, who
had been given several contracts as a visiting professor, claimed
that his contract had been renewed for five years, giving him *de
facto* tenure.[231] The court found that the contract clearly stated
that time under a visiting professor's contract could not be ac-
crued as contract years toward tenure. In another case, a faculty
member who refused a half-time, seventh-year contract offered
because of financial exigency could claim neither tenure nor the
right to a full-time contract because the part-time contract had been
offered.[232] These types of contracts and obligations were clearly
differentiated in the institution's policies and letters of appointment.

Breach of Contract

In nonrenewal cases, a breach of contract is usually based on
allegations that the terms of the contract have not been fulfilled.
An employer's alleged breached duties under the contract can
range from an expected duty of an award of tenure, to timely notice of nonrenewal of the contract, to a claim of due process rights.
A good example of a breach of duty under a contract was present
in the case *Gladney v. Thomas*,[233] decided by a federal district court
in Alabama. The plaintiff held a joint appointment that emphasized teaching. The College of Arts and Sciences recommended
denial of tenure after finding her research record, while substan-

---

[230] Hill v. Talladega College, 502 So.2d 735 (Ala. 1987).
[231] Tetlow v. Loyola Univ., 483 So.2d 1242 (La. Ct. App. 1986).
[232] Sacchini v. Dickinson State College, 338 N.W.2d 81 (N.D. 1983).
[233] 573 F. Supp. 1232 (W.D. Ala. 1983).

tial, to be deficient. The academic vice president, in a letter granting a one-year extension, stated that an improvement in her research record would yield a positive decision in her quest for tenure. She had two more articles published the next year, but was still denied tenure. The court found that the year extension was either a bad faith contract or a breach of contract. If the institution entered into the contract for the extension year with the opinion that it was impossible to improve the research record in one year, they formulated a bad faith contract. Since she had improved her research record in the time stipulated in the contract, denial of tenure was a breach of that agreement. However, this case should not be interpreted as obligating institutions to formalize the criteria with which to evaluate performance. In New York, a state court of appeals found that the formalization of the criteria used to evaluate performance of probationary faculty did not limit the right of the institution to elect nonrenewal of the contract.[234] Nor did the formalized procedures result in a breach of the contract when the institution decided not to renew a contract.

Clarity of the institutional policy and appointment letters are the final arbitrator in breach of contract claims. In a University of Texas case, the court found that the plaintiff had not acquired tenure, as *de facto* tenure was specifically prohibited by institutional policy and the contract language gave no expectation of tenure.[235] However, in Illinois, an appeals court found that letters negotiating the terms of the employment offer stipulating that, based on satisfactory service, a tenure application would be submitted at the end of the first year, were part of the contract.[236] At the end of the year, the dean failed to submit the faculty member's credentials for tenure review, thereby breaching the contract. The court affirmed the lower court's award of a set amount for damages because the plaintiff should have been granted tenure, not sent a nonrenewal notice a year later.

The claim of a breach of contract, where tenure was denied to probationary faculty after a review, has been litigated on several occasions. At Fordham University, the federal district court found that the procedures followed, which conformed to the school's policies, and the reasons for denial (the department's tenure quota and the faculty member's poor relational skills) did not constitute a breach of contact.[237] However, in Arizona, a state appeals court

---

[234] Brumbach v. Rensselear Polytechnic Inst., 510 N.Y.S.2d 762 (N.Y. App. Div. 1987).
[235] LaVerne v. University of Tex. Sys., 611 F. Supp. 66 (S.D. Tex. 1985).
[236] Lewis v. Loyola Univ. of Chicago, 500 N.E.2d 47 (Ill. App. Ct. 1986).
[237] Waring v. Fordham Univ., 640 F. Supp. 42 (S.D.N.Y. 1986).

found that an institution had breached its contract when it failed to review the plaintiff in his sixth year as stipulated in institutional documents.[238] In two other cases, the court rejected the plaintiff's claim involving a breach of contract.[239] In one of these cases, the probationary faculty member was notified that his next contract would be his final contract, even though during that final contract year he would have become eligible for review, but had not been reviewed for tenure.[240]

Failure to give timely notice was another issue litigated under breach of contract claims. In an Oregon case, the court found a contract had not been breached when the written notice was received after the notice deadline stipulated in the contract.[241] The plaintiff's attendance and testimony before the board in the meeting where the nonrenewal decision was made, was determined by the court to be evidence of timely notice in this case. A Mississippi court found that a contract was breached when the notice of nonrenewal was twenty-eight days late, but failed to award damages because the plaintiff could not show that he could have maintained his current salary level in his new job if the notice had been timely.[242] Another court, however, found that a District of Columbia institution had breached its contract when it failed to give timely notice of nonrenewal, but reversed the lower court's decision awarding tenure and remanded the question of tenure, ordering a trial on the merits.[243]

Termination during the contract period also has resulted in breach claims. In Vermont, an institution attempted to force the resignation of a faculty member in the middle of a two-year contract. The court found that the contract had been breached by this action, but refused to award damages because a retraction of the termination took place before there was a material change in plaintiff's employment status.[244] In *Skehan v. State System of Higher Education*,[245] the court found that the dismissal of a nontenured faculty member for cause in the middle of the contract period, following adequate due process procedures, was not a breach of contract. The plaintiff in this case, litigated since 1972, claimed a

---

[238] Smith v. University of Ariz. *ex rel.* Bd. of Regents, 672 P.2d 187 (Ariz. Ct. App. 1983).
[239] Batla v. North Dakota State Univ., 370 N.W.2d 554 (N.D. 1985); Stensrud v. Mayville State College, 368 N.W.2d 519 (N.D. 1985).
[240] Batla, *supra* note 48.
[241] Boyce v. Umpqua Community College, 680 P.2d 671 (Cir. Ct. App. 1984).
[242] Robinson v. Board of Trustees of East Cent. Junior College, 477 So.2d 1352 (Miss. 1985).
[243] Howard Univ. v. Best, 484 A.2d 958 (D.C. 1984).
[244] Lowe v. Beaty, 485 A.2d 1255 (Vt. 1984).
[245] 815 F.2d 244 (3d Cir. 1987).

breach because the procedures used did not conform to those spelled out for the removal of tenured faculty for cause, an argument not endorsed by the court. This decision, however, would not be the end to this litigation. The court of Common Pleas of Pennsylvania ruled that the professor's legal action was barred by *res judicata*.[246] After the college attempted to get an injunction preventing him from coming to campus and teaching classes not assigned to him, Skehan sued.

Conclusions on Nonrenewal

A review of the case law surrounding the nonrenewal of probationary faculty illustrates the courts' search for a balance between the sometimes competing rights of the employer and the employee. While the nonrenewal decision usually does not require reasons for the decision unless required by institutional policy, cases involving discrimination under title VII mandate divulging the reasons surrounding the nonrenewal decision. Valid reasons free of discriminatory intent will free the institution from violating a probationary faculty member's civil rights. Courts use terms of the contract of probationary faculty to determine what rights exist in matters of nonrenewal. Courts have refused to give probationary faculty a property right requiring due process unless the terms of the contract so stipulate. Thus, in most cases, a probationary faculty member's contract does not require due process in nonrenewal except for timely notice. Further, the terms of the contract will determine whether a faculty member has acquired the right to an appeal or a tenure review process. Courts have exhibited caution in becoming involved in the nonrenewal decision, and have shown an interest in protecting the academic decision making process.

Denial of Tenure

Each year, probationary faculty who are at the end of their probationary period are reviewed for the possible award of tenure. In the last decade, the number of tenure positions at institutions have decreased, and the qualifications for the award of tenure have become more stringent. At the same time, institutional affirmative action policies and federal laws have opened

---

[246] Commonwealth *ex rel*. Bloomsburg State College v. Porter, 610 A.2d 516 (Pa. Comm. Ct. 1992).

the process of tenure review to court scrutiny.[247] Litigation surrounding the denial of tenure has been extensive. In light of this litigation, careful institutional review of policies is important to not only protect concepts of fundamental fairness, but also to improve managerial effectiveness in monitoring the tenure review process.

The Review Process

Courts have found that a probationary faculty member has no expectation of continuous employment implicating a liberty or property interest requiring due process in the denial of tenure.[248] Institutional policies and the particular contract in question dictate the requirements to be followed in a probationary faculty member's tenure review.

For example, a Minnesota court reversed a lower court ruling unfavorable to a probationary faculty member.[249] The probationary faculty member was supported at each level, but there were some negative votes and abstentions. The department in her case solicited letters from 40 external reviewers, when the usual number of solicitations was 3 to 6. The provost, when reviewing her dossier, interpreted the negative votes and abstentions as failure to prove a "compelling case for tenure." The court, reversing, found the tenure procedures to be improper and arbitrary and capricious.

On the other hand, the First Circuit Court of the United States Court of Appeals found no procedural or arbitrary or capricious action when a faculty member was denied tenure.[250] The tenure application came before the department faculty whose vote was evenly split for and against tenure. The college committee, following a subcommittee recommendation, voted to deny tenure and the administration, at the faculty member's request, refused to intervene. The court found that the faculty member failed to state a cognizable claim. In another case, an Oklahoma court found that under state law, the board was authorized to set policies for promotion and tenure and found that the institution could apply a new policy uniformly to all faculty members eligible for review, even if the faculty member's contract was executed under a dif-

---

[247] R. Hendrickson & B. Lee, ACADEMIC EMPLOYMENT AND RETRENCHMENT JUDICIAL REVIEW AND ADMINISTRATIVE ACTION (1983).

[248] E.g., Beville v. South Dakota Bd. of Regents, 687 F. Supp. 464 (D.S.D. 1988); Staheli v. University of Miss., 854 F.2d 121 (5th Cir. 1988).

[249] Ganguli v. University of Minn., 512 N.W.2d 918 (Minn. Ct. App. 1994).

[250] Spiegel v. Trustees of Tufts College, 843 F.2d 38 (1st Cir. 1988).

ferent policy.[251] A Wisconsin court found that an individual denied tenure in the sixth year was not entitled to another review in the seventh year under the institution's policies governing review.[252] An Alaska court found that tenure review decisions come under provisions of the state's sunshine laws. Failure to conduct the review in the sunshine resulted in a court order to reinstate the faculty member for one year with the appropriate opened tenure review to be conducted during that year.[253]

The entitlement to an award of tenure resulting from an institution's failure to conform to the policies governing the review process also has been litigated. The Fifth Circuit Court of Appeals found that consideration of a professor's lenient grading policy in denying tenure did not violate the Equal Protection Clause even where other faculty's grading policies were not considered in their tenure reviews.[254] However, in a state case where tenure was denied, on appeal, the hearing agent found that the tenure review was tainted because the plaintiff was not allowed to defend himself against letters detailing negative incidents with a social service agency. The state supreme court affirmed a hearing agent's order of reinstatement as a probationary faculty member for one year and reevaluation for tenure. The court agreed that while the faculty member was not entitled to an award of tenure he was entitled to a new and fair tenure review.[255] An Iowa court, however, found that the issue of award of tenure should be remanded for adjudication. A hearing panel had found that the actions of a probationary faculty member's peers were unreasonable and recommended the award of tenure, but the president awarded two more years of probationary status and a new evaluation within that period. On remand from the Iowa Supreme Court was the question of whether the tenure policies obligated the award of tenure based on the hearing agent's finding rather than another tenure review.[256] Several cases support the notion that a new tenure review free of procedural flaws will be upheld by the courts. In New York, a court ruled that a faculty member was given due process when the institution followed its review policies in a new tenure review negotiated in a settlement agreement.[257] In New Jersey, a court found the plaintiff's charges that the ordered review process was biased and, therefore, futile, could not be

---

[251] Randolph v. Board of Regents of Okla. Colleges, 648 P.2d 825 (Okla. 1982).

[252] Pfeiffer v. Board of Regents of Univ. of Wis. Sys., 328 N.W.2d 279 (Wis. 1983).

[253] University of Alaska v. Ceistauts, 666 P.2d 424 (Alaska 1983).

[254] Levi v. University of Tex. at San Antonio, 840 F.2d 277 (5th Cir 1988).

[255] State ex rel. Norton v. Stone, 313 S.E.2d 456 (W. Va. 1984).

[256] Black v. University of Iowa, 362 N.W.2d 459 (Iowa 1985)

[257] Chen v. Wharton, 492 N.Y.S.2d 494 (App. Div. 1985).

determined until the process was completed.[258] A South Carolina court found that tenure need not be granted where a faculty member was reinstated and a new review ordered when error was found by a grievance committee in the original tenure evaluation process.[259]

These cases point to the fact that absent a policy awarding tenure due to a faulty review process, the courts will not award tenure. These decisions are in keeping with other court rulings where a property right exists mandating due process. The contract gives the faculty member the right to a procedure consistent with institutional policy and fundamental fairness but not automatic tenure where the prescribed procedure is not followed.

Access to Review Materials

The issue of whether a probationary faculty member alleging civil rights violations can gain access to peer review materials (letters of evaluation of the candidate by peers in the field) was before the courts in a number of cases. The controlling case, decided by the United States Supreme Court in 1990, is *The University of Pennsylvania v. The Equal Employment Opportunity Commission*.[260] A faculty member alleged that she was denied tenure based on her gender and national origin. She maintained that she was better qualified than five male faculty members who received tenure. The University refused to comply with an Equal Employment Opportunities Commission (EEOC) order to grant the plaintiff and the EEOC access to confidential peer review files on the plaintiff and male faculty. The institution stated that it had denied tenure because it did not possess a need for a person with the plaintiff's research specialty: Chinese-related research. The University argued for a balancing approach "reflecting the constitutional and societal interest inherent in the peer review process." The institution contended that the intrusiveness of the EEOC's investigatory efforts needed to be minimized in the interest of protecting the integrity of the peer review process. This contention was based on the common law protection of the confidentiality of documents such as reference letters and the First Amendment right of academic freedom.[261]

---

[258] Snitow v. Rutgers Univ., 510 A.2d 1118 (N.J. 1986).
[259] Storrer v. University of S.C., 343 S.E.2d 664 (S.C. Ct. App. 1986).
[260] 110 S. Ct. 577 (U.S. 1990).
[261] *Id.* at 580.

The Court found that Congress, in formulating title VII, granted access to employment information at academic institutions and specifically chose not to exempt this information from the reach of the EEOC.[262] While agreeing that higher education institutions are important to society and that the confidentiality of references must be protected, the court found that the balance weighted more heavily toward the need to prevent discrimination in tenure decisions. The Court stated: "Indeed, if there is a smoking gun to be found that demonstrates discrimination in tenure decisions, it is likely to be tucked away in the peer review files."[263] The Court viewed as speculation the University's contention that the peer review process would be compromised. The Court, however, emphasized the continued endorsement of academic privilege in academic decisions: ...[C]ourts have stressed the importance of avoiding second-guessing in legitimate academic judgments. This Court itself cautioned that judges...should show great respect for faculty's professional judgment.... *Nothing we say today should be understood as a retreat from the principle of respect for legitimate academic decision making* (emphasis added).[264]

This Supreme Court ruling is consistent with an earlier ruling in a lower court involving Franklin and Marshall College.[265] A probationary faculty member of French origin was denied tenure, and subsequently filed a complaint with the EEOC, alleging discrimination on the basis of national origin. The EEOC asked for not only the confidential peer review materials, but also for the records of other tenure decisions made since 1977. The institution maintained that absent an impermissible consideration, the information was protected by academic privilege. It based this argument on two other federal circuit court decisions.[266] The EEOC, basing its argument on a decision in the Fifth Circuit Court of Appeals, argued that impermissible considerations could not be discovered without access to this information where discrimination has been charged.[267] The Third Circuit Court of Appeals, agreeing with the EEOC argument, ruled that the institution should be compelled to provide the requested relevant documentation under a court-monitored guarantee of confidentiality of personnel records.

---

[262] *Id*. at 582.

[263] *Id*. at 584.

[264] *Id*. at 587.

[265] EEOC v. Franklin and Marshall College, 775 F.2d 110 (3d Cir. 1985), *cert. denied*, 106 S. Ct. 2288 (1986).

[266] EEOC v. University of Notre Dame—Du Lac, 715 F.2d 331 (7th Cir. 1983); Gray v. Board of Higher Educ., City Univ. of N.Y., 692 F.2d 901 (2d Cir. 1982).

[267] *In re* Dinnan, 661 F.2d 426 (5th Cir. 1981), Dinnan v. Blaubergs, *cert. denied*, 457 U.S. 1106 (1982).

In a federal rules decision, the Seventh Circuit Court of Appeals further clarified occasions when academic privilege is superseded by the need for access to material used in the tenure decision. The court ruled that the files of other tenure decisions within a reasonable time frame were relevant information to which the regulatory agency should be given access.[268] Recently, the courts seem fairly consistent in their willingness to give access to peer review materials in cases alleging discrimination. For example, a federal district court ruled that in a case alleging gender discrimination in the denial of tenure, the plaintiff faculty member was entitled to discovery[269] of the identities of peer reviewers from her dossier and recently tenured male faculty.[270] A federal district court in New York, however, denied a law professor access to the review files of another probationary faculty member awarded tenure.[271] The court found access to the files to be irrelevant to his free speech retaliation claim.

Other recent cases have emulated these decisions. In a case involving allegations of discrimination on the basis of sex, a federal district court affirmed a magistrate's denial of access to non-faculty employment records and student records. The court stated that these records were irrelevant to the charges made, but did grant access to the tenure decisions of male faculty made within the past ten years, as these would be relevant to the allegations.[272] A Minnesota court found that a faculty member was entitled, during litigation, to discover tenure review files and relevant personnel files.[273] In a New Jersey case, a black probationary faculty member was granted access to review materials because access was important to the substantiation of a *prima facie* case. Confidentiality of outside reviewer's letters of recommendation, however, were protected by excision of the authors' names.[274] Two Pennsylvania cases affirmed a state labor relation department's ruling that tenure evaluations were "performance evaluations." The commonwealth court concluded that a faculty member should have the right to inspect such "performance evaluations," and

---

[268] Namenwirth v. Board of Regents of Univ. of Wis. Sys., 769 F.2d 1235 (7th Cir. 1985).

[269] Discovery Trial Practice: The disclosure by the defendant of facts, titles, documents, or other things which are in his exclusive knowledge or possession, and which are necessary to the party seeking discovery as part of a cause or action.... BLACK'S LAW DICTIONARY 466 (6th ed. 1990).

[270] Schnieder v. Northwestern Univ., 115 F.R.D. 319 (N.D. Ill. 1993).

[271] Blum v. Schlegel, 150 F.R.D. 38 (W.D.N.Y. 1993)

[272] Jackson v. Harvard Univ., 111 F.R.D. 472 (D. Mass. 1986).

[273] Orbovich v. Macalester College, 119 F.R.D. 411 (D. Minn. 1988).

[274] Dixon v. Rutgers Univ., A.2d 1315 (N.J. Super. Ct. 1987).

found no merit to the argument that disclosure should be blocked based on academic freedom privileges.[275]

Courts have granted access to materials where it is relevant to the pursuit of a claim of discrimination and involves records of other similarly situated employees. Confidentiality of the materials, however, is closely monitored by the courts. In this way, the courts continue to search for a balance between the concepts of peer review and the need to prohibit discrimination among faculty in higher education.

Access to Promotion and Tenure Committee Deliberations

Access to committee deliberations and the actual vote on the candidate's application for promotion or tenure has also been granted to plaintiffs. In the *University of Pennsylvania* and *Franklin and Marshall* cases, *supra*, both granted access to these materials. In the *Franklin and Marshall* case, the court cited *In re Dinnan*[276] as controlling. In *Dinnan*, the court ordered a member of the promotion and tenure committee to reveal his vote on the probationary faculty member's tenure decision. In *Franklin and Marshall*, the court stated:

> Clearly an alleged perpetrator of discrimination cannot be allowed to pick and choose the evidence which may be necessary for agency investigation. There may be evidence of discriminatory intent and of pretext in the confidential notes and memorandum which the appellant seeks to protect.[277]

The Third Circuit Court of Appeals agreed that access to materials was essential to sustain a plaintiff's title VII claim, but that redaction of names of authors of the material was appropriate.[278]

A California suit brought against a private university by a black faculty member who had been denied tenure is the best example of how access to review committee deliberations facilitate a plaintiff's claim of discrimination. In *Clark v. Claremont Univer-*

---

[275] Lafayette College v. Commonwealth Dep't of Labor & Indus. Bureau of Labor Standards, 546 A.2d 126 (Pa. Commw. Ct. 1988); Pennsylvania State Univ. v. Commonwealth, Dep't of Labor & Indus. Bureau of Labor Standards, 536 A.2d 852 (Pa. Commw. Ct. 1988).

[276] Dinnan, *supra* note 63 at 427 (5th Cir. 1981), *cert. denied*, 457 U.S. 1106 (1982).

[277] EEOC v. Franklin and Marshall College, 775 F.2d 110, 116 (3d Cir. 1985), *cert. denied*, 106 S. Ct. 2288 (1986).

[278] EEOC v. University of Pa., 850 F.2d 969 (3d Cir. 1988), *aff'd*, 493 U.S. 192 (1990).

sity Center,[279] discussions by the departmental faculty were over-heard by the applicant. These discussions contained racial overtones. Previously, the tenure candidate had been subjected to racially motivated comments and incidents. When he was denied tenure, he filed a racial discrimination claim under the state's Fair Employment and Housing Act. A California Court of Appeals affirmed the lower court decision that the tenure process was tainted by racial discrimination. Without access to the review committee deliberations, the faculty member may not have prevailed in his claim. In a Massachusetts case, a federal district court granted the plaintiff access to deliberations and negative complaints discussed by faculty during the review process.[280]

The court will continue to balance plaintiffs' need for access to information against the protection of academic decision making. Courts, in these cases, expressed concern for the integrity of the academic employment decisions and the potential damage that these issues may have for the peer review process.

President or Board Authority

Another issue before the courts has been the level of the final authority to make the tenure decision when there is a discrepancy in the recommendations of various parties involved in the decision to award tenure. Typically, the president or the board is given "final authority" to award tenure. The Seventh Circuit Court of Appeals ruled that the board had authority to make the final decision at an Illinois institution where the tenure committee recommended denial of tenure. The president had found procedural error and ordered another review, and the board overruled the president's decision and denied tenure. The Seventh Circuit upheld the ultimate authority of the board to grant tenure based on state statute and institutional policy.[281] In Florida, the state court found that the president had the authority to deny tenure, even though the grievance committee ordered the award of tenure.[282] The president provided a valid reason for the denial (failure to meet the requirement of distinction in two of the following three areas: teaching, research, and service). In Washington, the state appeals court found that the president and the board had broad

[279] 8 Cal. Rptr. 2d 151 (Cal. Ct. App. 1992).

[280] Jackson v. Harvard Univ., 111 F.R.D. 472 (D. Mass. 1986).

[281] Ranyard v. Board of Regents, 708 F.2d 1235 (7th Cir. 1983).

[282] Remsen v. University of Fla., 429 So.2d 1228 (Fla. Dist. Ct. App. 1983).

authority to refuse to grant tenure, despite the findings of the university tenure committee who voted to award tenure.[283] However, a New York court found that the chancellor of a city university under institutional policy did not have the sole authority to deny tenure to a law school faculty member.[284] These cases indicate that ultimate authority is determined by institutional charter, policies, and state statutes. Where ultimate authority is vested in the president or the board, such authority will be supported where actions conform to policy, practice, and concepts of fairness.

Liability

Claims for damages in the denial of tenure have been before the courts; however, with regard to damages, the record is somewhat inconclusive. While in some cases damages were awarded to plaintiffs, the reviewing courts have remanded these cases due to errors.[285] Other liability cases have been based on a charge of defamation. For example, a probationary faculty member charged that a performance evaluation contained defamatory information. The Pennsylvania Supreme Court found that these performance evaluations were not defamatory and denied a damage award.[286] This ruling was based in part on qualified privilege, a defense against defamation. Qualified privilege was implicated because comments on job performance were within the necessary duties.

In another case, the court found that the evaluation of a department in which the plaintiff was chair was not defamatory, especially in light of the fact that it was not made public.[287] When two individuals, however, charged that a faculty member under a tenure review had mismanaged funds, plagiarized research, and violated professional ethics, they were not granted a summary judgment[288] by the lower court. The Texas Court of Appeals found that there were issues of material fact which necessitated a trial of this defamation claim.[289] Notice these charges went to the faculty member's good name, which indicated a liberty right.

---

[283] Amoss v. University of Wash., 700 P.2d 350 (Wash. Ct. App. 1985).

[284] Faculty of City Univ. o f N.Y. School at Queens College v. Murphy, 531 N.S.2d 665 (Sup. Ct. 1988).

[285] *See* Skehan v. Bloomsburg State College, 503 A.2d 1000 (Pa. Commw. Ct. 1986); Howard Univ. v. Best, 484 A.2d 958 (D.C. 1984).

[286] Baker v. Lafayette College, 532 A.2d 399 (Pa. 1987).

[287] Howard Univ. v. Best, 484 A.2d 958 (D.C. 1984).

[288] Summary Judgment: Procedural devices available for prompt and expeditious disposition of controversy without trial when there is no dispute to either material fact or influence to be drawn from undisputed facts, or if only question of law is involved. BLACK'S LAW DICTIONARY 1435 (6th ed. 1990).

[289] Goodman v. Gallerano, 695 S.W.2d 286 (Tex. Ct. App. 1985).

Conclusions on Denial of Tenure

In a review of the denial of tenure cases, one finds the courts stepping gingerly into the process. While they are willing to review the process and its conformity to policy, they are reluctant to circumvent the substance of the peer review decisions. Although courts have allowed access to review materials and comparative employment data in discrimination cases, judges continue to closely monitor this access. Many courts continue to seek to strike a balance between maintaining the integrity of the academic peer review judgment and review of the procedures by granting access to materials and committee deliberations.

Termination of Tenured Faculty for Cause

A faculty member's rights are established by the contractual relationship negotiated with an institution. Tenure, established to protect academic freedom, is a contractual right defined by the terms of the contract.[290] Although the United States Supreme Court, in *Perry v. Sindermann*,[291] established the control of the contact over tenure matters, it also pointed out in *dicta* that where other constitutionally based claims existed at public institutions, the terms of the contract would be immaterial. Constitutionally based tenure claims will be discussed in a later section of this chapter.

Termination of an existing tenure contract at public institutions implicates a property right requiring due process protections. Charges brought to remove a tenured faculty member that impugn one's good name or reputation involve a liberty right requiring due process. The existence of a property right based on the contract, or of a liberty right threatened by the nature of the charges, would require public institutions to guarantee due process to tenured faculty before terminating their services. The terms of the contract dictate what requirements are imposed on private institutions in the termination of tenured faculty. This section will clarify the specific requirements public institutions must meet to guarantee due process to tenured faculty and to avoid the infringement of faculty's constitutional rights. Contractual obligations to faculty at private institutions may logically be implicated in the course of analysis although these obligations are based on the provisions in the contract, not the imposition of other constitutional constraints.

---

[290] W. Kaplin, Black's Law Dictionary (1985), at 163.
[291] 408 U.S. 593 (1972).

The Tenure Contract

One of the first questions courts address is whether or not a tenured contract exists. In an Arizona case, a federal district court ruled that a faculty member given a contract with automatic tenure and an administrator's guarantee that there would be no tenure review procedure constituted *de facto* tenure requiring due process when the faculty member was terminated at the end of the first year of employment.[292] The issue of whether existence of a tenured contract at a branch campus gave a faculty member a claim to tenure on the main campus was before a court.[293] In 1975, a university's governing board changed its policy on tenure to state that a faculty member had tenure only on the campus of his or her appointment, not throughout the university. One faculty member who received tenure in 1979, claimed that she had acquired tenure on the main campus. The federal court found the claim to lack merit since the plaintiff received tenure after the change in policy. Further, the court found the claim, filed eight years after the change in policy, was time barred. In another case, the question arose as to whether an instructor employed in "academic support services" but who was not teaching full-time had tenure under the provisions of the community college employment contract.[294] The court found that the institution's regulations on tenure covered full-time employees engaged in "teaching or academic support services," but did not include a requirement that faculty have a full-time teaching assignment. Academic support service employees were faculty under the provisions of the contract. In Illinois, a community college faculty member who was dismissed in December of 1979 could not claim tenure under the Public Community College Tenure Act which went into effect on January 1, 1980.[295] All of these cases point to the importance of specific institutional policies in defining whether, in fact, a tenure contract exists.

The question of what constitutes a resignation from a tenured contract in termination cases also has been before the courts. A Georgia case involved a tenured faculty member who refused to sign an annual contract as required by institutional policy.[296] A faculty member who objected to an unchanged department assignment was given three opportunities to sign the contract, was

---

[292] Harris v. Arizona Bd. of Regents, 529 F. Supp. 987 (D. Ariz. 1981).

[293] Mulligan v. Hazard, 777 F.2d 340 (6th Cir. 1985).

[294] Dauel v. Board of Trustees of Elgin Community College, 768 F.2d 128 (7th Cir. 1985).

[295] Fleischer v. Board of Community College Dist. #519, 471 N.E.2d 213 (Ill. App. Ct. 1984).

[296] Jordan v. Board of Regents Univ. Sys. of Col. 582 F. Supp. 23 (S.D. Ga. 1983).

then given a fourth opportunity accompanied by notification that refusal to sign constituted resignation and that the department assignment was a grievable claim under the institution's grievance procedure. The teacher was given a hearing before the board on the resignation after failing to sign the contract and then sued for slander and breach of contract. The federal court found that failure to sign the contract in this case negated any claim of continued employment and was a resignation. In a similar case, a federal court found that the failure to sign and return a contract for the next year did not require additional notice by the institution and was abandonment of employment.[297] In Oklahoma, however, a faculty member who followed instructions enclosed with the contract (signed the contract, returned it on time but also included a note questioning the salary amount) had not reopened negotiation of the contract. The state appeals court found the signature to be acceptance and the note simply to be a reflection of the displeasure with the conditions of the contract rather than a counteroffer.[298] In California, a faculty member dictated a letter of resignation to the secretary of the institution's personnel officer but never signed the letter. The faculty member later told the president he did not intend to resign. The personnel officer, however, had forwarded a resignation notice to the board, and it was accepted. The state appellate court found that where formal policies required a resignation in writing from the employee, the phone message did not constitute legitimate resignation and further, the resignation had been withdrawn.[299]

Another case points out that an institution cannot be sporadic in the enforcement of institutional policy used to terminate tenured faculty members. In an Illinois case, a federal district court found that the institution acted in an arbitrary and capricious manner by enforcing a policy prohibiting full-time employees from holding two jobs. The institution, after a ten-year hiatus of non-enforcement, had sought to dismiss without notice faculty who were violating the policy.[300] When the board of a community college decided to commence termination proceedings against several tenured faculty members, the faculty resigned. The court ruled that the resignations were not procured under duress and were therefore valid.[301]

---

[297] McGhee v. Miller, 680 F.2d 1220 (8th Cir. 1982).
[298] Price v. Oklahoma College of Osteopathic Medicine and Surgery, 733 P.2d 1357 (Okla. Ct. App. 1986).
[299] Mahoney v. Board of Trustees of San Diego Community College Dist., 214 Cal. Rptr. 370 (Ct. App. 1985).
[300] Kaufman v. Board of Trustees, Community College Dist. #508, 552 F. Supp. 1143 (N.D. Ill. 1982).
[301] Allen v. Board of Trustees, Community College Dist. # 508, 675 N.E.2d 187 (Ill. Ct. App. 1996).

These cases indicate that an institution's policies and practices will influence terms and conditions as well as the existence of a contract. Policies that were ratified at the time of the award of tenure will be enforced during the contractual period. Further, an institution must be consistent in enforcing the terms of the contract. Decisions to enforce provisions after a period of clear nonenforcement probably require employee notification to avoid a charge of arbitrary or capricious action. A tenured faculty member who fails to sign an annual contract, which is the normal procedure followed in the institution, will be viewed by the court as abandoning employment. However, protest notes accompanying a signed contract have not been seen as a basis to assume the faculty member has reopened contract negotiations.

Liberty Interest

Charges brought to terminate tenured faculty members for cause that impugn their reputation would implicate a liberty interest mandating due process requirements.

A number of termination for cause cases brought forth the question of a liberty interest requiring due process. In one case, a musician was reassigned from a string ensemble to teaching. The musician claimed that the reassignment involved a liberty interest because it reflected on his reputation by impugning his musical skills. The state supreme court agreed that a liberty interest and a property right existed for the assignment to the wind ensemble as per a contract stipulating due process before reassignment. The court ordered a name-clearing hearing under 42 U.S.C. § 1983. However, the State Supreme Court acknowledged the plaintiff's right to file under section 1983 in federal court before exhausting administrative remedies, and reversed the lower court finding that pending administrative remedies provided adequate due process under a liberty claim.[302]

A terminated faculty member sued the president of an Alabama institution, claiming defamation in the contents of a letter the president sent him notifying him of the charges against him. The Alabama Supreme Court found that a letter written to notify a faculty member of charges as part of a quasi-judicial hearing was privileged communication.[303] Defamation charges could be sustained only if the communication was made public, that is, if it

---

[302] Kramer v. Horton, 371 N.W.2d 801 (Wis. Ct. App. 1985); *rev'd*, 383 N.W.2d 54 (Wis. 1986).
[303] Webster v. Byrd, 494 So.2d 31 (Ala. 1986).

was shared with people who were not part of the proceedings or who did not need to know in order to make sure the terminated faculty member did not get paid.

Procedural Due Process

The existence of a liberty interest or a property right requires due process in termination for cause. The procedures followed in termination have been heavily litigated in the past few years.

A number of cases involved both the notification procedures and the content of the notice. In terms of the content of the notice, two cases questioned the types of cause that can be used to remove tenured faculty. In both cases, the faculty alleged that only actions that affect faculty members' ability to teach should be a legitimate cause for termination. In these cases, courts rejected claims that private consensual sexual activity between a student and a faculty member[304] or moral turpitude[305] did not affect teaching, finding both termination causes to be valid. A Tennessee Court found that charges of "capricious disregard for accepted professional standards" used to terminate a tenured faculty member were not vague and were supported by the evidence.[306]

A faculty member successfully challenged the adequacy of notice when an institution failed to provide him with an explanation of the substance of the charges against him.[307] In this Wyoming case, the faculty member challenged the adequacy of the notification because it did not contain the names of witnesses who would be testifying against him. The state supreme court ruled that the notice did not have to contain the names of witnesses, since it advised him that such a list would be available upon request.[308] In a California case, a faculty member was able to sustain a claim of laches[309] under the state civil service code against charges of sexual harassment that took place five years earlier.[310] The court found that since the notice was based on a "linked set of events" and all but one was thrown out as time barred, the charges should be dropped and the faculty member reinstated because there was a lack of evidence in the remaining sexual harassment charge.[311]

---

[304] Korf v. Ball State Univ., 726 F.2d 1222 (7th Cir. 1984).

[305] Corstvet v. Boger, 757 F.2d 223 (10th Cir. 1985).

[306] Phillips v. State Bd. of Regents, 863 S.W.2d 45 (Tenn. 1993).

[307] Cotnoir v. University of Me. Sys., 35 F.3d 6 (1st Cir. 1994).

[308] White v. Board of Trustees of W. Wyo. Comm. College Dist., 648 P.2d 528 (Wyo. 1982).

[309] Laches, "Doctrine of Laches"... neglect to assert a right or claim which taken together with lapse of time and other circumstances causing prejudice to adverse party, operates as bar in court of equity. BLACK'S LAW DICTIONARY 875 (6th ed. 1990).

[310] Brown v. California State Personnel Bd., 213 Cal. Rptr. 53 (Ct. App. 1985).

[311] *Id.* at 61.

Procedural questions involving the termination hearing have been raised during litigation. Issues surrounding the selection of the hearing board, its membership, and the right of access to legal counsel have received particular attention. In a Georgia case, the court ruled that the plaintiff's due process rights to a hearing had been violated when the president, the executive vice president and board members decided not to hold a hearing.[312] The administrators and board members had argued that since the facts were not in dispute, there was no need for a hearing. In a Minnesota case, a court ruled that denying the appearance of student witnesses who had been intended to provide testimony about the faculty member's professional competence, was not a procedural error.[313] In this case involving dual academic appointments at two institutions, the student testimony was viewed as irrelevant. An Alabama case raised the question of whether due process procedures in the termination of a tenured faculty member required the right to legal counsel. The Alabama Supreme Court, citing several cases,[314] ruled that the plaintiff had been given the right to cross-examine witnesses and did not object to absence of counsel prior to the hearing.[315] While acknowledging that a right to counsel may exist, the court found that access to legal counsel was not essential to protect the due process rights of a faculty member during the employment termination hearing.[316] In this case, the plaintiff did not preserve this issue for review. Under Alaska's Administrative Procedures Act, however, a tenured faculty member would have the right to have legal counsel fully participate, which would include questioning witnesses in both pre-termination and post-termination hearings.[317] An Illinois court noted that the due process rights of a faculty member were not violated when an institution heard the case before the institution's hearing committee, denying the faculty member's request for an independent hearing agent.[318] In a Texas case, the court found that a plaintiff's claim of bias on the part of two members of the hearing committee was

---

[312] Savannah College of Art & Design, Inc. v. Nulph, 453 S.E.2d 80 (Ga. App. 1994).

[313] Zahavy v. University of Minn., 544 N.W.2d 32 (Minn. Ct. App. 1996).

[314] See Matthews v. Eldridge, 424 U.S. 319 (1976); Goldberg v. Kelly, 397 U S. 254 (1970). The nature of the property right in grievance procedures governs in these cases. While there is scant precedent for college professors, in one case the court upheld the institution's decision to allow counsel to be present to advise his client but counsel was not to participate in the hearing. See Frumkin v. Board of Trustees, Kent State Univ., 626 F.2d 19 (6th Cir. 1980).

[315] Johnson v. Alabama Agric. and Mechanical Univ., 481 So.2d 336 (Ala. 1985).

[316] Matthews v. Eldridge, 424 U.S. 319, 339 (1976).

[317] Odum v. University of Alaska, Anchorage, 845 P.2d 432 (Alaska 1993).

[318] Inwang v. Community College Dist. #508, County of Cook, 453 N.E.2d 896 (Ill. App. Ct. 1983).

based on "mere speculation and tenuous inferences."[319] The plaintiff alleged that two committee members were biased because: the plaintiff was involved in a decision to refuse one hearing committee member graduate faculty status, and the other's alleged bias stemmed from the failure to award funding to the plaintiff's research proposal.

In a Wisconsin case, a tenured faculty member requested a leave of absence without pay while a hearing was held to review charges that had been made concerning his teaching competence. The state court noted that the plaintiff was a tenured faculty member and therefore, had a property right in his position requiring a hearing as provided by institutional policy.[320] Attempts to address the grievances by letter were an inadequate means of protecting the plaintiff's employment rights.[321] In another case, a California appeals court ruled that certain procedures a faculty member selected in a termination proceeding, which allowed the president the right to disagree with the hearing committee's findings after a review of the proceedings, were not unfair.[322] A Tennessee court ruled that suspension without pay approved by the faculty senate executive committee, pending the decision of the hearing committee, was within prescribed institutional policy and did not violate the plaintiff's rights.[323] An Indiana court held that although an employee's termination hearing is subject to the "open door law," the institution's hearing complied with those laws.[324] No evidence was presented to indicate that interested parties had been denied access to hearings held behind closed doors, and review by the board of trustees met the provisions of the law. The court further noted that the evidence clearly substantiated the charges against the faculty member.[325] A California court upheld a hearing board's requirement that a faculty member conduct lab experiments during the hearing as an assessment tool to determine the validity of a charge of incompetence.[326]

In a West Virginia case, the hearing agent's failure to summarize the charges against the plaintiff and to present specific evidence substantiating those charges, was determined to be an error vio-

---

[319] Levitt v. Monroe, 590 F. Supp. 902, 907 (W.D. Tex. 1984); *aff'd*, Levitt v. University of Tex. at El Paso, 759 F.2d 1224 (5th Cir. 1985); *cert. denied*, 474 U.S. 1034 (1985).
[320] Patterson v. Board of Regents of Univ. of Wis. Sys., 350 N.W.2d 612 (Wis. 1984).
[321] *Id.* at 618.
[322] Samaan v. Trustees of Cal. State Univ. and Colleges, 197 Cal. Rptr. 856 (Ct. App. 1983).
[323] Josberger v. University of Tenn., 706 S.W.2d 300 (Tenn. Ct. App. 1985).
[324] Riggin v. Board of Trustees of Ball State Univ., 489 N.E.2d 616 (Ind. Ct. App. 1986).
[325] *Id.* at 628.
[326] Bevli v. Brisco, 212 Cal. Rptr. 36 (Ct. App. 1985).

lating the plaintiff's due process.[327] The plaintiff was unable, without more specific information, to make an adequate assessment of whether to request a review of the proceedings. The court also noted the inadequacy of the letter communicating the institution's decision.[328] The letter lacked detail and specificity about the nature of the substantiated charges against the faculty member.

Issues in several cases involved discrepancies in the decision of the hearing committee and the final decision of the board or executive officer. One case affirms the right to dismiss faculty where they are viewed as a threat to students.[329] An Alabama court ruled that the plaintiff's rights were not violated when a college / university president used both the hearing record and the employee's personnel file in making a dismissal decision contrary to the recommendation of the hearing committee.[330] The best example of a case where the president's decision is in conflict with the findings and recommendations of the hearing committee was a case involving the alleged fraudulent billing to a research grant.[331] The hearing committee found that the billing problem existed, but labeled it as error and recommended probation. The president, on review of the evidence, found the problem to constitute fraud and terminated the faculty member responsible. The court acknowledged the president's statutory power to disagree in writing with the hearing committee decision, and noted that the evidence clearly supported the president's conclusions and his findings.[332] A United States District Court ruled that the terminated faculty member was not entitled to another hearing before the Board of Trustees because the board did not follow the punishment recommended by the faculty hearing committee.[333]

A Kansas case involved a board's rejection of a hearing committee's report and the board's subsequent decision to dismiss two faculty members. No statutory mandate compelled the board to adopt the hearing committee's report, and the state court ruled that as long as the rudiments of due process were maintained, the board's decision, contrary to the evidence that the hearing committee presented, did not violate the plaintiff's due process.[334] A District of Columbia case, however, had a different

---

[327] Clarke v. West Virginia Bd. of Regents, 301 S.E.2d 618 (W. Va. 1983).

[328] *Id.*

[329] Cockburn v. Santa Monica Community College Dist. Personnel Comm'n, 207 Cal. Rptr. 589 (Ct. App. 1984).

[330] Johnson v. Alabama Agric. and Mechanical Univ., 481 So.2d 336 (Ala. 1985).

[331] Samaan v. Trustees of Cal. State Univ. and Colleges, 197 Cal. Rptr. 856 (Ct. App. 1983).

[332] *Id.* at 866.

[333] Wexley v. Michigan State Univ., 821 F. Supp. 479 (W.D. Mich. 1993).

[334] Kelly v. Kansas City, 648 P.2d 225 (Kan. 1982).

result. A professor became embroiled in a controversy when a student made slanderous comments in his class. Referred for disciplinary action, the student refused to apologize to the professor despite an order of the disciplinary committee to do so, and continued to attend class. The university failed to follow up, and the professor refused to continue teaching his class. The institution charged the professor with neglect of duty and the grievance committee found him not guilty of the charge because of extenuating circumstances. After reviewing a summary of the grievance committee report, the board dismissed the professor. The federal district court issued a summary judgment in favor of the university, finding the board had final authority in these matters.[335] The Court of Appeals for the District of Columbia found that significant evidence existed to question whether the professor had neglected his duty, and that the plaintiff's allegations that the institution had breached its contract when it failed to follow through on the disciplinary action against the disruptive student had significant merit and should be reviewed. Further, the institution may have violated its due process procedures when the president transmitted a two-page summary of the grievance committee's report to the board when the faculty handbook stated that the full report must be transmitted. The appeals court concluded that it found no reason why, if a contractual relationship exists between a public or private university employee and the institution, university employee decisions should receive more "judicial deference" than business or other professions.[336]

Contracts and statutes control when constitutional rights are protected. The Fifth Circuit Court of Appeals noted that where due process requirements are met, any additional rights allegedly denied that are enumerated in the statutes of a state or in the contract should be adjudicated in state court.[337] For example, a Kansas court found that state statutory provisions required the board to follow a unanimous decision of the hearing committee.[338]

Procedural due process is required in the termination of tenured faculty for cause. These procedures govern proper notice of the charges, a hearing, and the decision. In a number of states, the Administrative Procedures Act clearly outlines the procedures to be followed in the termination of state employees (faculty holding tenure at public institutions). The form of the hearing and the ways used to evaluate specific charges contained in the notice are

---

[335] McConnell v. Howard Univ., 621 F. Supp. 327 (D.D.C. 1985).

[336] McConnell v. Howard Univ., 818 F.2d 58 (D.C. Cir. 1987).

[337] Levitt, *supra* note 104 at 1233.

[338] Keller v. Board of Trustees of Coffeyville Community College, 733 P.2d 830 (Kan. Ct. App. 1987).

points where the court appears to defer to academic judgments. The authority to make the ultimate termination decision depends on the nature of the contact and state statutes. In some cases, this authority is vested in the president or the board of trustees

Other Constitutional Claims

Although many tenured faculty termination cases involve due process questions, some involve other fundamental constitutional rights. Where these constitutional claims are involved, the courts look outside the contractual relationship for a resolution of the issues.

For example, one case raised the issue of a privacy right. A faculty member was terminated for having a homosexual relationship with a student not enrolled in the professor's class.[339] The professor maintained that the relationship was a private consensual matter between two adults and should be beyond consideration by his employer. The circuit court, noting that evidence showed that he had made sexual advances to other students, viewed his behavior as "exploitation" of students under the AAUP's Statement of Professional Ethics. The court rejected the privacy argument by saying that the faculty member's conduct in this case cannot be viewed as that of "an ordinary person on the street," but that this special student-faculty relationship mandates the observance of ethical standards.[340]

Cause for Termination

The case law provides a way of analyzing the types of cause used in termination cases. Cause is broken down into several areas: insubordination, neglect of duty, incompetence, moral turpitude, and, in some cases, violations of professional and ethical standards. The types of cause illuminated by the case law in each of these areas will be outlined to give a better understanding of the kinds of employment actions encompassed in each of these categories.

---

[339] Korf v. Ball State Univ., 726 F.2d 1222 (7th Cir. 1984).
[340] Id. at 1227.

Insubordination

Insubordination is the refusal to comply with the directives of a superior.[341] Synonymous with insubordination is uncooperative behavior. A number of cases enrich the description of what constitutes insubordination. Several of the cases involve employee speech regarding the skills and qualities of a superior. If the speech concerns an employee matter as opposed to a matter of public concern, First Amendment rights are not implicated, and the institution might be able to support a claim that the behavior had a disruptive or negative effect.[342] One such case involved a faculty member who refused to follow university procedures and exhibited uncooperative and disruptive behavior toward a dean, faculty, and students.[343] Another case involved a faculty member who continued to communicate with donors and retain possession of center artifacts after he was removed from his position as director of the American Heritage Center.[344] When the faculty member refused to cease contacting donors and surrender certain artifacts by order of the university's president, the institution terminated him. The court found that his termination was procedurally correct and did not violate his First Amendment rights since they were matters of personal, not public, concern. A department chair, however, terminated for insubordination because he refused to turn over to the president of the institution the grade book of an adjunct professor involved in grade fraud, successfully claimed a free speech violation.[345] The department chair had gone public with the grade fraud and sent a notarized copy of the grade book to the university president explaining that the actual book was available in his attorney's office. The Tenth Circuit Court of Appeals found that termination for insubordination was retaliation for speech on matters of public concern, grade fraud.

Some cases involved disrespectful and uncooperative behavior based on the abusive and threatening manner of the employee's expression.[346] Several other insubordination cases involved refusal to comply with a superior's orders. In one case, the faculty member was denied a request to be absent from campus to give an

---

[341] *See* BLACK'S LAW DICTIONARY 801 (6th ed. 1990).

[342] Protected speech presented in an abusive or threatening manner could serve in part as the basis of an adverse employment decision.

[343] Johnson v. Alabama Agric. and Mechanical Univ., 481 So.2d 336 (Ala. 1985).

[344] Gressley v. Deutsch, 890 F. Supp. 1474 (D. Wyo. 1994).

[345] Powell v. Gallentine, 992 F.2d 1088 (10th Cir. 1993).

[346] Russ v. White, 541 F. Supp. 888 (W.D. Ark. 1981); Kelly v. Kansas City, 648 P.2d 225 (Kan. 1982).

address abroad but went anyway.[347] Another case involved the refusal to teach a course as assigned by the academic unit.[348]

Neglect of Duty

Neglect of duty is defined in the case law as the failure to perform an obligation owed to an employer. Faculty terminations for neglect of duty were upheld in several instances where faculty failed to perform tasks that were part of their job descriptions.[349] However, where the institution owes a duty to the employee and the employee's nonperformance stems from the failed institutional duty, the court will reach a different result. For example, when a university failed to discipline a disruptive student, a faculty member's refusal to teach class may not be a neglect of duty.[350]

Incompetence

The legal definition of incompetence is the fitness to discharge required duties.[351] In *Dhuria v. Trustees of the University of the District of Columbia*,[352] a faculty member was dismissed under the school's incompetence provisions for repeated years of poor student evaluations of teaching. The faculty member was given notice of these problems, and his failure to improve over time brought charges of incompetence against him. The Federal District Court for the District of Columbia found that he had not been discriminated against in the termination nor had the charge of incompetence been a pretext for discrimination. In one case, the charges went to specific examples of incompetence such as failure to cover pertinent topics in the course syllabus, poor organization of lectures, failure to meet class regularly, and failure to provide opportunities for students to meet with the professor on an individual basis.[353] In another case, the allegations involved poor performance in teaching, research, and service to the university.[354] The court found, in another incompetence case, that it was appropriate to require the faculty member to demonsrate his teaching skills at the hearing as part of the decision to terminate.[355]

---

[347] Stastney v. Board of Trustees of Cent. Wash. Univ., 647 P.2d 496 (Wash. Ct. App. 1982).

[348] Smith v. Kent State Univ., 696 F.2d 476 (6th Cir. 1983).

[349] *See* Josberger v. University of Tenn., 706 S.W.2d 300 (Tenn. Ct. App. 1985); Fleischer v. Board of Community College Dist. #519, 471 N.E.2d 213 (Ill. App. Ct. 1984).

[350] McConnell v. Howard Univ., 818 F.2d 58 (D.C. Cir. 1987).

[351] BLACK'S LAW DICTIONARY, 765 (6th ed. 1990).

[352] 827 F. Supp. 818 (D.D.C. 1993).

[353] Riggin v. Board of Trustees of Ball State Univ., 489 N.E.2d 616 (Ind. Ct. App. 1986).

[354] King v. University of Minn., 774 F.2d 224 (8th Cir. 1985).

[355] Bevli v. Brisco, 212 Cal. Rptr. 36 (Ct. App. 1985).

Moral Turpitude

Moral turpitude is defined as conduct contrary to honesty, modesty, or good morals.[356] Several specific causes come under the umbrella of moral turpitude. One cause is fraud. The fraudulent certification of the completion of credits by students resulted in the termination of one faculty member.[357] Another involved the fraudulent signing of another faculty member's attendance report, resulting in a 60-day suspension.[358] A California case involved over 100 incidents of fraudulent billing to a research grant by a faculty member.[359] Another area of moral turpitude is plagiarism. A case involving plagiarism in the preparation of a laboratory manual resulted in the termination of a tenured faculty member.[360] A tenured faculty member at a community college was terminated after he was first convicted and then acquitted on charges involving in the sale of cocaine to students.[361] The faculty member claimed to have no knowledge of the sale of cocaine in his condominium by a friend who periodically stayed there. The court upheld the institution's termination decision. Finally, a case involving immoral conduct resulted from the arrest of a faculty member for solicitation of sexual activities in a rest room.[362]

Ethical and Professional Standards

Failure to uphold the professional and ethical standards of the profession has emerged as another area that institutions have incorporated into their termination for cause policies. Perhaps the most prominent recent case involved a faculty member who, for four years, disregarded the suggestion of his dean that he take a leave of absence as he held faculty appointments at two institutions simultaneously.[363] The court found that this unprofessional conduct, the holding of dual academic appointments, impaired his fitness in a professional capacity. An Ohio professional college found a faculty member who publicly criticized another faculty member's teaching and advising violated its professional

---

[356] BLACK'S LAW DICTIONARY, 1160 (5th ed. 1979).

[357] Ivey v. Board of Regents of Univ. of Alaska, 673 F.2d 266 (9th Cir. 1982).

[358] Inwang v. Community College Dist. #508, County of Cook, 453 N.E.2d 896 (Ill. App. Ct. 1983).

[359] Samaan v. Trustees of Cal. State Univ. and Colleges, 197 Cal. Rptr. 856 (Ct. App. 1983).

[360] Agarwal v. Regents of Univ. of Minn., 788 F.2d 504 (8th Cir. 1986).

[361] West Valley-Mission Community College Dist. v. Concepcion, 21 Cal. Rptr. 2d 5 (Cal. Ct. App. 1993).

[362] Corstvet v. Boger, 757 F.2d 223 (10th Cir. 1985).

[363] Zahavy v. University of Minn., 544 N.W.2d 32 (Minn. Ct. App. 1996).

standards. The court found that the institution, under its termination policy, could dismiss the critiquing faculty member for unprofessional conduct.[364]

Conclusions on Termination for Cause

The case law indicates that many institutions have been successful in terminating faculty for cause. However, examples also exist of duplicitous behavior on the part of institutions by attempting to eliminate faculty who were, in the institution's view, a nuisance. Although it may be important to police the ranks of faculty to eliminate those who violate AAUP standards, academic administrators must be careful to protect the rudiments of fair play and foster academic freedom. The basic claims for termination include insubordination, neglect of duty, incompetence, and moral turpitude. In recent years, ethical and professional standards violations have been added to the list of what constitutes termination for cause.

The First Amendment and Academic Freedom

When a faculty member at a public institution speaks out on matters of work conditions or decisions on educational policies of an institution, are these matters covered by the Constitution through the First Amendment? Certainly the hallowed concept of speech as part of academic freedom enjoys universal awareness as a hallmark of higher education, but when is the concept of academic freedom applied? Is it restricted to areas of one's expertise, or is it applied to comments on other work-related activities, such as academic standards or educational policies? To answer these questions and understand the distinction between employee speech and matters covered by the First Amendment, one needs to first understand the relationship between academic freedom and the Constitutional guarantees of First Amendment speech.

First Amendment Speech

While the faculty at public institutions must be guaranteed freedom of speech rights, a review of the case law will indicate that this guarantee is not a blanket coverage of all speech. Fur-

---

[364] Braham v. Ohio College of Pediatric Med., 651 N.E.2d 30 (Ohio Ct. App. 1994).

ther, while academic freedom is not a constitutional guarantee but rather a contractual right granted at most institutions, there is an overlap in the coverage of the two protections. The United States Supreme Court has acknowledged the importance of academic freedom on a number of occasions in cases dealing with the First Amendment's application. A review of the case law on the First Amendment will illuminate the distinctions and overlap of the speech guarantees and academic freedom.

The Supreme Court commented on speech rights in higher education in *Sweezy v. New Hampshire*,[365] stating:

> The essentiality of freedom in the community of American universities is almost self-evident. No one should underestimate the vital role in a democracy that is played by those who guide and train our youth. To impose a strait jacket upon the intellectual leaders would imperil the future of our nation. No field of education is so thoroughly comprehended by man that new discoveries cannot yet be made..... Teachers and students must always remain free to inquire, to study and to evaluate, to gain new maturity and understanding; otherwise our civilization will stagnate and die.[366]

The Court commented also on the existence of political freedom in this case involving investigations of the content of lectures and other associations under a law designed to route out subversive persons from public employment roles. However, deciding the case on technical grounds, the Court found that the state attorney general extended his investigation beyond the legislative authority under the law. While *Sweezy* is frequently cited in academic freedom cases, the Court's comments on these issues are dictum.[367]

In *Keyishian v. Board of Regents of the University of the State of New York*,[368] the Supreme Court rejected the idea that constitutional guarantees could be limited for public employees. The First Amendment right of a citizen to comment on matters of public concern was established in *Pickering v. Board of Education*.[369] The Court ruled that a letter written to the newspaper on a proposed school tax increase was a matter of public concern and could not

---

[365] 354 U.S. 234 (1957).

[366] *Id.* at 250.

[367] Dictum: The word is generally used as an abbreviated form of *obiter dictum*, "a remark by the way;" that is, an observation or remark made by a judge in pronouncing an opinion upon a cause, concerning some rule, principle, or application of law, or the solution of a question suggested by the case at bar but not necessarily involved in the case or essential to its determination; ... BLACK's LAW DICTIONARY 454 (6th ed. 1990).

[368] 385 U.S. 589 (1967).

[369] 391 U.S. 563 (1968).

be the basis for the dismissal of a school teacher. This First Amendment speech right was further defined in *Mt. Healthy City School District Board of Education v. Doyle*.[370] The Court found that while the protected speech on matters of public concern played a substantial part in the decision to dismiss a teacher, the lower court should have determined whether a preponderance of evidence showed that the decision to dismiss would have been reached absent the protected activity.[371] This standard is commonly referred to as the "but for" test.

The Court differentiated between matters of public concern and matters of interest only to the employee (employee speech) in *Connick v. Myers*.[372] In this case, the Court balanced the interests of the employee in commenting on matters of public concern against the interest of the public employer (the state) in promoting efficiency in employee public service.[373] The Court found that a questionnaire circulated to other employees seeking responses on office morale, the office transfer policy, and confidence in supervisors was not a matter of public concern, but rather a matter of personal interest to the employee. Speech on matters of personal interest by a public employee are not covered by First Amendment speech protections. It followed, therefore, that the public employer could dismiss the employee on grounds that the questionnaire, not protected speech, served as the basis for the dismissal decision since the questionnaire jeopardized the smooth operation of the office. This case established the distinction between protected speech by public employees on matters of public concern and employee speech that is not covered by constitutional guarantees. Some speech that falls within the academic freedom provisions may be outside the reach of First Amendment guarantees because it is viewed by the courts as employee speech.[374]

This point of differentiating First Amendment protected speech from speech governed by principles of academic freedom was set out in a Supreme Court decision involving "meet and confer" pro-

---

[370] 429 U.S. 274 (1977).

[371] *Id*. at 287.

[372] 461 U.S. 138 (1983).

[373] *Id*. at 139.

[374] *See* Clark v. Holmes, 474 F.2d 928 (7th Cir. 1972), *cert. denied*, 411 U.S. 972 (1973); denial of a faculty member's First Amendment right to disregard institutionally established curriculum. *See also* Hetrick v. Martin, 480 F.2d 705 (6th Cir. 1973), *cert. denied*, 414 U.S. 1075 (1973): nonrenewal for failure to conform to accepted institutional standards of pedagogy, and educational philosophy was not prohibited by the First Amendment.

visions of a collective bargaining agreement. In *Minnesota State Board for Community Colleges v. Knight*,[375] the Court stated:

> The academic setting of policy making at issue in this case does not alter this conclusion. [Appellees have no constitutional right as members of the public to a government audience for their policy views.] To be sure, there is a strong, if not universal or uniform, tradition of faculty participation in school governance, and there are numerous policy arguments to support such participation.... But this Court has never recognized a constitutional right of faculty to participate in policymaking in academic institutions.[376]

While it is true that this case involved the right to participate in policy making, not dismissal, because of policy pronouncements, the Court appears to be differentiating between some principles of academic freedom and rights as guaranteed by the Constitution.

More recently, the Supreme Court has attached qualifiers to speech on matters of public concern. In *Waters v. Churchill*,[377] the Court ruled that public employers could dismiss a public employee for protected speech that was disruptive. It stated:

> The key to First Amendment analysis of government decisions, then, is this: The government's interest in achieving its goals as effectively and efficiently as possible is elevated from a relatively subordinate interest when it acts as sovereign to a significant one when it acts as employer. The government cannot restrict the speech of the public at large just in the name of efficiency. But where the government is employing someone for the very purpose of effectively achieving its goals, such restrictions may well be appropriate.[378]

In this case, the Court found that statements made by a nurse were found to be disruptive, and, therefore, could serve as the basis for dismissal. They also found that the disruptive pronouncements were not on matters of public concern and were not protected speech. The Court commented that even if the speech was protected, the disruptive nature of the speech gave the employer a

---

[375] 465 U.S. 271 (1984).
[376] *Id.* at 1067.
[377] 511 U.S. 661 (1994).
[378] *Id.* at 1888.

legitimate basis to dismiss the employee. The Court noted that "this potential disruptiveness was enough to outweigh whatever First Amendment value the speech might have had."[379]

Case law on the dismissal of faculty where First Amendment violations are alleged further defines the degree of differentiation between academic freedom principles and First Amendment protections. It also clarifies that the presence of disruptive but protected speech will still allow the employer to dismiss an employee for disrupting the effective functioning of the organization.

Faculty Termination or Nonrenewal

Faculty termination or nonrenewal allegedly motivated by First Amendment protected speech also has been litigated within higher education. The case law not only elaborates the distinction between protected speech and employee speech but also further defines the relationship between constitutional protection and academic freedom. In cases involving dismissal of faculty allegedly for protected speech, the Court has prescribed a proof strategy. In *Mt. Healthy*, the burden of proof initially is with the plaintiff to demonstrate that protected speech was a factor in a dismissal. The burden then shifts to the institution to show by a "preponderance of evidence" that the dismissal decision would have been reached absent the protected speech.[380] Other courts have used this proof strategy.[381] The case law can be grouped according to when speech has been used as a motivating factor in the denial of tenure or termination, the types of speech as alleged constitutional violations, and employee speech not on matters of public concern, which is not protected.

Speech as a Motivating Factor

Examples of allegations that protected speech was a motivating factor in the nonrenewal of a university employee's contract are numerous. In *Montgomery v. Boshears*, the Fifth Circuit Court of Appeals found that a librarian's speech about the qualifications

---

[379] *Id.* at 1891.
[380] Mt. Healthy, *supra* note 148.
[381] *See* Hamer v. Brown, 831 F.2d 1398 (8th Cir. 1987); Honore v. Douglas, 833 F.2d 565 (5th Cir. 1987); Leachman v. Rector and Visitors of Univ. of Va., 691 F. Supp. 961 (W.D. Va. 1988).

of her newly hired supervisor and criticism of the new library computer system were matters of public concern and, therefore, protected speech.[382] The plaintiff, however, did not meet her burden to show that protected speech was a motivating factor in the non-reemployment decision. On the other hand, the plaintiff in *Roos v. Smith*[383] was able to prove that speech was the motivating factor in her claim against the university. The court found that the decision not to renew the probationary faculty member's contract was in retaliation for her exercise of protected speech. In a California case, where the court vacated a summary judgment, they found that the plaintiffs' statements regarding law school admissions policies, administration of budgets, and failure to certify law school graduates as eligible for the state bar exam were matters of public concern and protected speech.[384] The plaintiff showed that this speech was a substantial and motivating factor in his denial of tenure. The case was remanded to determine, by a preponderance of evidence, whether other reasons existed to reach the denial of tenure decision. A Massachusetts faculty member alleged that his refusal to reduce the academic standards he utilized in his course was a motivating factor in his nonrenewal.[385] Noting the institution's prerogative to set academic standards and citing several cases to that effect,[386] the court did not reach the question of whether the speech over a grading incident involved protected speech, finding the speech was not the substantial motivating factor in the nonrenewal decision. A decision by the Sixth Circuit Court of Appeals, however, puts a unique twist on the premise of institutional control over academic standards.[387] The federal appeals court found that protected speech, a professor's refusal to change a grade assignment after institutional demands, may have been the motivating factor in the dismissal decision. However, the court differentiated between the forced change and the institution's prerogative to change the grade for the course from the one assigned by the instructor. The case was remanded to determine whether the protected speech was a motivating factor in the nonrenewal decision.

---

[382] 698 F.2d 739 (5th Cir. 1983).
[383] 837 F. Supp. 803 (S.D. Miss. 1993).
[384] Honore v. Douglas, 833 F.2d 565 (5th Cir. 1987).
[385] Lovelace v. Southeastern Mass. Univ., 793 F.2d 419 (1st Cir. 1986).
[386] E.g., Keyishian v. Board of Regents, 385 U.S. 589 (1967).
[387] Parate v. Isibor, 868 F.2d 821 (6th Cir. 1989).

An Arkansas court found that while discussion of the expenditure of funds was protected speech, the speech was not the substantial and motivating factor in the termination of a faculty member's contract.[388] The court found that a preponderance of the evidence substantiated mismanagement and declining enrollment in the program operated by the faculty member as the basis for the termination decision. In a faculty member's termination, the federal appeals court remanded the case because evidence existed to substantiate whistle blowing, which was protected speech, as a motivating factor in the termination decision.[389] The terminated employee had informed the administration of improprieties regarding the way a faculty member was expending funds.

As these cases demonstrate, protected speech must be on matters of public concern. The success of the plaintiffs' claims in these cases also hinges on showing that protected speech, not other reasons, served as the basis of the negative employment decisions. However, there are indications that some matters dealing with academic standards or educational policy may be within the institution's prerogative, and would not fall under the ambit of protected speech. Other First Amendment claims will help to ascertain the nature of First Amendment protections.

Protected Speech in Dismissal or Termination

An analysis of the type of protected speech litigated in the courts will serve to define the scope of First Amendment protections. *Scallet v. Rosenblum*[390] is a good example of the differentiation between "protected speech" and "employee speech." A probationary professor's contract was not renewed and he claimed a violation of his First Amendment rights. The court found that classroom speech about diversity issues at the university disrupted the pedagogical mission of the institution and was not protected speech. But, speech about diversity issues at faculty meetings and the placement of cartoons outside his office door were both protected speech under the First Amendment. The plaintiff, however, was unable to show that the protected speech was the motivating factor for the university's decision not to renew his contract.

A number of cases involve findings that the speech involved was not protected speech under the First Amendment. Most of these cases hinge on the institutional prerogative to maintain cer-

---

[388] Hamer v. Brown, 831 F.2d 1398 (8th Cir. 1987).
[389] Brown v. Texas A & M Univ., 804 F.2d 327 (5th Cir. 1986).
[390] 911 F. Supp. 999 (W.D. Va. 1996)

tain academic standards. A Texas faculty member's use of profanity in the classroom to improve student performance, which ultimately resulted in his termination, was not protected speech.[391] The court reasoned that profanity or offensive speech can be regulated and the speech used to motivate his students was not a matter of public concern. In Ohio, a faculty member's refusal to teach a course assigned to him and his petition for the removal of the department chair became the basis for his termination. The court found that the faculty member did not meet his burden in proving that these activities were protected speech, and that the activities did interfere with the administration of the department.[392] An Indiana faculty member was dismissed because he failed to cover the prescribed material in class and spent an inordinate amount of class time on discussions of "nonpertinent matters."[393] The court acknowledged the authority of the institution to set the curriculum and refused to recognize a faculty prerogative to use the classroom as a forum to discuss noncourse related, personal matters of tenure.[394] These cases indicate that the institution does maintain control over curricular matters and academic standards in the classroom.

Speech involving the institution's research policies also comes before the courts. In Mississippi, the court denied a motion for summary judgment, finding that a nontenured professor's comments on the disposal of laboratory waste at a community landfill was protected speech.[395] At trial, the court would have to determine whether the speech was the motivating factor in the denial of tenure decision. In Virginia, a faculty librarian alleged that his dismissal from the faculty resulted from his pronouncements to the state legislative audit committee on the library's materials procurement procedures.[396] The court found that the institution's decision to dismiss him was not motivated by protected speech. Further, the court found his use of the institution's grievance procedures to object to the reduction of his contract length from three years to one year was not protected speech.

In Texas, the court found that a faculty member's denial of tenure may have been based on public pronouncements on the misuse of research funds, in violation of First Amendment pro-

---

[391] Martin v. Parrish, 805 F.2d 583 (5th Cir. 1986).

[392] Smith v. Kent State Univ., 696 F.2d 476 (6th Cir. 1983).

[393] Riggin v. Board of Trustees of Ball State Univ., 489 N.E.2d 616, 629 (Ind. Ct. App. 1986).

[394] Mayberry v. Dees, 663 F.2d 502 (4th Cir. 1981), *cert. denied*, 459 U.S. 830 (1982).

[395] Staheli v. University of Miss., 621 F. Supp. 449 (N.D. Miss. 1985).

[396] Leachman v. Rector and Visitors of Univ. of Va., 691 F. Supp. 961 (W.D. Va. 1988).

tected speech.[397] In Indiana, a professor denied research funds by a federal agency alleged First Amendment speech violations and commenced a protracted controversy that eventually involved the top institutional officers, the governor, a United States Senator, and agents from the Federal Bureau of Investigation and state police.[398] The faculty member continued his pronouncements and the controversy over a period of nine years, with threatening and near slanderous behavior resulting in the initiation of institutional procedures to censure and dismiss him. While the court acknowledged the existence of First Amendment speech, the court also found that the faculty member's unprofessional conduct, not the protected speech, served as the basis for dismissal.[399] The court noted that the controversy was disruptive and, if continued, could prove to be destructive to a major research university.[400] This is similar to another court's finding that speech conducted in a threatening and unbusiness-like manner was not protected speech.[401] A dispute over the terms and conditions of a faculty member's contract, specifically the departmental assignment of the faculty member, was not protected speech.[402] Failure to execute three contracts and to meet assigned classes was, the courts said, abandonment of employment, not protected speech. Other cases similarly involved a failure to establish a claim of activities involving protected speech.[403]

Faculty pronouncements about institutional research policies that involve the expenditure of funds or the relationship between the institution and federal or state agencies are viewed as matters of public concern and are, therefore, protected speech. In *McCann v. Ruiz*,[404] a seismologist raised questions about the construction of an electric generating plant on a seismic fault. With pressure from the power company, the institution decided not to renew his contract as director of the Seismic Network or his probationary associate professor's contract. A federal district court found that the seismologist's First Amendment rights had been violated, issued an injunction reinstating him, and awarded damages. They labeled the violation "whistle blowing." However, speech that involves harassment (e.g., frequent calls at all hours), threats to ones safety or good name, or bordering on slander can result in

---

[397] Goodman v. Gallerano, 695 S.W.2d 286 (Tex. Ct. App. 1985).
[398] Fong v. Purdue Univ., 692 F. Supp. 930 (N.D. Ind. 1988).
[399] *Id.* at 959.
[400] *Id.* at 958.
[401] Russ v. White, 541 F. Supp. 888 (W.D. Ark. 1981).
[402] Jordan v. Board of Regents, Univ. Sys. of Ga., 583 F. Supp. 23 (S.D. Ga. 1984).
[403] Carley v. Arizona Bd. of Regents, 737 P.2d 1099 (Ariz. Ct. App. 1987); Weinstein v. University of Ill., 628 F. Supp. 862 (N.D. Ill. 1986); Stastney v. Board of Trustees of Cent. Wash. Univ., 647 P.2d 496 (Wash. Ct. App. 1982).
[404] 802 F. Supp. 606 (P.R. 1992).

the loss of speech rights or could be viewed as unprotected speech.

Speech on matters of public concern has also been protected. For example, a faculty member's employment was terminated after he advised a group of students to seek legal counsel. This was the sole basis for his termination. The court found the advice was was protected.[405] But when a Stanford faculty member publicly encouraged student activism to shut down the university, the court found that while the faculty member's speech was protected, it was also disruptive and could serve as the basis for dismissal.[406] Nondisruptive pronouncements on public matters are protected speech and cannot serve as the basis for a dismissal.

In a case not involving dismissal or termination, a federal court found that the removal of art work to a less strategically located art gallery did not violate a faculty member's First Amendment rights.[407] The art work was moved from a display at the main entrance of the college to a less heavily traveled area because the art work, depicting explicit sexual activities, was viewed as obscene and racially offensive. The institution, under certain standards, can control the content of speech where that speech is viewed as legally obscene or offensive. It should be noted, however, that in this case, the speech was not denied but rather it was relocated to a less public area.

Disruptive Protected Speech

As *Waters* demonstrates, protected speech that is disruptive to the effective operation of the organization can serve as the basis for an adverse employment decision. A recent renowned case on this point is *Jeffries v. Harleston*.[408] The black studies department chair and a tenured professor gave a speech that raised a firestorm of controversy. As a result, the chair was removed from his position. He sued, claiming his First Amendment speech had been violated when he made a speech on matters of political, sociological, and economic issues. Specifically, his speech contained numerous anti-Semitic comments. A jury verdict in federal district court found that the chair had been removed because of his speech, which violated First Amendment rights. The Second Circuit Court of Appeals affirmed the First Amendment violation finding that the administrators were not protected from liability

---

[405] Stern v. Shouldice, 706 F.2d 742 (6th Cir. 1983), *cert. denied*, 464 U.S. 993 (1983).
[406] Franklin v. Leland Stanford Junior Univ., 218 Cal. Rptr. 228 (6th Cir. 1985).
[407] Piarowski v. Illinois Community College Dist. # 515, 759 F.2d 625 (7th Cir. 1985).
[408] 828 F. Supp. 1066 (S.D.N.Y. 1991), jury verdict for the professor; *aff'd in part, vacated in part, and remanded*, 21 F.3d 1238 (2d Cir. 1994); *granted cert., vacated and remanded*, 511 U.S. 661 (1994).

due to qualified immunity, but vacated the award of punitive damages. After the Supreme Court vacated and remanded the case in light of *Waters*, the Second Circuit Court of Appeals found for the university.[409] The court found that it was reasonable for the administrators to base their decision to remove Dr. Jeffries as department head on a finding that his speech about Jewish people created a disruptive atmosphere for the effective operation of the university. The disruptive nature of his speech supersedes any First Amendment claim he could raise.

Employee Speech

Speech involving employment conditions is not considered to be protected speech and can be the basis for termination or dismissal where it is viewed as disruptive or insubordinate. An analysis of the alleged speech found to be unprotected employee speech will illuminate the definition of such speech in higher education.

Employee speech involving matters of public concern will be protected by the First Amendment. For example, the Third Circuit Court of Appeals found that while part of a controversy in a chemistry department may have been personal disputes, the record indicated that matters of educational standards and academic policy were applied broadly to the institution, not just within the department.[410] The court found that controversies over these standards were matters of public concern covered by the First Amendment and vacated the lower court summary judgment for the institution on the First Amendment claim.

Other cases demonstrate that some forms of employee speech are not matters of public concern and, therefore, are not protected speech. For example, in one case, the court found that the filing of a grievance over a question of denial of promotion to an associate professor was not a matter of public concern and was not protected speech.[411] In Arizona, the court found that complaints about the hiring of a particular individual as an assistant professor within the department was not a matter of public concern, but rather employee speech not covered by the First Amendment.[412] In Kentucky, a federal district court found that complaints about the staffing and support of a program, the administrative skills of the dean and his department chair, the circulation of a course outline

---

[409] Jeffries v. Harleston, 52 F.3d 9 (2d Cir. 1996).

[410] Johnson v. Lincoln Univ. of Commw. Sys. of Higher Educ., 776 F.2d 443 (3d Cir. 1985).

[411] Singh v. Lamar Univ., 635 F. Supp. 737 (E.D. Tex. 1986).

[412] Harris v. Arizona Bd. of Regents, 528 F. Supp. 987 (D. Ark. 1981).

on management in which he insisted several administrators should enroll, and derogatory comments about a particular academic program by a faculty member were viewed as employee speech not covered by First Amendment protections.[413]

These cases point out that speech which is not of public concern will not be protected by First Amendment speech provisions. Such topics as management criticism, involving matters mainly of interest to the employee will be beyond the reach of protected speech. However, matters which go to the overall health of the institution, application of academic standards, or expenditure or misuse of resources will be viewed by the courts as protected speech. Dismissal or termination for protected speech is an unacceptable constitutional violation when it is the reason for this employment action.

Other First Amendment Faculty Speech Claims

Outside the context of employment decisions, faculty have raised other First Amendment speech violations. *Burnham v. Ianni*[414] raises the question of whether the removal of a display of pictures of the history faculty dressed in period costumes, holding guns and knives in keeping with their areas of interest, violated the faculty's First Amendment rights. The chancellor of the university ordered the display removed after anonymous threats had been made to another faculty member's life, creating a violent environment. The Chancellor reasoned that the display added to the current unsettled situation on the campus. Reversing the lower court decision, the Eighth Circuit Court of Appeals found that even if the faculty First Amendment rights had been violated, the Chancellor was protected by qualified immunity. The Chancellor was given qualified immunity because he removed what he viewed as "potentially disruptive and inappropriate subject matter" and "officers of reasonable competence could disagree on this issue"[415] (the issue being the removal of the display as disruptive).

Loving v. Boren[416] involved the issue of access by faculty to Internet services. Fearing that those under 18 would have access to adult newsgroups on the Internet, the university blocked ac-

---

[413] Landrum v. Eastern Ky. Univ., 578 F. Supp. 241 (E.D. Ky. 1984).
[414] 98 F.3d 1007 (8th Cir. 1996).
[415] *Id.* at 1020.
[416] 956 F. Supp. 953 (W.D. Okla. 1997).

cess to those newsgroups. However, computer-savvy users still had access through alternative routes. Later, the university set up two servers: one server to which anyone had access but on which no adult newsgroups were available; the other server had all existing news groups available but had restricted access to those over 18 years who agreed to certain terms of usage. A faculty member sued, claiming his First Amendment rights had been violated. A federal district court ruled that any First Amendment claim was moot, both by the alternative route to access newsgroups in the first policy, and the accessibility to newsgroups in the new policy. The court also held that university computer service and the Internet service is not a "public forum" requiring heightened First Amendment protection.[417]

Conclusions on First Amendment Speech

While there is an overlap between them, academic freedom is a contractual right and First Amendment protections are constitutional guarantees granted to employees at public institutions. Protected speech of public employees under the First Amendment covers only pronouncements on matters of public concern, not matters of mere personal interest to the public employee. The manner within which the speech is conducted will also determine whether it is protected. Protected speech that is viewed as disruptive to the functioning of a public organization can serve as the basis for adverse employment decision. In the last analysis, the court will balance a public employer's right to operate an efficient and effective organization against the employee's protected speech rights. An indication of the existence of the employer's rights are those cases which give the institution the prerogative to regulate academic standards and curriculum content and prevent disruption of the effective functioning of the organization. That is not, however, meant to diminish the importance the courts have placed on the free speech rights of public employees and the particular emphasis on the need for academic freedom in higher education.

Chapter Conclusions

This review of faculty employment cases has implications for institutional policy. These implications can be most clearly stated by discussing them under each of the issue areas previously reviewed.

---

[417] *Id.* at 955.

Terms of the Contract

The contract terms include the letter of employment, policy manuals, and institutional employment practices. If the contract clearly states that the contract is a one-year contract, renewal can not become obligatory by the development of a review process during the probationary period or by language that indicates that the probationary faculty member will be considered for reappointment.

Where policies clearly put employment action in the hands of the board, the board may be obligated to officially decide to either renew or not renew employment contracts. In some cases, depending on the language of state statutes, this authority may not be delegated to another institutional officer, either through institutional policies or a collective bargaining agreement.

De facto tenure will not be awarded by the court where an institution has clearly spelled out the procedures to achieve tenure. Added protection against *de facto* tenure would be a clear statement that the achievement of *de facto* tenure is not possible. The development of evaluation procedures for probationary faculty during the period of employment, but prior to the tenure review, would not obligate the institution in question to renew the one-year contract.

If the institution has a policy of reviewing a probationary faculty member after a specified number of years of employment, it will breach the contract if it fails to evaluate the probationary faculty member in the specified year. However, a review would not have to be conducted if the probationary faculty member was notified that the review year contract was a terminal contract. A contract will be breached if notification of nonrenewal does not conform to specified time constraints.

Nonrenewal

In court, a probationary faculty member can sustain neither a claim of a property right requiring due process in the nonrenewal decision nor a claim of a liberty interest because of the nonrenewal decisions. Further, providing reasons to the probationary faculty member in confidence does not implicate a liberty interest, unless those reasons impugn the probationary faculty member's good name (i.e., charges of plagiarism, cheating, etc.)

Denial of Tenure

Tenure reviews, if conducted consistent with fundamentally fair institutional policies, will withstand challenges in court. Where tenure policies have been violated or a decision is found to be unreasonable, arbitrary, or capricious, the court will usually order a new review purged of the error. In unusual circumstances, however, based on the nature of the institution's policies, the court may be compelled to award tenure.

In charges of violation of protected rights under federal EEO regulations, the regulatory agency (i.e., EEOC) or the plaintiff will be given access to materials reviewed in the tenure decision plus access to the materials used for other probationary faculty tenure decisions within a relevant time frame. Further, the courts have granted access to the deliberations of the promotion and tenure committee. The courts, where clearly stated in institutional policies or state statutes, have supported the president's or the board's ultimate decision authority in matters of tenure. However, it is clear that the decision must be supported by valid reasons and would not be upheld if it was found to be arbitrary, capricious, or discriminatory in nature.

Termination of Tenured Faculty for Cause

Insubordination, uncooperative behavior, neglect of duty, incompetence, moral turpitude, and violations of ethical and professional standards will be accepted by the courts as valid causes for termination but must be substantiated at the hearing. The specific charges must be clearly stated in the letter of notification to the tenured faculty member. The letter should also advise faculty members of their rights under the due process procedures as outlined in institutional policy. The question of the right to legal counsel is yet unsettled. While the court may hold that the institution could not deny counsel the right to attend the hearing, the institution may be able to limit counsel's participation in the proceedings. The institution should ensure adherence to the procedures outlined in the faculty handbook during termination proceedings. The written findings of the hearing committee should provide a clear link between the charges, the evidence, and the conclusions and should be made available to the charged faculty member and those who must render a final decision. The institution can have a procedure that allows the president or the board to review the hearing committee report and render a final decision contrary to the recommendation of the hearing committee. However, the rudiments of fair play and due process must be followed and the evidence should support the conclusion. Further, it is essential that the institution comply with any policies governing the manner in which a hearing report is transmitted to the president or the board. A letter to the faculty member communicating the results should describe the link between the charges, the supporting evidence, and the decision where termination is the selected action.

First Amendment Speech

Speech surrounding issues of employment that are not on matters of public concern are not covered by First Amendment guarantees. Denial of tenure due to pronouncements on matters of public concern are impermissible and violate First Amendment rights. The burden would fall on the institution to show that denial of tenure would have taken place even if no pronouncements were made. Protected speech disruptive to the effective operation of the institution can serve as the basis for an adverse employment decision.

Liability Claims

Liability claims for damages have been made for violations of contract rights or Constitutional rights. It can be said with certainty that the court will, at minimum, order a new evaluation and another probationary year of employment when violations of employee rights have been clearly established. Damage awards could include the award of tenure where the institutional policy so stipulates.

Defamation claims based on evaluations of job performance have not withstood court scrutiny. However, claims that allege violations of ethical codes or laws may stand up under defamation charges and should be viewed carefully in light of liberty interest claims. Due process procedures should be implemented in these types of claims in order to protect rights and avoid later litigation.

Institutions of higher education need to review their policies to determine the intent of the policies and to make sure they uphold the concepts of fundamental fairness and maintain the institution's academic integrity. Institutions have been given great latitude by the courts in these matters, but individual rights cannot be ignored.

CHAPTER V

The Quest for Equity and Diversity in Employment in Higher Education

Introduction

The evolution of the concept of equity in American higher education emanates from the Fifth and Fourteenth Amendments to the Constitution. While the Fifth Amendment helps define the relationship of a citizen to the federal government, the Fourteenth Amendment uses similar language to define the relationship of a citizen to the state. The Fourteenth Amendment, which applies the Bill of Rights to citizens in a relationship with the state, reads:

> All persons born or naturalized in the United States, and subject to the jurisdiction thereof, are citizens of the United States and of the State wherein they reside. No State shall make or enforce any law which shall abridge the privileges or immunities of citizens of the United States; nor shall any State deprive any person of life, liberty, or property, without due process of law; nor deny to any person within its jurisdiction the equal protection of the laws.[418]

Public institutions of higher education are agents of state government and must guarantee to state citizens' due process and equal protection under the law. Historically, the concept of equity has evolved from the concept of slavery to the concept of segregation through the separate but equal doctrine,[419] and on to today's standard of integration and equality.[420] Appended to this notion is also the concept of diversity; an attempt to insure that the employees of an institution come from a multiplicity of racial, gender, religious, and ethnic backgrounds, which more closely mirror society at large. The quest for both equity and diversity have at times resulted in clashes between legal notions of equal protection under the law and plans to achieve diversity. The notion of racial neutrality in admissions and scholarships are endemic of this clash, and will be discussed in the chapter on student issues.

---

[418] U.S. Const. Amend. XIV § 1.
[419] Plessy v. Ferguson, 163 U.S. 537 (1896).
[420] Civil Rights Cases, 109 U.S. 3 (1883).

The concept of equal protection under the law implies that if the state guarantees certain rights, these rights must be guaranteed to each person equally. At the same time, certain privileges could be awarded based on merit. As long as the criteria used to determine merit are free of bias or preference based on race, sex, national origin, and religion, then equity has been achieved. Institutions of higher education award grades, degrees, and employment positions based on merit, and the assurance of equity in these awards has resulted in legislation to protect basic rights. Legislation has helped to further define the concept of equity and reinforce the constitutional guarantees. Litigation emanating from this legislation has further defined the concept of equity.

Federal Legislation to Insure Equity

Federal legislation on the concept of equity in the decades of the 1960s and the 1970s significantly changed the ways employers and employees interacted. For example, the Civil Rights Act of 1964 contains two significant sections prohibiting discrimination. One, title VI, prohibits discrimination in programs receiving federal financial assistance and states, "No person in the United States shall on the grounds of race, color, or national origin, be excluded from participation in, be denied the benefits of, or be subjected to discrimination under any program or activity receiving federal financial assistance."[421]

The other, title VII of the Civil Rights Act of 1964, covers discrimination in employment based on race, color, religion, sex, or national origin. Employment includes hiring and other employment practices such as tests used to evaluate employment status. Title VII, amended by the Equal Opportunities Act of 1972, states:

(a) It shall be an unlawful employment practice for an employer: (1) to fail or refuse to hire or to discharge any individual, or otherwise to discriminate against any individual with respect to compensation, terms, conditions, or privileges of employment because of such individuals race, color, religion, sex, or national origin; (2) to limit, segregate, or classify his employees or applicants for employment in any way which would deprive or tend to

---

[421] Title VI of the Civil Rights Act of 1964, 42 U.S.C. 2000I et. seq.

deprive any individual of employment opportunities or otherwise adversely affect his status as an employee, because of such individuals race, color, religion, sex, or national origin.

(b) It shall be an unlawful employment practice for an employment agency to fail or refuse to refer for employment, or otherwise to discriminate against, any individual because of his race, color, religion, sex, or national origin, or to classify or refer for employment any individual on the basis of his race, color, religion, sex, or national origin.[422]

Employment discrimination was also regulated to prevent discrimination in the award of pay. The Equal Pay Act states:

No employer having employees subject to any provision of this section shall discriminate, within any establishment in which such employees are employed, between employees on the basis of sex by paying wages to employees in such establishments at a rate less than the rate at which he pays wages to employees of the opposite sex in such establishment for equal work or jobs the performance of which requires equal skill, effort, and responsibility, and which are performed under similar conditions, except where such payment is made pursuant to (I) a seniority system; (II) a merit system; (III) a system which measures earnings by quantity or quality of production; or (IV) a differential based on any other factor other than sex; Provided, that an employer who is paying a wage rate differential in violation of this subsection shall not, in order to comply with the provisions of this subsection, reduce the wage rate of any employee.[423]

Several other federal statutes make it unlawful to discriminate on the basis of age[424] and disability[425] in programs receiving federal financial assistance. These laws are patterned after title VI as is title IX of the Education Amendments of 1972. Title IX stimulated a controversy, whose resolution would reinforce a number of these provisions. Title IX simply reads: No person in the United States shall, on the basis of sex, be excluded from participation in, be denied the benefits of, or be subjected to discrimination under

---

[422] Title VII of the Civil Rights Act of 1964 (as amended by the Equal Opportunities Act of 1972), 42 U.S.C. 2000e et. seq.

[423] The Equal Pay Act of 1963, 29 U.S.C. 206(d) et. seq.

[424] The Age Discrimination in Employment Act of 1967, 29 U.S.C. 621-34 et. seq.

[425] The Rehabilitation Act of 1973, 29 U.S.C. 701 et. seq.

any educational program or activity receiving federal financial assistance.[426]

While title VII and The Equal Pay Act were written for business organizations, their application to higher education has become routine.[427] From its inception title IX, written for the academic enterprise, was embroiled in controversy involving its application to higher education. This controversy would eventually become the catalyst for reform.

The Saga of Title IX and the Reform of Civil Rights

The method by which Congress passed title IX was somewhat unique and may have contributed to the ongoing controversy. Title IX was presented as an amendment to the Education Amendments on the floor of Congress without prior hearings. The result was a number of post enactment hearings to define the scope of the law. Further, the regulations[428] to administer the law written by HEW and later under the jurisdiction of the Department of Education were embroiled in controversy over their scope. A number of issues would be debated into the 1990s and included questions surrounding intercollegiate athletics, single-sex programs and institutions, and employment. It was the employment issue that eventually resulted in the reform of the civil rights laws.

The Department of Education assumed in the regulations that title IX covered not only students, but also employees. However, the courts were reluctant to include employment under the scope of title IX throughout most of 1970s.[429] It appeared from the litigation of that decade that the administrative agency's regulation had exceeded the scope of the law.

Two cases decided in 1980 by separate federal circuit courts of appeals would change the interpretation of the law's regulatory authority over employment. The Second Circuit Court of Appeals ruled that the scope of title IX covered employment.[430] The court

---

[426] Title IX of the Education Amendments of 1972, 20 U.S.C. 1681(a).

[427] R. Hendrickson & B. Lee, ACADEMIC EMPLOYMENT AND RETRENCHMENT: JUDICIAL REVIEW AND ADMINISTRATIVE ACTION, ASHE-ERIC Higher Education Research Report No. 8, p. 66 (1983).

[428] 34 C.F.R. 1-106.71 (1980).

[429] See Seattle Univ. v. United States, 621 F.2d 992 (9th Cir. 1980), vacated sub nom, United States Dept. of Educ. v. Seattle Univ., 456 U.S. 986 (1982); Romeo Community School v. HEW, 600 F.2d 581 (6th Cir. 1979), cert. denied, 444 U.S. 972 (1979); University of Toledo v. HEW, 464 F. Supp. 693 (N.D. Ohio 1979).

[430] North Haven Board of Educ. v. Hufstedler, 629 F.2d 773 (2d Cir. 1980).

reached this conclusion through an analysis not only of the debate during passage of the amendment, but also through postenactment debate and legislative actions by Congress concerning title IX. The Fifth Circuit Court of Appeals reached a similar conclusion but limited coverage to those programs where the employee's compensation was paid fully or in part through federal funds.[431] The Supreme Court agreed to hear a case in order to resolve the questions of the scope of the law.

In addition to the question of the law's coverage of employment, two sub-issues faced the Court.[432] One surrounded the question of the definition of what constituted federal aid. Clearly, moneys paid directly to the institution in the form of loans, grants, or contract performance would be covered under the law, but was money given to students in the form of loans and grants also considered to be direct federal financial assistance? Further, the scope of the law's coverage within the institution receiving federal money required resolution. This question focused on the definition of the word "program." The Court needed to determine whether the institution was a program under the law or if the word was intended to refer to only the specific unit or activity within an institution that was supported wholly or in part by direct federal financial assistance. The resolution of these issues by the Court would determine the scope of title IX.

In *North Haven Board of Education v. Bell,*[433] the United States Supreme Court addressed the issue of whether title IX covered employment. The Court adopted the Second Circuit's method of analyzing post-enactment legislative actions on the title to arrive at a finding that title IX was intended by Congress to cover employment. However, the Court disagreed with the lower court, concluding that the law covers only specific programs receiving federal financial assistance and left the definition of a program to subsequent litigation.

In 1982, the Court finally resolved these questions of the definition of a program and direct financial assistance while significantly narrowing the scope of title IX in *Grove City College v. Bell.*[434] The case involved a controversy over the fact that Grove

---

[431] Dougherty City School Sys. v. Harris, 622 F.2d 735 (5th Cir. 1980).

[432] *See* R. Hendrickson & B. Lee, *supra* note 10; Note, *Title IX of the Education Amendments of 1972: Does It Protect Employment of Educational Institutions?*, 47 BROOK. L. REV. 1075 (1981); D. Murphey, *Title IX: An Alternative Remedy for Sex-Based Employment Discrimination for Academic Employees?*, 55 ST. JOHNS L. REV. 329 (1981); R. Salamone, *Title IX and Employment Discrimination: A Wrong in Search of A Remedy*, 9 J. OF L. & EDUC. 433 (1980).

[433] 456 U.S. 512 (1982).

[434] 465 U.S. 555 (1984).

City College refused to complete compliance forms required by the Department of Education. Grove City maintained that since they received no direct federal funds, that the college was not required to complete the forms. The Department of Education maintained that the College received federal aid in the form of federal student loans and grants to students. The Court ruled that student aid was direct federal financial assistance under the law but that a program was defined as only the program or activity directly receiving the funds (i.e., the financial aid office at Grove City College), not the institution itself. This ruling, in effect, rendered title IX impotent since it narrowed the scope of its coverage to those offices within an institution receiving direct federal financial assistance. The case had implications for the scope of other civil rights statutes that were also based on the receipt of federal money and had similar program specific language. The case stimulated the United States Congress to reconsider the scope of these statutes.

In 1988, Congress passed and then overrode a presidential veto to enact the Civil Rights Restoration Act.[435] While some might argue that the word restoration is a misnomer, the law redefined the meaning of the word "program" to cover the whole institution where direct federal financial assistance is received by any part of that organization. The law also specifies that "program" means any state system of education where any part of the system receives federal financial assistance.

Other Title IX Cases

Most of the early litigation involving title IX surrounded the scope of coverage of the law, and the number of cases which address specific discriminatory actions under the statute were scant until the 1990s. However, the statute could prove to be an effective tool in the quest for equity because it allows direct access to a court. Unlike title VII which requires the pursuit of administrative remedies through the Equal Employment Opportunities Commission, the Supreme Court in *Cannon v. University of Chicago*,[436] ruled that a private right of action existed under title IX. This means that a private individual can take their case directly to a court for adjudication.

---

[435] The Civil Rights Restoration Act, P.L. 100-259 (1987); 102 Stat. 28 (1987).
[436] 441 U.S. 677 (1979).

Subsequent litigation on *Cannon* addressed the merits of whether there was evidence based on sex discrimination. On remand from the Supreme Court, the Seventh Circuit Court of Appeals ruled, that in title IX cases, as in title VI cases, the "disparate treatment" test (requiring proof of intent to discriminate) rather than "disparate impact" test (which only looks at outcome) should be applied in cases where the punishment would be the loss of federal funds.[437] A decision on the merits in the *Cannon* case resulted in a finding that the medical schools to which Ms. Cannon had applied had not discriminated against her on the basis of sex.[438] This protracted litigation ended with a court issued contempt order based on what the court termed frivolous appeals causing excessive harassment to the defendants,[439] and the assessment of fines emanating from violations of the court order to cease litigation.[440]

In the decade following the passage of the Civil Rights Restoration Act, title IX litigation began to address gender discrimination issues in higher education. In *Bowers v. Baylor University*,[441] a United States district court in Texas ruled that a private cause of action for damages existed under title IX. When a female, women's basketball coach was removed, she brought an exclusive claim under title IX of gender discrimination. The court denied the university's motion to dismiss. A United States District Court in Ohio reached a different conclusion in *Wedding v. University of Toledo*.[442] The court found that no private right of action existed under title IX for sex discrimination in employment. The court stated, "Thus, if an employee could maintain an implied private right of action under title IX, the very expressed provisions of title VII could be avoided. See *Storey v. Board of Regents*, 604 F. Supp. 1200, 1205 (W.D. Wis. 1985). This Court is not persuaded that Congress intended such a result."[443]

There is no indication which of these positions would emerge, but cases have been adjudicated which involve both title IX and title VII claims of gender discrimination. For example, the Fifth

---

[437] Cannon v. University of Chicago, 648 F.2d 1104 (7th Cir. 1981), *cert. denied*, 454 U.S. 811 (1981).

[438] Cannon v. University Health Sciences/Univ. of Chicago, 710 F.2d 777 (7th Cir. 1983).

[439] Cannon v. Loyola Univ. of Chicago, 784 F.2d 777 (7th Cir. 1986).

[440] Cannon v. Loyola Univ. of Chicago, 116 F.R.D. 244 (N.D. Ill.1987); *see also* Cannon v. Loyola Univ. of Chicago, 676 F. Supp. 823 (N.D. Ill. 1987); Cannon v. Loyola Univ. of Chicago, 687 F. Supp. 424 (N.D. Ill. 1988).

[441] 862 F. Supp. 142 (W.D. Tex. 1994).

[442] 862 F. Supp. 201 (N.D. Ohio 1994).

[443] *Id* at 203.

Circuit Court of Appeals ruled that a terminated women's athletic director had a private right of action under title IX in a claim of retaliation.[444] Further, the court held that the lower court abused its discretion when it denied her motion to add a title VII claim to her complaint. A Kansas federal district court ruled that a former women's basketball coach had a private right of action to claim retaliatory discharge under title IX.[445] The court also found, that the plaintiff was not required to exhaust administrative remedies before bringing a title IX claim.

In *Nelson v. University of Maine*,[446] two professors spoke out on gender discrimination against particular administrators at the institution who discriminated against women. The institution retaliated against the two professors by raising allegations of sexual harassment against one of the professors but never investigated these allegations, and denied tenure to the other professor. The professors filed both First Amendment free speech claims and retaliation claims under title IX. The court, ruling on several preliminary motions, found that the professors' First Amendment speech claims were subsumed into their title IX claim. Maine's six-year statute of limitations on liability claims also covered title IX claims, and the time within which the professors' title IX claim could be filed commenced on the date he was notified that he would be denied tenure.[447]

It appears that the court will use the shifting burden of proof strategy[448] used under title IX based on several sexual harassment cases[449] brought under title IX. Further, a private right of action appears to exist under title IX in claims of gender discrimination in employment and plaintiffs do not have to exhaust administrative remedies before proceeding to court.[450]

---

[444] Lowery v. Texas A & M Univ. Sys.,117 F.3d 242 (5th Cir. 1997).

[445] Clay v. Board of Trustees of Neosho County Community College, 905 F. Supp. 1488 (D. Kan. 1995).

[446] 914 F. Supp. 643 (D. Me. 1996).

[447] *Id.*

[448] The shifting burden of proof in title VII cases involves the following: The plaintiff establishes a prima facie case, the burden shifts to the employer or institution to establish valid reasons for its action, the burden then shifts back to the plaintiff to establish that the reasons were a pretext for discrimination. McDonnell Douglas Corp. v. Green, 411 U.S. 792 (1972).

[449] See chapter VI on sexual harassment.

[450] See discussion of student litigation under title IX in chapter VII.

Discrimination Under Title VII

Title VII of the Civil Rights Act of 1964 covers discrimination in employment. While it seemed clear that this title, along with other equal protection statutes, covered race, gender and religious discrimination, questions remained as to whether these provisions covered ethnic discrimination. The Supreme Court in *Saint Francis College v. Al-Khazraji*[451] ruled that ethnic origin, in this case Arabian ancestry, was covered by the statutes governing equal protection.

Religious educational institutions and institutions supported or controlled by a religious organization are exempt from title VII. In *Killinger v. Samford*,[452] a professor of a Baptist university sued claiming religious discrimination under title VII when he was removed from a position in the divinity school. A federal district court granted a summary judgment to the institution finding that the divinity school was exempt as a religious educational institution and the university was exempt as an organization substantially supported by the state Baptist Convention. Some religious affiliated private institutions not permeated with religious doctrine would probably not meet this exemption except in their divinity or theological programs. Institutions like Northwestern University or the University of Denver are examples of this type of institution.

Title VII is enforced by the Equal Employment Opportunities Commission (EEOC) which is an administrative adjudicative agency designed to resolve title VII disputes. A plaintiff alleging discrimination under the statute does not have a direct private right of action in court but rather must file a complaint with the EEOC. The agency will issue a right to sue letter only after it has established that discrimination may have occurred and after all attempts to settle the dispute have failed. Failure to seek administrative remedies through EEOC within the time period specified in the regulations (300 days from the date of the unlawful employment practice) will bar any attempt to litigate under the statute.[453] Litigation and precedents have evolved around the concept of counting or tolling the number of days before the statute

---

[451] 481 U.S. 604 (1987).

[452] 113 F.3d 196 (11th Cir. 1997).

[453] Casavantes v. California State Univ., Sacramento, 732 F.2d 1441 (9th Cir. 1984).

of limitations bars litigation. The doctrine of "equitable tolling" involves an attempt to start tolling from the time the plaintiff became aware of the discriminatory employment practice as opposed to when it actually occurred.[454] Along with tolling is the procedural issue of immunity of the state from the law. States have been unsuccessful in claiming immunity from prosecution under the protection of the Eleventh Amendment in title VII litigation[455]

Title VII allows litigation to proceed in two ways. One is a "disparate impact" suit in which the plaintiff attempts to prove that a particular employment practice has a negative impact or effect on minority opportunities. If the plaintiff is successful, then the burden shifts to the defendant's employer to prove that the employment practice serves a necessary business purpose.[456] The other is "disparate treatment," which as a prosecution device, requires intent to discriminate. The United States Supreme Court prescribed in *McDonnell Douglas Corporation v. Green*[457] a three-part shifting burden of proof strategy in "disparate treatment" cases. First, the plaintiff shoulders the burden to establish a prima facie case of discrimination (on the face of it, discrimination appears to have occurred). The burden then shifts to the defendant to articulate valid job related reasons for the contested employer action. Finally, if the employer meets the burden, then the burden shifts back to the plaintiff to prove that the reasons given were a pretext for discrimination. The case law is organized around these two strategies.

Disparate Impact

Donnelly v. Rhode Island Board of Governors for Higher Education[458] demonstrates the principles behind the concept of disparate impact theory. Faculty at the university brought this title VII claim alleging that the university's new minimum salary schedule for faculty had a disparate impact on women who were concentrated

---

[454] Mauro v. Board of Higher Educ., Kingsbourgh Community College, 658 F. Supp. 322 (S.D. N.Y. 1986), *aff'd*, 819 F.2d 1130, *cert. denied*, 108 S. Ct. 189 (1987); Ohemeng v. Delaware State College, 643 F. Supp. 1575 (D. Del. 1986); Shockley v. Vermont State Colleges, 793 F.2d 478 (2d Cir. 1986).

[455] Gehrt v. University of Ill. At Urbana-Champaign Coop Extension Serv., 974 F. Supp. 1178 (C.D. Ill. 1997); Stefanovic v. University of Tenn., 935 F. Supp. 944 (E.D. Tenn. 1996).

[456] W. Kohlburn, *The Double Edged Sword of Academic Freedom: Cutting the Scales of Justice in Title VII Litigation*, 65 Wash. Univ. L.Q. 445, 451 (1987).

[457] 411 U.S. 792 (1973).

[458] 110 F.3d 2 (1st Cir. 1997)

in the lower salary tier. The plan set up three salary tiers: the humanities tier, the natural sciences tier, and the business tier. The minimum salaries in the humanities tier, with high concentrations of women, were much lower than the other two tiers. A federal district court found for the university and the First Circuit Court of Appeals affirmed. The court stated:

> As the district court found in *Donnelly,* 929 F. Supp. at 591-92, the professor's choice of academic field and the workings of the national market, not Plan A, as such, are basically responsible for compensatory differences between the tiers within Plan A, these differences being generally established by reference to nationwide faculty salaries within disciplines. Most, if not all, higher education institutions in this country display a similar discipline based compensatory disparities; without Plan A, faculty members in Tier B [the humanities tier] would on the whole continue to earn less (probably even less than currently) than those in the higher tiers.[459]

Since the plaintiffs' failed to establish a prima facie case (the plan having an adverse impact on women) of disparate impact, the court found it unnecessary to address the issue whether the salary schedule meets the requirements as a business necessary as the lower court had done.[460]

An Alabama decision is another example of a "disparate impact" case.[461] The plaintiff, a white female, was passed over for a position at a predominantly black institution in favor of a black female returning from a doctoral leave. While hiring from within is a facially neutral employment practice, it has a disparate impact on white applicants because historic preference for black applicants at this institution has skewed the work force racially.[462] The federal appeals court noted that "disparate impact" claims could be filed not only in class action claims, but also by individuals. The institution failed to show that it had a compelling business purpose to give preference to employees on study leaves. The institution had argued that hiring those on study leave allowed the institution to improve the quality of the staff and hire staff at reduced salaries.[463] While laudable, these objectives do not overcome the past practice of preference in hiring for those from one

---

[459] *Id.* at 5.

[460] *Id.* at 6

[461] Craig v. Alabama State Univ., 804 F.2d 682 (11th Cir. 1986).

[462] *Id.* at 685. *See* Craig v. Johnson, 451 F. Supp. 1207 (M.D. Ala. 1978); the court found that the institution had discriminated against whites in employment decisions.

[463] *Id.* at 689.

race. Since the university failed to show job relatedness or the use of an "essential" business practice, the court saw no need to address the question of whether the practice was a pretext for discrimination.

In *Peters v. Lieuallen*,[464] the plaintiff failed to show that the hiring requirements of good written and oral communication skills, while racially neutral, had a disparate effect on minority applicants. The plaintiff failed to establish a prima facie case of discrimination. In *Hassan v. Auburn University*,[465] an unsuccessful applicant for a faculty position claimed that the requirement of English fluency had a disparate impact based on national origin discrimination. A federal district court found that English fluency, a valid criterion for teaching, would not necessarily have a disparate impact based on national origin.

Several cases involved allegations of religious discrimination because a Catholic college refused to hire a non-Catholic applicant to a theology position. In one of these cases, the court found that preference for a person of the religious faith of the affiliated college was a bona fide occupational practice essential to the operation of the theology department.[466] In another, the court found a disparate impact analysis unreachable because of First Amendment separation of church and state provisions.[467]

One case involving the failure of four female faculty members to achieve promotion or tenure is instructive of how disparate impact might be applied to the faculty promotion and tenure process.[468] The plaintiff must substantiate a discriminatory effect in criteria used for promotion and tenure. The female plaintiffs failed to substantiate the discriminatory effect when they used a broad sample of faculty outside their respective discipline, which showed that 65 percent of the men achieved tenure while only 42 percent of the women achieved tenure. Statistical sampling fails to take into account the decentralized nature of the decision, the varying criteria across various disciplines, and the number of available tenure positions within specific departments.[469] Further, the plaintiffs failed to show that the "facially neutral" tenure review process, using subjective peer reviews and criteria such as publication quality, had a discriminatory effect on female candidates.[470]

---

[464] 568 F. Supp. 261 (D. Or. 1983), *aff'd*, 746 F.2d 1390 (9th Cir. 1984).

[465] 833 F. Supp. 866 (M.D. Ala. 1993).

[466] Pime v. Loyola Univ. of Chicago, 585 F. Supp. 435 (N.D. Ill. 1984), *aff'd*, 803 F.2d 351 (7th Cir. 1986).

[467] Maguire v. Marquette Univ., 627 F. Supp. 1499 (E.D. Wis. 1986), *aff'd*, 814 F.2d 1213 (7th Cir. 1987).

[468] Zahorik v. Cornell Univ., 729 F.2d 85 (2d Cir. 1984).

[469] *Id.* at 92.

[470] *Id.* at 96.

Disparate Treatment

Cases based on this title VII theory involve the three-part burden of proof strategy discussed above. Many of the disparate treatment cases brought by individuals revolve around the denial of tenure or promotion of faculty. To establish a prima facie case, the plaintiff must show that the person is a member of a protected class, the person was qualified for the position sought, and that a person not from the protected class was hired. For example, in *Langland v. Vanderbilt University*,[471] an assistant professor failed to establish a prima facie case of discrimination in her denial of tenure. The assistant professor failed to establish that she was qualified to be promoted. The Eleventh Circuit Court of Appeals reached a similar conclusion in a case involving a woman who was not promoted to a full professorship.[472] In *Luxemburg v. Texas A & M University System*,[473] a member of the Jewish faith who was a tenure track professor claimed his salary had been reduced in retaliation for religious and national origin discrimination complaints he had filed against his department head and other administrators. The court found that he failed to establish a prima facie case of disparate treatment when his salary was reduced to the level negotiated at the time he was hired because he failed to receive a grant negotiated as part of his salary.

However, in *Field v. Clark University*,[474] the First Circuit Court of Appeals found that the plaintiff was able to establish a prima facie case when she provided evidence that the unanimous decision to deny tenure was made by an all-male faculty department. The plaintiff was also able to show that the reason (poor teaching) was pretextual because two male faculty with poor teaching evaluations and scholarship less substantial than hers were granted tenure.

When a prima facie case is established, the court moves on to the defendant employer's burden to establish a viable reason for the employment decision. For example, the Fourth Circuit Court of Appeals found that the lack of a terminal degree and poor scholarship demonstrated how the plaintiff had failed to meet the tenure

---

[471] 589 F. Supp. 995 (M.D. Tenn. 1984). For a similar result, *see* Edwards v. Interboro Inst., 840 F. Supp. 222 (E.D.N.Y. 1994).

[472] Wu v. Board of Trustees of the Univ. of Ala., 847 F.2d 1480 (11th Cir. 1988), *cert. denied*, 409 U.S. 1006 (1989). *See* Edwards v. Wallace Community College, 49 F.3d 1517 (11th Cir. 1995); as another example of a failure to establish a prima facie case of discrimination under disparate treatment theory.

[473] 863 F. Supp. 412 (S.D. Tex. 1994).

[474] 817 F.2d 931 (1st Cir. 1987).

standards of the institution and were valid reasons.[475] The Fifth Circuit Court of Appeals found that strong scholarship was not measured by a count of publications, but rather by the comprehensiveness and direction of research.[476] The Ninth Circuit Court of Appeals found that discrepancy in the award of tenure between women in the all-female nursing school and the all-male pharmacy school were due to differences in the two fields of study and not based on gender.[477] In New York, a federal district court found that the decision to not renew a tenure track faculty member was legitimately based on failure to demonstrate excellence in teaching and failure to construct an experimental laboratory on solid state mechanics.[478] In another case involving religious discrimination, the university provided legitimate reasons that the candidate was not qualified and the decision not to hire the applicant had nothing to do with his Jewish faith.[479] There was no evidence that anti-Semitic postings on the campus influenced the university's decision. Similarly, in another case, the institution provided legitimate reasons for not hiring a Hispanic applicant as director of the Spanish language program.[480]

In a Nebraska case, a federal district court found that the job assignments made to the plaintiff were no heavier than those made to other new faculty, either male or female. The institution refused to grant tenure for a valid and substantiated reason: negligence in the performance of duties.[481] In another case, the institution's reasons—the filled quota of tenured faculty, and poor interpersonal skills—were accepted as valid by the court.[482] Finally, a court found, based on the institution's policy, it would be valid to look at the potential promise of other probationary faculty not yet ready for tenure review. However, because of affirmative action statements in the policy, the plaintiff's gender should have been given additional consideration.[483]

Establishing valid job reasons shifts the burden back to the plaintiff to prove that the reasons are a pretext for discrimination.

---

[475] Ritter v. Mount St. Mary's College, 814 F.2d 986 (4th Cir. 1987), *cert. denied*, 484 U.S. 913 (1987).

[476] Merrill v. Southern Methodist Univ., 806 F.2d 600 (5th Cir. 1986).

[477] Rios v. Board of Regents of the Univ. of Ariz., 811 F.2d 1248 (9th Cir. 1987).

[478] Spencer v. City Univ. of N.Y./College of Staten Island, 932 F. Supp. 540 (S.D.N.Y. 1996). The faculty member of the Jewish faith had claimed religious discrimination motivated the nonrenewal decision.

[479] Shipowitz v. Board of Trustees of Univ. of D.C., 914 F. Supp. 1 (D.D.C. 1996).

[480] Stern v. Trustees of Columbia Univ., 903 F. Supp. 601 (S.D.N.Y. 1995).

[481] O'Connor v. Peru State College, 605 F. Supp. 753 (D. Neb. 1985).

[482] Waring v. Fordham Univ., 640 F. Supp. 42 (S.D.N.Y. 1986).

[483] Sola v. Lafayette College, 804 F.2d 40 (3d Cir. 1986).

Negating the employer's reasons as pretextual has been difficult in most cases. For example, hiring a female systems analyst as an affirmative action officer when no systems analyst jobs were available was not a pretext for discrimination.[484] Denying a black female clerk at the college bookstore a promotion based on previous poor work and attendance records was not pretextual, according to the Third Circuit Court of Appeals.[485]

LaFleur v. Wallace State Community College[486] is an excellent example where the plaintiff was able to prove that the employer's reasons were a pretext for discrimination. The plaintiff was one of a few black faculty members in a predominantly white community college in Alabama. The plaintiff became embroiled in a controversy over her salary and was deemed an uncooperative employee. As a result, her probationary faculty contract was not renewed. She sued, alleging racial discrimination under the disparate treatment theory of title VII. The Federal District Court for the Middle District of Alabama found that she had established a prima facie case for discrimination since she was a member of a minority group, qualified for the position, and had received an adverse employment decision. The burden then shifted to the community college to provide valid reasons for the employment decision. The college alleged that her academic credentials (a doctorate from a nonaccredited institution), non-adherence to her work schedule, and incompatibility with college administrators were the reasons for the nonrenewal decision. The burden then shifted back to the plaintiff to show that the reasons were a pretext for discrimination or that there was evidence of an intention to discriminate. The court found that her academic credentials were pretextual since the faculty position she held required a master's degree. Furthermore, while she was not a cooperative employee, there was other evidence of a discriminatory intent. Her immediate supervisor had made discriminatory and racial threats to the plaintiff, and other evidence indicated that the employment decision was motivated by a discriminatory intent. Thus, the plaintiff was able to meet her burden of showing that the employment action was a pretext for discrimination. The court awarded her back pay, attorney's fees, right to a declaratory judgment, but not reinstatement. The court ruled that because the reinstatement would result in bumping the current occupant of the position, and result in undue hardship to that occupant, reinstatement was not a viable solution.

---

[484] Sweeney v. Research Found. of State Univ. of N.Y., 711 F.2d 1179 (2d Cir. 1983).
[485] Lewis v. University of Pittsburgh, 725 F.2d 910 (3d Cir. 1984).
[486] 955 F. Supp. 1406 (M.D. Ala. 1996).

Pretext can be substantiated in several other ways. One would be to attack the employer's motives and substantiate other motives. Another would be to offer comparative evidence that shows comparability to males who were promoted. In *Namenwirth v. Board of Regents of University of Wisconsin System*,[487] the Seventh Circuit Court of Appeals rejected the pretext argument where the female faculty failed to show comparability with the records of male faculty. The court concluded that the evidence indicated that men similarly situated would not be promoted. In another case, a federal district court concluded that the sociology department acted on the legitimate interests of the university when it reopened a search. The object, to place a highly qualified scholar in an endowed chair rather than hire the female applicant who ranked third but well behind the other two in the original search, was not a pretext for discrimination.[488]

In Massachusetts, a federal district court ruled that where discrimination based on sex was found in a denial of tenure decision, title VII mandated reinstatement as an associate professor with tenure.[489] In *Roebuck v. Drexel University*,[490] a court found that the jury could reach a determination based on the evidence that race was a factor in a denial of tenure. Under the institution's policies, the plaintiff had met the criteria of outstanding performance in two areas: teaching and service. However, the federal appeals court affirmed the district court order of a new trial based on a finding that the jury verdict was against the great weight of evidence.

Retaliation

Retaliation for filing a title VII complaint is another way that cases can be brought before the court. For example, in *Smart v. Ball State University*,[491] the plaintiff was unable to show that poor job performance evaluations constituted "adverse employment action" or retaliation for filing a title VII complaint with the EEOC. In *Johnson v. University of Wisconsin—Eau Claire*,[492] the institution

---

[487] 769 F.2d 1235 (7th Cir. 1985), *cert. denied*, 474 U.S. 1061 (1986).

[488] Lamphere v. Brown Univ., 690 F. Supp. 125 (D.R.I. 1988). *See* Lamphere v. Brown Univ., 613 F. Supp. 971 (D.R.I. 1985), *vacated and remanded*, 798 F.2d 532 (1st Cir. 1986). For original consent decree which affects this ruling, *see* Lamphere v. Brown Univ., 491 F. Supp. 232 (D.R.I. 1980), *aff'd*, 685 F.2d 743 (1st Cir. 1982).

[489] Brown v. Trustees of Boston Univ., 674 F. Supp. 393 (D. Mass. 1987).

[490] 852 F.2d 715 (3d Cir. 1988).

[491] 89 F.3d 437 (7th Cir. 1996).

[492] 70 F.3d 469 (7th Cir. 1995).

had changed the base salary for part-time teachers and instituted a policy to increase the teaching of tenured faculty by decreasing the number of part-time positions. The court found the nonrenewal of a female part-time faculty member's one-year contract was not in retaliation for her filing of a complaint with EEOC over salary reductions.

Class Action Cases

Class action cases involving title VII disputes tend to rely on statistical analysis to establish discrimination under either a disparate impact or disparate treatment theory. Multiple regression analysis has been used not only to establish a prima facie case of discrimination, but also to prove that the reasons given for the job decisions were a pretext for discrimination. Litigation surrounds the variables included in the regression analysis and the validity of the process. Since the Equal Pay Act cases also use this same proof strategy, the discussion of the issues surrounding statistical analysis will be presented under the Equal Pay Act.

Title VII Cases Conclusion

These title VII cases point to the fact that it is difficult under title VII regulations for a plaintiff to survive the proof strategies required by the court. When institutions provide non-discriminatory reasons, the plaintiff has found it difficult to prove a pretext for discrimination. However, the courts have acted on cases of blatant discrimination. Title VII cases demonstrate the dichotomy the court finds itself in where it is upholding the law while attempting to protect the integrity of the faculty-peer review process. Title VII and title IX cases involving claims of sexual harassment have grown in frequency and importance over the last few years; therefore, these claims have been given prominence as a separate chapter.

The Equal Pay Act

The Equal Pay Act is designed to ensure equal pay for equal work. While the concept seems quite simple, it has resulted in some highly complex litigation. Hendrickson and Lee noted: "Yet the concept of equal pay for college faculty has spawned some of the most complex litigation encountered by the federal courts during the past decade."[493] They cite the reasons for this complexity as the very nature of colleges and universities, variations in individual talent among the faculty, differences in prestige across disciplines, and measurement of scholarly productivity. These problems, some of which are similar to those encountered in the promotion and tenure litigation, are exacerbated by the lack of consistent procedures to determine salaries across the various academic units within colleges and universities. These factors make the litigation in this area complex and, at times, protracted.

The procedures to file an Equal Pay Act claim are similar to those under title VII. In fact, in many cases the plaintiffs have filed both an Equal Pay Act and title VII claim in pay disputes. One of the procedural questions is whether the application of the Equal Pay Act to private church affiliated institutions violates the "free exercise" or "establishment" clause of the First Amendment. A Tennessee federal district court ruled that there was no violation of the First Amendment when the Equal Pay Act was applied to salaries at private church related institutions.[494] The second procedural question has to do with Eleventh Amendment sovereign immunity based on *Seminole Tribe of Florida v. Florida*.[495] The Federal District Court of Northern Alabama recently ruled, based on *Seminole*, that Congress did not have the power to abrogate the state's Eleventh Amendment sovereign immunity with regard to the Equal Pay Act provisions of the Fair Labor Standards Act.[496] Whether this decision is followed by other courts, remains to be seen. If it is, it will have a significant limiting effect on the application of the Equal Pay Act to state institutions of higher education.

The issue of the time frame or tolling within which a complaint can be filed has also been litigated under the Act. The normal tolling period to file a complaint is 300 days from either the time of the violation or the time the plaintiff should have been aware of the violation. Complaints will be time barred if they are not brought within the period allowed.[497] However, since the EEOC is the agency authorized to bring action, tolling will not commence where it failed to advise the plaintiff to file a civil complaint.[498] Finally, application of the Equal Pay Act to state organizations is

---

[493] Hendrickson & Lee, *supra* note 10 at 45.
[494] Russell v. Belmont College, 554 F. Supp. 667 (M.D. Tenn. 1982).
[495] 517 U.S. 44 (1996). For a full discussion of this issue see chapter II.
[496] Larry v. Board of Trustees of Univ. of Ala., 975 F. Supp. 1447 (N.D. Ala. 1997).
[497] Billings v. Wichita State Univ., 557 F. Supp. 1348 (D. Kan. 1983).
[498] Erickson v. New York Law Sch., 585 F. Supp. 209 (S.D.N.Y. 1984).

controlled by whether or not a state will allow a citizen to sue it in federal court. Where states have elected to supersede the Eleventh Amendment prohibition of suit in federal court, a citizen may sue a public college or university for a violation of the Equal Pay Act.[499]

Criteria for Equal Pay

The Regulations governing the Equal Pay Act set out criteria or conditions under which pay should be equal.[500] Salaries must be equal where "equal skills," "equal effort," and "equal responsibility" exist. These criteria are related to the job, not the individual in the position, and are used to establish a prima facie case, the first stage in the burden of proof strategy. For example, the plaintiff must show that the two jobs in question require equal skill, effort and responsibility. However, where the jobs require equal skill, effort and responsibility, the court may look at individual attributes such as experience, training and ability as determinants of salary differential.[501] Courts have allowed employers to differentiate pay for jobs where substantially similar services are performed but one of the positions requires differences in the expertise and level of responsibility of the worker. In Georgia, the court found that while registered nurses and physician's assistants in a university hospital performed similar services, the physician's assistants had greater training, expertise, and responsibilities which justified the pay differential.[502]

These questions of equality of job skill, effort, and responsibility gave rise to the resultant legal concept of comparable worth. Comparable worth attempts to show that two different jobs involving different services are of the same worth within the organization and should receive equitable compensation. Some states enacted state statutes on comparable worth; also, the Equal Pay Act and title VII were used as the basis for a comparable worth argument on the federal level. The controlling federal case was decided in Washington and served to defeat comparable worth

---

[499]Billings v. Wichita State Univ., 557 F. Supp. 1348 (D. Kan. 1983).

[500] 29 C.F.R. 800.125 (1980).

[501] EEOC v. McCarthy, 768 F.2d 1 (1st Cir. 1985). On appeal, the court found that the issue of ability was never contested in the district court. This means that if it was not a contested issue, it could be inferred that the male and female faculty members in this case were of equal ability.

[502] Beall v. Curtis, 603 F. Supp. 1563 (M.D. Ga. 1985); *see also* Adams v. University of Wash., 722 P.2d 75 (Wash. 1986).

arguments on the federal level. The case, *Spaulding v. University of Washington*,[503] involved the claim of female nursing faculty that their jobs were comparable to jobs in other academic departments with predominantly male faculty. They alleged that salary differentials between academic units were discriminatory based on sex. The federal court of appeals ruled that the jobs between various academic units within the university were not comparable. The academic units placed varying degrees of emphasis on teaching, research, and community service. Other factors could account for salary differences: time in rank, prior job experience and academic rank. These factors were not considered in the plaintiff's multiple regression analysis. The court refused to take the position that market value differentials in pay would be discriminatory. The court stated, "Every employer constrained by market forces must consider market value in setting his labor costs. Naturally, market prices are inherently job-related, although the market may embody social judgments as to the worth of some jobs."[504] The court noted that market value factors are not something within an employer's control, and the law was designed to "combat culpable discrimination."[505] With this decision the comparable worth arguments receded from litigation under the Equal Pay Act.

Once the plaintiff has shown that a differential in pay exists for comparable jobs, the burden shifts to the employer to prove that the salary results from factors other than the sex of the plaintiffs. The law provides an employer with several justifications for a salary differential across comparable jobs. These include a seniority system, a merit pay system, a quantity or quality of production pay system, and a system which is based on factors other than sex. For example, a federal appeals court, finding that the female litigants held jobs equal to comparably skilled males within the academic unit of the institution, threw out the institution's claim of salary differential based on a merit system and market value factors.[506] The institution provided no evidence of the existence of a merit system nor that market factors resulted in salary differentials at the time of hiring let alone the award of salary increases.

It is in the areas of productivity and the criterion of teaching, research, and service used to determine pay that most of the higher education litigation has centered. A pay system based on quality

---

[503] 740 F.2d 686 (9th Cir. 1984), *cert. denied*, 469 U.S. 1036 (1984).
[504] *Id.* at 708.
[505] *Id.*
[506] Brock v. Georgia Southwestern College, 765 F.2d 1026 (11th Cir. 1985).

of production in higher education goes to issues similar to those argued in the area of promotion and tenure. The same subjective standards that applied in the peer review process for promotion and tenure apply when one measures the quality of publications, teaching, and services for the purpose of determining salary.

Training and experience also serve as valid factors in salary differential cases. For example, a plaintiff in Illinois was unsuccessful in claiming that she was discriminated against when she was hired as a faculty member at a salary lower than her male predecessor.[507] The male predecessor had received a higher salary based on his five years of experience in an academic position and the possession of a terminal degree, both valid reasons for the salary differential.

Market value factors have also been used to justify salary differentials. The market value factors have been litigated most frequently in cases involving multiple regression analysis.[508] An example of this type of argument involved a reverse discrimination case.[509] A male faculty member complained that he had been discriminated against because a female faculty member in a comparable job had been awarded a higher salary. The court found that the higher salary award was not gender based, but resulted from a job offer from another institution. The institution, under a court order to retain and acquire female faculty based on a previous finding of discrimination,[510] acted in concert with the court order by offering the woman a salary increase in order to keep her on the faculty. Her ability to remain competitive in the labor market resulted in the salary differential. While the courts have allowed market value factors based on salary differential across disciplines, they continue to reject the argument that certain classes of workers, such as women or foreigners, are willing to work for less as a market factor. For example, the use of lower salary demands by foreigners to justify the pay differential was a pretext for discrimination at a West Virginia institution.[511]

In the shifting burden of proof strategy, after the institution has supplied valid reasons for the salary differential, the burden shifts to the plaintiff to prove that the reasons are a pretext for

---

[507] Covington v. Southern Ill. Univ., 816 F.2d 317 (7th Cir. 1987), *cert. denied*, 484 U.S. 848 (1987). *See also* Strag v. Board of Trustees, Craven Community College, 55 F.3d 943 (4th Cir. 1995); reached a similar result but the comparator was a similarly situated male faculty member rather than the previous male occupant of the faculty position.

[508] *See* Chang v. University of R.I., 606 F. Supp. 1161 (D.R.I. 1985); Ottaviani v. State Univ. of N.Y. at New Paltz, 679 F. Supp 288 (S.D.N.Y. 1988), *aff'd*, 875 F.2d 365 (2d Cir. 1989).

[509] Winkes v. Brown Univ., 747 F.2d 792 (1st Cir. 1984).

[510] Lamphere v. Brown Univ., 491 F. Supp. 232 (D.R.I. 1980).

[511] West Virginia Inst. of Tech. v. West Virginia Human Rights Comm'n, 383 So.2d 490 (W. Va. 1989).

discrimination. Plaintiffs will try to show that a variety of actions (hiring, recruitment, degree held, productivity, promotion and tenure processes) collectively have had an adverse impact on the protected class. In faculty cases, however, plaintiff's have been unsuccessful in arguing that publication rates, rank, and market value factors are gender based and discriminatory against women and should be viewed as a pretext for discrimination.[512] Just as in title VII cases, meeting the pretext burden has been difficult if not insurmountable.

Class Action Suits

Under the Equal Pay Act, a class of employees could sue for wage disparity. The litigation would proceed in the usual manner after the class of individuals had been certified. Then statistical evidence, anecdotal information about the institution's activities plus individual claims would be reviewed to determine a prima facie case for discrimination. The shifting burden of proof outlined above would be followed in these cases.

Typically, female faculty are certified as a class of employees at an institution of higher education.[513] However, there is an exception to the certification of female faculty as a class. An Ohio federal district court found that the decision making process for faculty at a university was decentralized to various academic units. This decentralization prevented the use of statistical and anecdotal evidence showing a common pattern of discrimination across the institution.[514] If this court's position had been adopted, statistical analysis would be within each academic unit thereby creating statistical problems with sample size and other methodological issues. The court's action of decertifying the class based on the decentralization of decisions has important implications although it does not appear at this time that other courts have followed this argument. However, even if the courts adopted the argument, it would only apply to certain higher education institutions. Colleges and universities vary in the degree to which decision making is centralized or decentralized. At some institutions, where a centralized

---

[512] *See* Melani v. Board of Higher Educ. of City of N.Y., 561 F. Supp. 769 (S.D.N.Y. 1983); Sobel v. Yeshiva Univ., 566 F. Supp. 1166 (S.D. N.Y. 1983), *cert. denied*, 109 S. Ct. 3154 (1989).

[513] *See* Coser v. Moore, 587 F. Supp. 572 (E.D.N.Y. 1983); Chang v. University of R.I., 606 F. Supp. 1161 (D. R.I. 1985).

[514] Rosenberg v. University of Cincinnati, 118 F.R.D. 591 (S.D. Ohio 1987).

structure for decision making exists, the result may be the certification of faculty women as a class at that institution.[515]

Once the class of workers has been certified, the analysis moves to a showing that the class of workers is being treated differently than other workers, substantiating a prima facie case of discrimination. This analysis usually includes the presentation of statistical evidence, anecdotal evidence about the institution and its practices, and analysis of individual cases to prove that the class is being discriminated against. Usually, the plaintiffs will attempt in this analysis to anticipate the institution's reasons that justify the salary differential. The plaintiffs will either include them in their statistical analysis or argue that they should be disallowed because they are discriminatory.[516] Early in the history of equal pay litigation, this effort proved very successful for the plaintiffs but later defendant institutions learned how to counter this approach.

The use of statistical analysis in equal pay and title VII cases involved statistical procedure called multiple regression analysis. In multiple regression analysis, the dependent variable "salary" is predicted by analyzing scores on a number of independent variables.[517] These independent variables could include such factors as gender, age, rank, time in rank, degrees, publications, quality of productivity, and any other factors which are thought to have relevance in the determination of salary. The accuracy of multiple regression analysis is only as good as the comprehensiveness of the list of variables used and the sophistication of the quantification of variables so as to adequately account for their effect. For example, should publications be a variable in the regression equation to predict salary? Further, if publications are used, how are they quantified? Does a simple count of numbers capture the variable's effect on salary or must there be differentiation based on the type of publication? What about the issue of quality of publication or a measure of a publication's contribution to the field? The complexity of these issues turn what appears to be a simple and accurate mathematical analysis into a complex issue for the courts.

---

[515] R. Hendrickson and J. Bartkovich, *Organizational Systematics: Toward a Classification Scheme for Postsecondary Institutions*, 9 Rev. of Higher Educ. 303 (1986). A continuum of different levels of centralization of decision making was found. Centralization was not a function of the institution's classification under the Carnegie Classification Scheme.

[516] D. Stacy and C. Holland, *Legal and Statistical Problems in Litigating Sex Discrimination Claims in Higher Education*, 11 J.C. & U.L. 107, 116 (1984).

[517] R. Jaeger, Statistics As Spectator Sport, 301 (1983).

In the early use of multiple regression analysis, plaintiffs were quite successful in showing that salary differentials between men and women were based on sex.[518] This early success was due in part to the exclusion of certain variables in the regression analysis. In fact, the EEOC recommended the exclusion of certain variables such as rank (one of the strongest predictors of salary) in the regression analysis.[519] However, another reason for their early success appears to be the way the institutions chose to counter the regression analysis. The defendant institutions attacked the regression analysis and argued that certain variables, when excluded, bias the analysis. What occurred was the presentation of the regression analysis results by the plaintiffs and highly technical arguments by the defendant's statistical experts attempting to refute the validity of the analysis because of the exclusion of variables.[520] However, the defendant institutions were more successful when they began to present their own regression analysis containing the variables they wanted included (in these analyses, sex as a predictive variable was either minimized or eliminated). Faced with conflicting statistical results, the courts refused to base their rulings solely on the regression analysis and moved on to the review of anecdotal and individual cases to arrive at a decision.[521]

The result of the evolution in the use of regression analysis by both defendants and plaintiffs is that some institutions were found not to have discriminated against women as a class on the basis of sex, either in the award of salaries or the granting of other benefits.[522] Another outcome was litigation by males claiming reverse discrimination based on sex. For example, in an Illinois case, the court found for the female class and awarded salary adjustments. Male plaintiffs sued unsuccessfully in a claim of discrimination where salary determinations based on sex were the result of the

---

[518]*See* Craik v. Minnesota State Univ. Bd., 731 F.2d 465 (8th Cir. 1984); Melani v. Board of Higher Educ. of City of N.Y., 561 F. Supp. 769 (S.D.N.Y. 1983).

[519]Stacy and Holland, *supra* note 75 at 132.

[520]Mechlenburg v. Montana State Univ., 13 Empl. Pract. Dec. 11, 438 (D. Mont. 1976); Melani, *supra* note 100.

[521]Sobel v. Yeshiva Univ., 566 F. Supp. 1166 (S.D.N.Y. 1983), *cert. denied*, 109 S. Ct. 3154 (1989); Chang v. University of R.I., 606 F. Supp. 1161 (D.R.I. 1985); Ottaviani v. State Univ. of N.Y. at New Paltz, 679 F. Supp. 288 (S.D.N.Y. 1988).

[522]Sobel v. Yeshiva Univ., 566 F. Supp. 1166 (S.D.N.Y. 1983), *rev'd and remand*, 797 F.2d 1478 (2d Cir. 1986); on remand original decision adhered to in district court, *aff'd*, 839 F.2d 18 (2d Cir. 1988), *cert. denied*, 109 S. Ct. 3154 (1989); Penk v. Oregon State Bd. of Higher Educ., 816 F.2d 458 (9th Cir. 1987), *cert. denied*, 484 U.S. 853 (1987); Chang v. University of R.I., 606 F. Supp. 1161 (D. R.I. 1985); Coser v. Moore, 587 F. Supp. 572 (E.D.N.Y. 1983), *aff'd*, Coser v. Moore, 739 F.2d 746 (2d Cir. 1984).

previous finding of discrimination against females.[523] The most recent example of this type of case is *Smith v. Virginia Commonwealth University.*[524] Virginia Commonwealth University (VCU) set up a study committee to determine if salary disparity based on gender existed at the institution. VCU had been awarding merit pay based on teaching load, teaching quality, and quality and quantity of publications. However, the VCU study committee chose not to use those variables in their multiple regression analysis finding them to difficult to quantify. Based on a regression analysis, the committee found that salary differential was based on gender and VCU awarded appropriate salary increases to female faculty. Male faculty sued claiming gender discrimination in the award of salaries. A federal district court granted summary judgment to the University, and the male faculty appealed. The Fourth Circuit Court of Appeals reversed, finding that the regression analysis, absent the merit salary increase factors among other factors, was flawed. The courts found it was not valid for VCU to assume that men and women were equally productive and, therefore, eliminate productivity measures from their regression analysis.

The use of multiple regression in discrimination cases continues to be a complex judicial problem. Expert testimony by statisticians creates confusion. Judges appear to move quickly beyond the statistical data and look at anecdotal information associated with individual plaintiffs in order to make a determination of whether discrimination has taken place against a class. Courts also have refused to accept the argument that two standard deviations away from the mean in statistical analysis should automatically yield a finding of a prima facie case for discrimination.[525] The United States Supreme Court decisions point to the use of a full array of information rather than just statistical analysis to arrive at a determination of whether discrimination has occurred.[526]

---

[523]Ende v. Board of Regents of N. Ill. Univ., 565 F. Supp. 501 (N.D. Ill. 1983), *aff'd*, 757 F.2d 176 (7th Cir. 1985).

[524] 62 F.3d 659 (4th Cir. 1995).

[525] Ottaviani v. State Univ. of N.Y. at New Paltz, 679 F. Supp. 288 (S.D.N.Y. 1988), *aff'd*, 875 F.2d 365 (2d Cir. 1989), *cert. denied*, 493 U.S. 1021 (1990).

[526] Bazemore v. Friday, 478 U.S. 385 (1986); Watson v. Fort Worth Bank & Trust, 487 U.S. 977 (1988).

Age Discrimination

The Age Discrimination in Employment Act (ADEA) of 1967 states:

It shall be unlawful for an employer; (1) to fail or refuse to hire or to discharge any individual or otherwise discriminate against any individual with respect to his compensation, terms, conditions, or privileges of employment because of such individual's age; (2) to limit, segregate, or classify his employees in any way which would deprive any individual of employment opportunities or otherwise adversely affect his status as an employee, because of such individual's age; or (3) to reduce the wage rate of any employee in order to comply with this act.[527]

Subsequently, the age discrimination act was "uncapped," meaning that it now protected people over 70 years of age from discrimination.[528] Thus, mandatory retirement requirements violated the Act with one exception: tenured faculty in higher education.[529] Mandatory retirement of tenured faculty was allowed until December 31, 1993. The uncapping of mandatory retirement for higher education faculty has not seen a flood of case law and problems as predicted by some in the higher education community. Most of the cases that do exist since the uncapping of mandatory retirement have been brought as termination of tenured faculty for cause cases, not as ADEA cases.

There are several litigation issues under ADEA. These issues include: (1) the question of the jurisdiction of the ADEA over certain employees; (2) the question regarding procedural issues in the prosecution of an age discrimination case; (3) the actual allegations of age discrimination in employment; (4) the question of whether secession of fringe benefits at age 70 is retaliation for making a claim.

Jurisdictional issues involve two areas: one is the reach of the law in terms of state sovereignty, and the second involves the question of which employees are covered under the Act. The United States Supreme Court ruled on the former in *EEOC v. Wyoming*.[530] A game warden, employed by the state of Wyoming, retired at 55

---

[527] 29 U.S.C. § 621-634 (1982).

[528] *See* J. Burton, *Tenured Faculty and the 'Uncapped' Age Discrimination In Employment Act*, 5 YALE L. & POL'Y REV. 450 (1987).

[529] The Age Discrimination in Employment Act of 1986 6(a) and 6(b); Pub. L. No. 99-592.

[530] 460 U.S. 977 (1988).

under the state's mandatory retirement policy. The retiree sued alleging a violation of the ADEA. The state maintained that as a state it had the right to regulate public employees and the Act violated this state right. The specific question before the Supreme Court was whether ADEA violated the state's sovereignty under the Tenth Amendment to the Constitution. Citing *Hodel v. Virginia Surface Mining and Reclamation Association*, the Court outlined the three-part test used to determine whether the federal statute was a legitimate use of federal power in the face of the Tenth Amendment.

> ...First, there must be a showing that the challenged statute regulates the "states as states." Second, the federal regulation must address matters that are indisputably "attribute[s] of state sovereignty" [a]nd third, it must be apparent that the states' compliance with federal law would directly impair their [states] ability "to structure integral operations in areas of traditional governmental functions."[531]

The court, while not reaching the second part of the test, ruled that the statute did not impair a state's ability to "structure integral operations in areas of traditional governmental functions."[532] The state's objective is to maintain the preparedness of game wardens, a valid job criteria under ADEA. The federal statute allows the state the opportunity to prove that age may be a factor in preparedness and, therefore, a valid job criterion for game wardens. The court found that the federal interest in preventing age discrimination does not impinge on the state's right to perform a specific governmental function. This case served to remove the possibility that higher education institutions' exemption for tenured faculty should be maintained on the grounds that ADEA violated the Tenth Amendment. State sovereignty to provide higher education to its citizens would not be impinged by subsequent application of the ADEA to tenured faculty.[533]

Another jurisdictional question concerned the scope of higher education's exemption to ADEA. A university professor at age 65 had lost his tenure status but continued employment as a nontenured professor. At age 70, the institution reduced his employment status from full time to part time based solely on his age. In a suit alleging age discrimination, the Third Circuit Court of Appeals

---

[531] Hodel v. Virginia Surface Mining and Reclamation Assoc., 452 U.S. 264 (1981), at 287-288 (citations omitted, emphasis in original).
[532] EEOC v. Wyoming at 980.
[533] *See* discussions in chapter II which reinforce the notion that, under ADEA, Congress has abrogated state claims to sovereign immunity.

ruled that the ADEA exemption covers only tenured faculty.[534] Since the professor was not a tenured faculty member (an exempt employee) at the time, his employment status had been changed from full time to part time, the institution was in violation of ADEA and had discriminated on the basis of age.

Several other jurisdictional questions have been decided. The Sixth Circuit Court of Appeals found that the president of an institution falls within the ADEA exemption of "policy makers"[535] under the provision of the act.[536] Another federal court found that the ADEA statute did not violate the First Amendment separation of church and state provisions.[537] Private church related institutions are not exempt from the application of ADEA.

Procedurally, EEOC receives the plaintiff's claims, is responsible for investigating violations of ADEA, and issuing a right to sue letter. The concept of tolling also applies to ADEA, and the tolling period is 180 days. A North Carolina professor lost his claim in court because the violations which he alleged—loss of secretarial support, fringe benefits, and salary adjustments—took place more than 180 days prior to filing the claim with EEOC.[538]

Shifting Burden of Proof

The Age Discrimination in Employment Act litigation involves the same shifting burden of proof strategy used in title VII cases under the disparate treatment theory. The burden is on the plaintiff to establish a prima facie case of discrimination based on age. The burden shifts to the defendant institution to show that it had a valid reason for its employment action.[539] Finally, the burden shifts back to the plaintiff to show that the reason was a pretext for discrimination based on age.

Disparate treatment is not always reached by employees alleging age discrimination. For example, a Maryland private college did not commit age discrimination when they failed to renew a faculty member's one-year contract.[540] *Fisher v. Asheville-Buncombe Technical Community College*[541] reached a similar result. The insti-

---

[534] Levine v. Fairleigh Dickinson Univ., 646 F.2d 825 (3d Cir. 1981).

[535] Age Discrimination in Employment Act of 1967, 29 U.S.C. 630(f) (1976).

[536] EEOC v. Board of Trustees of Wayne County Community College, 753 F.2d 509 (6th Cir. 1983).

[537] Soriano v. Xavier Univ., 687 F. Supp. 1188 (S.D. Ohio 1988).

[538] Sanders v. Duke Univ., 538 F. Supp. 1143 (M.D. N.C. 1982).

[539] Note that this could be age under certain circumstances. *See* EEOC v. Wyoming, 460 U.S. 977 (1988).

[540] Blistein v. St. John's College, 860 F. Supp. 256 (D. Md. 1994).

[541] 857 F. Supp. 465 (W.D. N.C. 1993).

tution decided not to renew his contract after a faculty member refused to adapt to curricular changes. The court found that it is a violation of ADEA for an employee to be terminated based on his age, but not a violation of the law if the employee is terminated for unsatisfactory work. Under disparate treatment theory, the plaintiff established a prima facie case of age discrimination; the institution provided valid reasons (poor job performance) for the nonrenewal decision; and the plaintiff failed to show that those reasons were a pretext for discrimination. In *Senner v. North Central Technical College,*[542] an unsuccessful applicant for a faculty position was unable to show that the candidate screening committee discriminated on the basis of age. The court found that age was not a factor when only one other candidate over 40 was one of the top three candidates. However, in an Iowa case, the court denied summary judgment to a community college.[543] The plaintiff, whose job performance was satisfactory, charged that changing her library work schedule was constructive discharge as it forced her resignation because she had night blindness. Material issues need to be adjudicated surrounding the questions of whether a supervisor's query about her date of retirement, made before the schedule change, motivated the employment action.

Federal and State Claims

Age Discrimination in Employment Act cases will usually contain pendent state claims under state statutes.[544] These claims could involve state statues concerning age discrimination, but also include various breach of contract claims. The United States Supreme Court ruled in *Carnegie-Mellon University v. Cohill,*[545] that the District Court had authority to remand pendent state claims to a state court where the federal claims had been deleted.

Litigation on the merits point to what will be viewed as valid reasons for termination and what will be viewed as age discrimination under the law. In *Leftwich v. Harris Strowe State College,* when control of a Missouri community college located in St. Louis was transferred to the state college system, the new board did not

---

[542] 113 F.3d 750 (7th Cir. 1997).

[543] Schwartz v. Northwest Iowa Community College, 881 F. Supp. 1323 (N.D. Iowa 1995).

[544] For a good example of a claim of age discrimination brought under state law, *see* The Florida State Univ. v. Sondel, 685 So.2d 923 (Fla. Dist. Ct. App. 1997).

[545] 484 U.S. 343 (1988).

rehire the tenured associate professor. He sued, alleging that the hiring of a nontenured faculty member was age discrimination. A federal district court ruled that the board had not substantiated that the policy to improve the quality of the faculty was achieved by hiring nontenured faculty.[546] The court found that the institution's policy had a disparate impact on former tenured faculty at the institution over 40.

A decision by the Minnesota governor to eliminate a personnel position was not age discrimination when the 44-year-old plaintiff was terminated. The court found that the plaintiff had failed to establish a prima facie case of age discrimination.[547] In Oklahoma, a woman proved at trial that she was not promoted to chief of the cartographic section solely because of her age.[548] However, a Wisconsin university's decision to terminate an employee because she was not able to complete work, performed work incorrectly, and attempted to avoid work was a valid reason for termination and was not age discrimination.[549]

Another question involves whether the secession of the institution's contribution to a fringe benefit package at a specific age even though the employee continues employment violated ADEA. In one case, the university discontinued its contribution to fringe benefits at age 65, but continued the individual's employment at the institution. The federal district court ruled that the secession of payments into a fringe benefit plan at a certain age did not violate ADEA as long as the employee had been given proper advance notice of the employer's intent to cease the contribution.[550]

Retaliation

To retaliate against individuals because they file age discrimination claims is a violation of ADEA. For example, in *Hansen v. Vanderbilt University*,[551] the court found that it was not retaliation

---

[546] 540 F. Supp. 37 (E.D. Mo. 1982); *aff'd in part and rev'd in part*, 702 F.2d 686 (8th Cir. 1983). The court reversed the failure of the District Court to calculate back pay award on year-by-year basis.

[547] Reddemann v. Minnesota Higher Educ. Coordinating Bd., 811 F.2d 1208 (8th Cir. 1987).

[548] The District Court granted judgement notwithstanding the jury verdict, EEOC v. University of Okla., 554 F. Supp. 735 (W.D. Okla. 1982); *rev'd and remanded*, EEOC v. University of Okla., 774 F.2d 999 (10th Cir. 1985), *cert. denied*, 475 U.S. 1120 (1986).

[549] Johnson v. University of Wis., Milwaukee, 783 F.2d 59 (7th Cir. 1986).

[550] Kadane v. Hofstra Univ., 682 F. Supp. 166 (E.D.N.Y. 1988); *see* Bell v. Trustees of Purdue Univ., 658 F. Supp. 184 (N.D. Ind. 1987).

[551] 961 F. Supp. 1149 (M.D. Tenn. 1997).

to require the plaintiff to withdraw an EEOC claim before a settlement award was made on a state Human Rights Act claim. An Illinois collective bargaining agreement contained a clause that an employee could be dismissed if he/she filed a grievance through the appropriate grievance procedures in the contract, and then sought a remedy elsewhere.[552] A faculty member had filed a grievance after the president decided not to recommend him for tenure. Later, he filed a claim of age discrimination with EEOC and was subsequently terminated by the board. The court found that the provision in the collective bargaining agreement constituted retaliation in violation of ADEA. The court noted that provisions in a collective bargaining agreement do not insulate the institution from the reach of this federal age discrimination statute.[553]

In summary, while higher education tenured faculty were exempt from the provisions of ADEA until 1993, other employees of the institution fell under its provisions. After 1993, faculty came under the reach of ADEA. It would serve institutions well to become cognizant of the requirements of ADEA and to ensure that employment decisions are free of age discrimination. While mandatory retirement has ended for tenured faculty, institutions have adapted with early retirement programs and used termination for cause procedures only as a last resort.

Discrimination Based on Disability

The Rehabilitation Act of 1973 states, "No otherwise qualified handicapped individual shall, solely by reason of his handicap, be excluded from participation in, be denied the benefits of, or be subject to discrimination under any program or activity receiving federal financial assistance."[554]

Because the law involves provisions similar to those in the title VI of the Civil Rights Act of 1964 and title IX of the Education Amendments of 1972, it was also affected by the *Grove City College* case, *supra*. Thus, the law was rendered applicable only to very specific programs within an institution. In the decade since the Civil Rights Restoration Act of 1988 the case law has continued to refine the issues surrounding the Rehabilitation Act. Further, the Americans with Disabilities Act of 1990 (ADA)[555] has further de-

---

[552] EEOC v. Board of Governors of State Colleges and Univs., 665 F. Supp. 630 (N.D. Ill. 1987).

[553] *Id.* at 636.

[554] Rehabilitation Act of 1973, 29 U.S.C. 701 (1986).

[555] 42 U.S.C. § 12101 et seq.

fined the requirements institutions face in complying with the accommodation provisions of these acts. The ADA states, "No individual shall be discriminated against on the basis of disability in the full and equal enjoyment of the goods, services, facilities, privileges, advantages, or accommodations of any place of public accommodation by any person who owns, leases (or leases to) or operates a public accommodation."[556]

One of the controlling cases in handicap discrimination is *Southeastern Community College v. Davis*.[557] The United States Supreme Court ruled that an otherwise qualified handicapped individual "is one who could meet all the program admission requirements in spite of their handicap."[558] The admission requirements must go to the individual's ability to perform the job. In the *Davis* case, the court found that, because the applicant was deaf, only through close supervision would the person be able to function on the job.[559] Before the court was the question of whether a deaf applicant for a nursing degree program was qualified to enroll in the program in spite of her handicap. The state board of nursing found that her inability to rapidly respond to emergency situations made her unqualified for a nursing position, or not "otherwise qualified." The Court held that § 504 requires the accommodation of the needs of otherwise qualified handicapped individuals, but does not require affirmative action toward handicapped individuals.[560] However, academic institutions should not have to eliminate important aspects of the curriculum in an effort to accommodate to the needs of a handicapped student. Admissions and accommodations within academic programs will be discussed in the chapter on students. The other controlling Supreme Court decision is *Alexander v. Choate*,[561] which indicates that reasonable and nondiscriminatory modifications to a program would be determined in part by the cost of such modifications. The state reduced its hospital days for Medicaid recipients in order to reduce costs. The court noted that the reductions applied to both handicapped and non-handicapped Medicaid recipients equally and was therefore facially neutral. Section 504 does not require that states receiving federal financial

---

[556] 42 U.S.C.A. § 12182(1) (West Supp. 1995).
[557] 442 U.S. 397 (1979).
[558] *Id.* at 406.
[559] *Id.* at 409.
[560] *Id.* at 411.
[561] 469 U.S. 287 (1985).

assistance make distribution decisions in ways most favorable or with the least disadvantage to the handicapped.

While most of the litigation surrounding handicapped individuals involves admissions decisions, the law also covers employment. In *Carter v. Bennett*,[562] the federal court of appeals ruled that the employer, the United States Department of Education, had made reasonable efforts to accommodate the plaintiff, who was a blind employee. The Department had provided him with readers, and special equipment and office space, but the plaintiff was still unable to perform the work. The court found that the employer had dismissed the individual based on poor performance after reasonable accommodations for the plaintiff's handicap.[563] The implication for employment is that an employer must make some modifications for a handicapped individual who is "otherwise qualified" for the position. The degree to which modifications will be required will go to the cost of those modifications. It should be noted that the requirements for the federal government's compliance are viewed by the courts as much more onerous since the federal government is expected to be the model of compliance.

An Illinois appeals court decision gives some idea of how discrimination based on a handicap would be reached in hiring. The failure of the university to hire an amputee for a building and grounds position was handicap discrimination under a state statute similar to The Rehabilitation Act.[564] The university never inquired as to whether the applicant could perform the work required in the job, but assumed that he could not because of his handicap. The court found that the university was unable to support its position with evidence and found that the amputee with a prosthesis could safely perform the job tasks.

In summary, the Rehabilitation Act and ADA requires that in employment practices, an "otherwise qualified handicapped individual" cannot be refused employment solely on the basis of a handicap. Employers are expected to make reasonable modifications in the position in order to employ the individual. Courts will use cost as a factor in order to decide whether those modifications are reasonable for the employer to make.

---

[562] 840 F.2d 63 (D.C. Cir. 1988).

[563] *Id.* at 68.

[564] Board of Trustees of Univ. of Ill. v. Human Rights Comm'n, 485 N.E.2d 478 (Ill. App. Ct. 1985).

Conclusions

The quest for equity and diversity in employment in higher education is surrounded by questions of discrimination based on race, gender, age, and disability. Institutions need to set goals to strive for diversity in employment while ensuring that suspect criteria do not result in violations of federal statutes. The use of race, gender, age or disability as the sole or primary determinant of employment could result in litigation at significant expense. While institutions need to be proactive in seeking diverse employees, they also need to ensure that such policies do not increase the risk of charges of reverse discrimination. An informed review of the litigation under title VI, title VII, the Equal Pay Act, the Age Discrimination in Employment Act, and the Rehabilitation Act will aid institutions in developing policies that protect individual rights while achieving institutional and educational objectives.

Institutional practices in the quest for equity should be based on the following general guidelines:

- Criterion involved in hiring, promotion and tenure and the award of salaries or other rewards should be based on merit that is free from race, gender, or national origin bias.
- While institutions may seek diversity in employment, they must insure that decisions are made based on valid criteria and not solely on the basis of one's race. Using race as one of several criteria is currently a question the court needs to resolve.
- Valid measures of job performance are based on criteria that is bias free.
- Criteria used for faculty promotion, tenure, and salary should be valid measures of teaching, research, and service. The emphasis placed on any of these three areas ought to be consistent with the institutional mission.
- The quality of publications as assessed as part of a peer review and market value factors affecting salary have not been found to be biased by gender and therefore, continue as valid measures of merit.
- Age cannot be used to determine merit in hiring or promotion unless it can be shown to be a valid criterion which goes to job performance. One of few jobs where

ages might be used is a police officer or where strenuous physical exercise is required.
- Handicapped discrimination is prohibited where the person is "otherwise qualified." An "Otherwise qualified" individual is one who can perform tasks of the job with reasonable modification. Modification of essential job performance criteria is not required but modification of the work environment would be necessary to meet the accommodation requirements of ADA.

CHAPTER VI

Sexual Harassment

Sexual harassment is a recent employment issue in higher education. Its origins are in title VII of the Civil Rights Act of 1964, which prohibits certain forms of workplace discrimination. Under title VII, it is an unlawful employment practice for employers to discriminate against individuals with respect to their "compensation, terms, conditions or privileges of employment, because of such individual's race, color, religion, sex, or national origin." While the Act expressly prohibits gender discrimination, among other types of discrimination, it did not provide for a cause of action for sexual harassment. However, ten years after the passage of title VII, the Fifth Circuit Court of Appeals ruled that workplace harassment in the form of racial harassment was prohibited by law.[565] In 1976, a Federal District Court held that "sexual harassment" of a female employee by a supervisor was recognized as a title VII violation.[566] This concept of sexual harassment as a violation of title VII was incorporated into the Equal Employment Opportunities Commission (EEOC) Guidelines on Discrimination because of Sex, and in 1986, the Supreme Court embraced the concept in *Meritor Savings Bank v. Vinson*.[567] The Court recently reaffirmed the ban on gender-based harassment within the gender discrimination prohibitions of title VII in *Harris v. Forklift Systems, Inc.*[568]

Sexual harassment is defined as "unwelcome sexual advances, requests for sexual favors or other verbal or physical conduct of a sexual nature"[569] targeted toward one gender and not the other. There are two types of sexual harassment: *quid pro quo* sexual harassment and hostile work environment. *Quid pro quo* sexual harassment is the coercion of an employee into performing an unwelcome sexual act as part of a bargain to obtain favors or to avoid punitive actions. This type of sexual harassment does not

---

[565] Rogers v. EEOC, 454 F.2d 234 (5th Cir. 1971), *cert. denied*, 406 U.S. 957 (1972).
[566] Williams v. Saxbe, 413 F. Supp. 654 (D.D.C. 1976) at 657.
[567] 477 U.S. 57 (1986).
[568] 510 U.S. 17 (1993).
[569] 29 C.F.R. § 1604.11(a).

have First Amendment workplace speech problems associated with it. The other type of sexual harassment, hostile work environment, exists when employees because of their gender experience a work environment "permeated with discriminatory intimidation, ridicule, and insult which are sufficiently severe or pervasive to alter the conditions of employment and create an abusive working environment."[570] Unlike *quid pro quo* sexual harassment, hostile work environment does involve workplace speech, which raises First Amendment issues.

First Amendment speech for public employees, defined as speech on matters of public concern, is considered protected speech.[571] Public employee speech on matters of private concern, however, is not protected speech. In the private sector, employers are free to regulate the speech of their employees without fear of implicating the particular First Amendment speech rights that public employees enjoy. However, private employers are obligated to regulate or prevent harassing workplace speech under the prohibitions of a hostile work environment under title VII. In this way, private employers act under color of federal law. Acting under color of state or federal law makes the private employer an agent of government under the doctrine of state action, thereby bringing the private employer's regulation of workplace speech under the umbrella of First Amendment speech rights. This issue of whether a private employer's regulation of workplace speech violates employee First Amendment speech rights has been debated in a number of law journal articles, but the issue has yet to be addressed by the courts.[572] Not only are there constitutional questions surrounding workplace speech, but there is also the question of what a "sufficiently severe and pervasive" hostile work environment is.

Hostile Work Environment

In order to prove that a hostile work environment exists, courts have found that the following standards must be met. First, the plaintiff must show that the conduct is unwelcome. Second, it must be shown that the harassment was based on the gender of

---

[570] *Id.* at 20; *see* D. Epstein, *Can a "Dumb Ass Woman" Achieve Equality in the Workplace?* 84 GEO. L.J. 399 (1996), 410.

[571] Connick v. Myers, 461 U.S. 138 (1983).

[572]*Id.* Epstein; C. L. Estlund, *Freedom of Expression in the Workplace and the Problem of Discriminatory Harassment*, 75 TEXAS L. REV. 687, (1997); E. Volokh, *What Speech Does "Hostile Work Environment" Harassment Law Restrict?* 85 GEO. L.J. 627 (1997).

the harassed. Third, the harassment must be "sufficiently severe and pervasive" to create an abusive work environment. Finally, the plaintiff must show that a basis exists for imputing liability to the employer. Put another way, in order for employer liability to result, the employer must have knowledge of the harassing behavior and either fail to remedy the unwarranted behavior or outright condone the harassment. The question still remains as to what type of "sufficiently severe and pervasive" activity, creates a hostile work environment. To answer that question, one needs to look at case law to determine what constitutes harassing activity. In *Harris v. Forklift Systems, Inc.*, the United States Supreme Court found that these activities constitute harassment:

> [T]hroughout Harris' time at Forklift, Hardy (the president of the company) often insulted her because of her gender and often made her the target of unwanted sexual innuendoes. Hardy told Harris on several occasions in the presence of other employees, "You're a woman, what do you know" and "we need a man as the rental manager"; at least once, he told her she was "a dumb ass woman." Again in front of others, he suggested that the two of them "go to the Holiday Inn to negotiate a raise." Hardy occasionally asked Harris and other female employees to get coins out of his front pants pocket. He threw objects on the ground in front of Harris and other women and asked them to pick the objects up. He made sexual innuendoes about Harris' and other women's clothing. [After telling Harris he would stop upon receiving her complaint, he continued his harassment.] While Harris was arranging a deal with one of Forklift's customers, he asked her in front of other employees, "What did you do, promise the guy...some Saturday night?"[573]

The *Harris* Court clearly saw that the company president's behavior created a "severe and pervasive" hostile work environment. The Court not only found that a hostile work environment existed, but also found that the other elements necessary to prove sexual harassment were satisfied: the employee clearly communicated that the conduct was unwelcome; it was shown that the harassment was based upon the employee's gender; and the employer knew of and condoned the harassment by failing to remedy the unwarranted behavior. It should be noted that the employer could have avoided liability by taking remedial action, but an employer's failure to act on the knowledge of harassment will be

---

[573] 510 U.S. 17, 19 (1993).

viewed by the courts as condoning the harassment. *Harris* gives one a clear definition of "severe and pervasive" sexual harassment. Behavior less than that in *Harris* may meet the "severe and pervasive" standard, depending upon the circumstance of the particular past situation. Cases in higher education will help to illuminate where the boundaries of the standard lie.

Severe and Pervasive Standard

Several hostile work environment cases in higher education will shed some light on defining a "severe and pervasive" hostile work environment. In a case involving a Wyoming proprietary technical school, the court found that harassment of either gender constituted sexual harassment.[574] A supervisor harassed a husband and his wife, both employees at the institute. Another husband and wife, both employees of the institute, also were harassed in a similar fashion, and the husband was fired after he interceded on behalf of other women that the supervisor harassed. The supervisor made comments about the sexual prowess of the husbands and also made abusive comments to other females. The court found that the sexual harassment was clearly unwelcome, was "severe and pervasive," was condoned by the employer, and did not fall outside the boundaries of title VII simply because both genders were harassed.

During the 1982-83 academic year, a female college student had an affair with a faculty member of a Wisconsin college that she later characterized as an exploitive and abusive relationship. In the 1986-87 academic year, she enrolled in two courses taught by the faculty member, her former lover. Later she dropped both courses due to his "harassing behavior" toward her. She alleged that he missed an appointment, gave her a lower grade than she deserved, and criticized and demeaned her in such a way as to cause personal injury. Since she did not file her claim until March of 1992, any claim raised before March of 1986 was time barred. The court found her claims involving the courses did not establish a valid claim of sexual harassment. The court noted that the college did not have a policy prohibiting amorous relationships between students and faculty, and further, the professor's actions were personal actions, not discriminatory actions against women.[575]

---

[574] Chiapuzio v. BLT Operating Corp., 826 F. Supp. 1334 (D. Wyo. 1993).
[575] Ruh v. Samerjan, 816 F. Supp. 1326 (E.D. Wis. 1993).

The actions of the professor, therefore, did not meet the "severe and pervasive" standards necessary to support a sexual harassment claim. This case also seems to allude to the fact that sexual harassment prohibitions were not designed to protect either gender from the realities of life or the consequences of life's bad decisions.

At a university in New York, at the end of a counseling session, a counselor allegedly kissed his client as she left the session.[576] She filed a complaint, which was investigated by the university. The investigation concluded that no action should be taken since, without a corroborating witness, the incident could not be substantiated. The student pursued her complaint in the press, and two other women stepped forward proclaiming similar incidents, which occurred several years earlier in 1988. The president issued a memorandum of just cause, in which he gave a detailed accounting of the facts surrounding each incident. The purpose of the memorandum was to justify reopening the hearing process in this case. The court ruled that the hearing procedures were biased by the president's "memorandum to show cause," which created a fatal flaw in the due process proceedings and, therefore, made the institution's dismissal an arbitrary and capricious action. The case points out not only the limits of the "severe and pervasive" standard, but also the procedures required when the institution seeks a remedy to avoid liability. If the president had raised issues to show cause rather than reaching conclusions, the process would have been correct. Perhaps if the institution had developed a remedy short of dismissal and addressed the employee's unacceptable and unprofessional behavior from a remedial perspective it could have avoided litigation.

Academic Freedom and the Hostile Work Environment

Two cases dealt with sexual harassment arising from a hostile environment in the classroom. In New Hampshire, the instructor of a writing course used a sexual relationship between two people as an analogy to illustrate how one would focus on a thesis statement in technical writing.[577] Sexual intimacy was used to describe how one selects a topic, and a definition of belly dancing was used

---

[576] Starishevsky v. Hofstra Univ., 612 N.Y.S.2d 794 (Sup. Ct. 1994).
[577] Silva v. University of N.H., 888 F. Supp. 293 (D. N.H. 1994).

to elaborate on how to write a good definition for a technical report. The instructor used the analogy of belly dancing to putting a vibrator under a plate of Jell-O as an example of a good definition of belly dancing. Six women complained that he had created a hostile environment in the classroom. Using the hearing procedures under the institution's sexual harassment policy, the hearing panel found the instructor to be in violation of university policy. The panel recommended a one-year suspension without pay, reimbursement to the University for costs incurred due to his behavior, one year of counseling at his expense, refraining from retaliation against those bringing this claim, and providing a written public apology for his behavior. The instructor challenged the panel's findings in court. The court found that the sexual harassment policy at the university employed an "impermissible subjective standard of what constituted sexual harassment in the classroom in violation of academic freedom and First Amendment rights." The instructor's classroom statements, the court said, "were made for legitimate pedagogical, public purposes of conveying certain principles related to the subject matter of his course."[578] The court found that, but for this protected speech, the instructor would not have been disciplined. Given these findings, the professor was likely to succeed on his First Amendment claim. Further, the court found that his contract was breached because the institution failed to follow the termination grievance procedures spelled out for tenured faculty. Instead, the institution opted to use the formal procedures prescribed under the sexual harassment policies. The court found that the professor demonstrated that material issues of fact existed as to whether in the formal sexual harassment procedures he received adequate notice of all the charges against him and was offered a hearing before an unbiased panel. The court awarded a preliminary injunction to the plaintiff and ordered that he be returned to the classroom.

In another classroom case also involving academic freedom, a tenured professor was disciplined upon being accused of creating a hostile classroom environment. The professor alleged that his First Amendment rights were violated when he was disciplined.[579] The professor, who taught a remedial English class, required the students to write about provocative topics such as pornography, obscenity, cannibalism, and consensual sex with children. He

---

[578]*Id*. at 316
[579]Cohen v. San Bernadino Valley College, 92 F.3d 968 (9th Cir. 1996).

would use a "devil's advocate" style of teaching that sometimes included the use of profanity. The grievance committee found him guilty of creating a hostile classroom environment under the school's sexual harassment policy. With the president's and board's concurrence, he was ordered to provide students and the department with a course syllabus which outlined the content and teaching style of the course. He was also required to attend a sexual harassment seminar, undergo a formal evaluation as prescribed in the collective bargaining agreement, become sensitive to the particular needs of students in his class, and modify his teaching style to meet student needs. The court found the sexual harassment policy to be vague in that it "prohibited conduct that has the 'effect' of unreasonably interfering with an individual's academic performance or creating an intimidating, hostile, or offensive learning environment."[580] The court specifically noted that it was not deciding whether the college could punish speech if it had a more precisely crafted policy, but it was deciding that the existing policy was too vague. The professor's confrontational style, viewed over time by the college as pedagogically sound, could not result in punishment based on a vague definition of sexual harassment within the college's new policy. Therefore, the court found that the punishment violated the professor's First Amendment speech rights.

An Illinois case commented extensively on academic freedom issues surrounding a claim of classroom sexual harassment. A University of Illinois education professor's use of sexual commentary, inquiries, and jokes in a social studies teaching methods course resulted in a sexual harassment complaint by two female students.[581] After a meeting with university officials, the professor acknowledged the inappropriateness of his comments and agreed to be relieved of his duties as the instructor of the course for the remainder of the semester. The students received a letter from the university provost that acknowledged the investigating committee found sexual harassment and that remedial action had been taken. The professor sued, claiming denial of due process in the resolution of the students' grievance against him. The court rejected the professor's claim that academic freedom required substantive due process. The court stated:

> Academic freedom is not an independent First Amendment right.... As a type of speech, academic freedom

---

[580]*Id.* at 972.
[581] Rubin v. Ikenberry, 933 F. Supp. 1425 (C.D. Ill. 1996).

> receives some protection from governmental abridgement by the First Amendment. (citations omitted)
>
> Academic freedom refers to the freedom of university professors and university administrators to function autonomously, without interference from government.... It also refers to the freedom of individual teachers to not suffer interference but academic freedom does not license uncontrolled expression which is detrimental to the institution's proper functioning. (citations omitted)[582]

Thus, while academic freedom is "an extremely important academic right," it "is not a fundamental right" requiring substantive due process protection. The court granted the institution's summary judgment motion on all claims, including the due process claim.

The two cases above involving termination point out that it may be difficult to overcome the protected rights which faculty possess under First Amendment protected speech and under contractual provisions of academic freedom. However, actions involving remediation, short of suspension or termination, which assert the institution's right to control curricular content in keeping with sound educational principles appear to survive First Amendment or academic freedom challenges. Further, sexual harassment policies must be narrowly crafted to prohibit only those behaviors truly "severe and pervasive" under title VII of the Civil Rights Act of 1964.

Same-Sex Sexual Harassment

A female program coordinator for the women's resource center on a university campus brought a same-sex hostile work environment claim against the female director of the resource center.[583] For two years, from 1986 to 1988, she was subjected to harassing behavior from the director. This behavior included frequent touching, pressing against her body and breasts, obstructing her passage in narrow hallways, standing close to and putting her arm around the plaintiff, and making lewd and suggestive gestures and comments. In 1988, after transferring to the university's school of social work, the former program coordinator observed the women's resource center director hugging a woman in the school of social work in a suggestive way. The court, failing to

---

[582]*Id.* at 1433.
[583] Purrington v. University of Utah, 9996 F.2d 1025 (10th Cir. 1993).

mention the issue of same-sex sexual harassment which was before the Supreme Court in the 1997-98 term, ruled that the claim of sexual harassment was untimely filed. The court said that the 1986 to 1988 sexual harassment was time barred, and the incidents observed in 1989 were separate and unrelated harassment which did not support the existence of a continuing violation to establish equitable tolling.

Two years later the Federal District Court of Puerto Rico ruled that a same-sex sexual harassment claim could be brought under title VII.[584] A female librarian alleged that her female supervisors sexually harassed her by creating a hostile work environment. The harassment claim, which involved touching and sexually explicit comments and propositions, resulted in the court resolving a number of preliminary motions. The implication was that courts would recognize same-sex claims of sexual harassment. The Supreme Court of the United States affirmed the validity of same-sex sexual harassment claims under title VII in *Oncale v. Sundowner Offshore Services, Inc.*[585]

In summary, hostile work environment claims indicate that the court will not use the law to protect individuals from their own poor life decisions, nor will it protect young adults from being exposed to controversial topics. However, if the harassment is unwelcome, severe, and pervasive, aimed at one gender and condoned or ignored by the institution, the court will find that a hostile work environment exists. Further, the issue of whether same-sex sexual harassment is a valid claim under title VII was settled by the Supreme Court, and same-sex sexual harassment is a valid issue to be litigated under title VII.

Quid Pro Quo Sexual Harassment

Quid pro quo sexual harassment is based on the concept of exchange: an offer of sexual favors for a benefit (or other favor). A Georgia case involved *quid pro quo* sexual harassment culminating in rape.[586] A male employee of the medical college propositioned a female secretary, who eventually entered into a consensual relationship with the employee because he said he had influence with her supervisor. After she terminated the relationship, the employee began to verbally harass her, both in private

---

[584] Nogueras v. University of P.R., 890 F. Supp. 60 (D.P.R. 1995).

[585] 118 S. Ct. 998 (1998).

[586] Simon v. Morehouse School of Med., 908 F. Supp. 959 (N.D. Ga. 1995).

and public settings. Eventually, her supervisor began to harass her and ask personal questions about the terminated relationship with the employee. After the male employee raped her in her office, the plaintiff had difficulty coming to work and was plagued with headaches, nausea, loss of appetite and sleeplessness, which eventually resulted in her constructive discharge. Her supervisor was informed of the alleged rape within a month of the occurrence, but failed to investigate, because he refused to believe that the employee would do such a thing. The court refused to grant a summary judgment to the institution, the supervisor and the employee on the female's *quid pro quo* sexual harassment, constructive discharge, Georgia workers' compensation, intentional infliction of emotional distress, invasion of privacy, and negligent retention and supervision claims. In all of these areas the court said that genuine issues of material fact required litigation on the merits.

The issue of institutional liability for failure to investigate or remedy a claim of sexual harassment was before the court in a case involving Columbia University. An employee of the university entered into a sexual relationship with her supervisor.[587] After several years, she terminated the relationship and brought a claim for *quid pro quo* sexual harassment. While she had talked with several university officials about the relationship, her discussions did not center on sexual harassment but rather problems within the relationship. When she finally went to the affirmative action officer, she discussed the relationship as sexual harassment, but labeled the conversation as confidential. The court ruled that, because it had not reached a finding of sexual harassment by the supervisor, the institution could not be held liable. Further, the institution had not received adequate notice of a sexual harassment claim requiring investigation and remediation.

Title XI Sexual Harassment Claims

A number of claims brought by students alleging sexual harassment claims under title XI have emerged in the courts. The same concepts that surround title VII claims are used in these claims. These claims typically involve sexual harassment by professors serving in their official capacity with the institution. In one case, a federal court found that the student could sustain a *quid pro quo* claim of sexual harassment under title IX.[588] The court found

---

[587] Kariban v. Columbia Univ., 930 F. Supp. 134 (S.D.N.Y. 1996), *on remand*, 14 F.3d 733 (2d Cir. 1994).
[588] Slater v. Marshall, 906 F. Supp. 256 (E.D. Pa. 1995).

merit in her claim that even though she graduated with a 4.00 GPA, after refusing to have sexual relations with a faculty member, she was excluded from meaningful course work at the college based on her gender.

However, a Missouri case points out that title IX will not apply to harassment which occurs outside the academic program.[589] A dental student claimed that a professor sexually harassed her while she was employed in his private dental practice. She also alleged that in his class at the dental school he showed an instructional video which contained sexual innuendoes. The Eighth Circuit ruled that the presentation of a video containing sexual innuendoes, standing alone, did not create a pervasive hostile environment. Further, the court said that *quid pro quo* sexual harassment taking place in the course of employment in a private dental practice was "not a program or activity" covered by title IX. While title IX emerges as a vehicle for students to claim sexual harassment, it only covers educational programs or activities.

Conclusion

Sexual harassment claims under title VII are brought under both hostile work environment and *quid pro quo* theories. The clash between faculty First Amendment rights and academic freedom protections and institutional policies on sexual harassment continue to develop. The balance of these conflicting rights will continue to play itself out in the courts. Also, same sex claims have been established as valid under title VII sexual harassment provisions. Further, cases involving sexual harassment claims by students in educational programs under title IX have recently emerged and appear to follow the same legal theories as title VII cases.

The sexual harassment law continues to evolve. In formulating a sexual harassment policy, administrators should consider:

- Institutions should develop policy that outline the prohibition of sexual harassment mechanisms that are sensitive to the needs of the victim and facilitate the reporting of claims of sexual harassment.

---

[589] Lam v. Curators of the Univ. of Mo. at Kan. City Dental Sch., 122 F.3d 654 (8th Cir. 1997).

- Supervisors who are aware of harassing behavior but fail to report or take adequate corrective action put both themselves and their institution at risk.
- Sexual harassment claims brought against faculty for pronouncements in the classroom need to be carefully reviewed in order to insure that the faculty member's academic freedom or First Amendment protected speech are not trampled.
- Attempts to remove employees based on sexual harassment claims should utilize the procedures spelled out under institutional procedures for termination and not the procedures used to determine punishment under the sexual harassment policy.
- Policies should set guidelines and procedures for student-to-student sexual harassment.
- Just as with employees the student-to-student sexual harassment policies should rely on the school's disciplinary procedures in cases that may result in dismissal.

CHAPTER VII

Collective Bargaining in Higher Education

Introduction

The National Labor Relations Act[590] (NLRA), passed in the 1930s, was designed to allow employees in private industry to bargain collectively on matters of wages, benefits, and working conditions. The NLRA receives authorization from the Commerce Clause,[591] allowing the federal government to regulate businesses involved in interstate commerce.[592] The NLRA has provisions for an administrative adjudicatory agency authorized to settle disputes emanating from the provisions of the Act.[593] The National Labor Relations Board (NLRB) is the administrative adjudicatory agency with jurisdiction over labor disputes in private industry. The law makes distinctions between managers or supervisory employees who are outside the bargaining unit and workers who can organize and bargain collectively. While public institutions are not covered under the Act, states that allow public employees to bargain collectively model their state collective bargaining laws after the NLRA.

Initially, the NLRB viewed private higher education as being outside the scope of the NLRA. In 1970, however, the NLRB ruled that the faculty of Cornell University came under the provisions of the Act and could organize and bargain collectively.[594] Because the law was written to cover private industry, its application to private higher education raised significant issues of the scope of the law, especially with respect to whether employees within collegiate institutions were covered under the bargaining provisions of the Act.

---

[590] 29 U.S.C. §§ 151 - 169 (1982).
[591] U.S. Const. Art. 1, § 8, cl. 3.
[592] *See Note*: *Church-Affiliated Universities and Labor Board Jurisdiction: An Unholy Union Between Church and State?* 56 GEO. WASH. L. REV., 558 (1988).
[593] 29 U.S.C. § 153.
[594] Cornell University, 183 NLRB 329 (1970).

The involvement of faculty in decision making in higher education has long been a hallmark of the industry.[595] Millett's description of the "community of scholars" typifies not only the early notions of faculty control over academic decision making, but also the nature of the faculty role at some higher education institutions.[596]

This difference between the nature of the collegiate enterprise and business organizations prompted considerable litigation. This litigation concerned the establishment and membership of the bargaining unit, the specific aspects of the job that are subject to negotiation, the relationship between grievance procedures under collective bargaining and existing institutional tenure provisions, and First Amendment rights of both members of the bargaining unit and those employees who chose not to join the union. Each of these issues is discussed in this chapter.

The Organization of a Bargaining Unit

Since the NLRB decided that private higher education came under the provisions of the Act, a question at issue has been certification of the bargaining unit. One certification issue was whether faculty qualified as members of the bargaining unit in light of their involvement in institutional decision making. Another issue was whether department heads were supervisors and, therefore, excluded from membership in the bargaining unit. The NLRB used a ruling involving faculty at Fordham University to decide that the collective nature of faculty decision making would not yield a finding that faculty were managers instead of employees.[597] The Board extended the position of faculty membership in the bargaining unit in a case involving Adelphi University.[598] The NLRB further refined its position by holding that faculty acted in their own interest and not in the interest of the employer.[599] At the same time, the NLRB determined that an analysis at each institution based on the decision making authority of department chairs

---

[595] *See* J. Baldridge, et. al. (Eds.), GOVERNING ACADEMIC ORGANIZATIONS, (1971); J. Baldridge, et. al., POLICY MAKING AND EFFECTIVE LEADERSHIP, (1978); J. Baldridge, POWER AND CONFLICT IN THE UNIVERSITY, (1971); J. Millett, NEW STRUCTURES OF CAMPUS POWER, (1978); K. Mortimer and T. McConnell, SHARING AUTHORITY EFFECTIVELY, (1978).

[596] J. Millett, THE ACADEMIC COMMUNITY, (1962).

[597] Fordham Univ., 183 NLRB 329 (1970).

[598] Adelphi Univ., 189 NLRB 904 (1971); the NLRB concluded that the institution's Board of Trustees manages the institution and that the faculty have "policy making and quasi-supervisory authority."

[599] Northeastern Univ., 218 NLRB 247 (1975).

would determine whether department chairs were either supervisory, and therefore excluded from bargaining, or employees with full bargaining rights.[600] The NLRB position would hold firm on these issues throughout the 1970s.

The NLRB assumption that faculty were not managerial employees was challenged in the landmark case *National Labor Relations Board v. Yeshiva University*.[601] Yeshiva University claimed that because of the decision-making authority of faculty, they would fall under the managerial exclusion of the National Labor Relations Act. The NLRB, without analysis of the specific situation at Yeshiva University, simply certified the faculty at Yeshiva University as a bargaining unit based on previous rulings involving faculty in higher education.[602] The University appealed this NLRB ruling to the Second Circuit Court of Appeals.[603] That court found that while the faculty were professional employees, they were "in effect substantially and pervasively operating the enterprise,"[604] and under the labor law were managers removed from coverage. The United States Supreme Court affirmed the Circuit Court decision. The Court found that faculty at Yeshiva University had significant involvement in an array of decisions including determining salaries and fringe benefits, hiring, promotion and tenure, working conditions that included teaching load and teaching subject matter, academic policies involving curriculum, the grading system, admissions standards, the academic calendar; and course schedules—making them supervisory personnel.[605] This case forced the NLRB to evaluate decision making at each institution to determine whether faculty are managers or employees. Subsequent litigation has resulted in the decertification of faculty bargaining units at 28 institutions where faculties were found to be managers. Fifty-four institutions in total have been affected by the *Yeshiva* decision.[606] Courts and the NLRB have also found that

---

[600] *See* C. W. Post Center of Long Island Univ., 189 NLRB 109 (1971), Fordham Univ., 193 NLRB 23 (1971), University of Detroit, 193 N.L.R.B. 95 (1971).

[601] 444 U.S. 672 (1980).

[602] Yeshiva Univ., 221 N.L.R.B. 1053 (1975); *see also* 231 N.L.R.B. 597 (1977).

[603] N.L.R.B. v. Yeshiva Univ., 582 F.2d 868 (2d. Cir. 1978).

[604] 444 U.S. 672, 698.

[605] *Id.* at 672.

[606] J. Douglas, Directory of Faculty Contracts and Bargaining Agents In Institutions, (1987); *see* NLRB v. Lewis Univ., 765 F.2d 616 (7th Cir. 1985); Boston Univ. Chapter, AAUP v. NLRB, 836 F.2d 399 (1st Cir. 1987); Bradford College, 261 N.L.R.B. 565 (1982); Catholic Univ. of America Law School, 89 Lab. Cas. (CCH) 12,157 (1980); College of Osteopathic Medicine and Surgery, 265 N.L.R.B. No. 37, 111 L.R.R.M. (BNA) 1523 (1982); Duquesne Univ., 261 N.L.R.B. 587 (1982); Ithaca College, 261 N.L.R.B. 577 (1982); Polytechnic Inst. of New York, No. 29-UC-136 (1981); Pratt Inst., 256 N.L.R.B. 1166 (1981); Stephens Inst.v. NLRB, 620 F.2d 720 (9th Cir. 1980); Thiel College, 261 N.L.R.B. 580 (1982).

at some institutions faculty are employees, not managers.[607] These contrasting court decisions reflect the diversity of institutional type and mission in higher education and point to the fact that the application of the *Yeshiva* decision is limited to certain types of private colleges and universities where faculty involvement in decision making is extensive.

The ability of employees at public colleges and universities to bargain collectively will depend on whether the specific state in question allows public employees to bargain collectively. Where states have provided for public employee bargaining by law, they have typically modeled their provisions after the National Labor Relations Act and have established a state labor relations board to adjudicate disputes. Questions before these state boards are similar to those on the federal level. There are cases that attempt to determine the types of employees who qualify for membership in the bargaining unit.[608] For example, an Illinois court ruled that two bargaining units, the professional/technical employee unit and the faculty unit of a college, could institute a self determination petition to merge into one bargaining unit.[609] State cases also involve the certification of the bargaining unit.[610] Questions of whether specific categories of public employees qualify for membership are also at issue. For example, an Illinois court ruled that adjunct faculty who are assigned as part-time faculty to courses on a semester-by-semester basis could not, under state law, organize to bargain collectively.[611] Faculty hired on a semester-by-semester basis did not have reasonable assurance of rehiring. However, at another Illinois college, adjunct faculty who taught at least twelve credits in an academic calendar year and had an expectation of rehiring were eligible members of the faculty bar-

---

[607] Florida Memorial College, 263 N.L.R.B. No. 160 (1982), *aff'd*, NLRB v. Florida Memorial College, 820 F.2d 1182 (11th Cir. 1987); Loretto Heights College, 264 N.L.R.B. No.149, 111 L.R.R.M. (BNA) 1680 (1982), *aff'd*, Loretto Heights College v. NLRB, 742 F. 2d 1245 (10th Cir. 1984).

[608] Board of Regents of Regency Univ. System v. Illinois Educ. Labor Relations Bd., 520 N.E.2d 1150 (Ill. App. Ct. 1988), Directors of research units were managers; Regents of Univ. of Cal. v. Public Employment Relations Bd., 715 P.2d 590 (Cal. 1986), students in a residency program as medical house staff were part of the bargaining unit.

[609] Black Hawk College Professional Technical Unit v. Illinois Educ. Labor Relations Bd., 655 N.E.2d 1054 (Ill. Ct. App.1995).

[610] *See* Hawaii Gov't Employees Ass'n, AFSCME v. Armbruster, 681 P.2d 587 (Hawaii Ct. App. 1984), and Univ. of Or. Chapter, AFT v. University of Or., 759 P.2d 1112 (Or. Ct. App. 1988), professional academic employees did not have the right to form a separate bargaining unit under the state labor law.

[611] William Rainey Harper Community College v. Harper College Adjunct Faculty Ass'n, 653 N.E.2d 411 (Ill. Ct. App. 1995).

gaining unit under state law.[612] Another state court found that college or university employees were not city employees who would be exempt from the state labor relations statute,[613] and a state system of public higher education was a public employer authorized to bargain collectively with professional employees.[614] Finally, there is the issue of whether graduate research and teaching assistants may organize to bargain collectively. New York law allows them to organize and bargain collectively,[615] while in California it was thought unwise to allow "students" to organize a collective bargaining unit.[616]

Collective bargaining issues also include questions regarding organizing procedures and what constitutes unfair labor practices. The United States Supreme Court ruled that an institution could refuse to allow a union to use campus mail for purposes of organizing the institution's employees.[617] The Court found that the union's use of the institution's mail service did not fit within the provisions of the Private Express Statutes[618] because it was a matter of interest to the union, not a matter of "current business" of the institutional carrier.[619] Other state cases deal with issues of alleged but unfounded charges of an unfair labor practice where the institution failed to recognize informal meetings of employees as the formation of a bargaining unit,[620] or where the institution ceased bargaining with one group when another group began petition procedures to become the bargaining agent.[621]

There is extensive litigation on what constitutes unfair labor practices in both the organizational and contract negotiations

---

[612] Elgin Community College v. Illinois Educ. Labor Relations Bd., 660 N.E.2d 265 (Ill. Ct. App. 1996).

[613] City of Philadelphia v. Local 473, 508 A.2d 628 (Pa. Commw. Ct. 1986).

[614] Board of Governors of State Sys. of Higher Educ. v. Commonwealth of Pa., 514 A.2d 223 (Pa. Commw. Ct. 1986), the court found that the state system of higher education was the employer and was not to be joint public employer with the Commonwealth of Pennsylvania even though the Commonwealth had control over aspects of the employment relationship.

[615] State v. New York State Pub. Employment Relations Bd., 586 N.Y.S.2d 662 (N.Y. App. Div. 1992).

[616] Association of Graduate Student Employment v. Public Employment Relations Bd., 8 Cal. Rptr. 2d 275 (Cal. Ct. App. 1992).

[617] Regents of Univ. of Cal. v. Public Employment Relations Bd., 108 S. Ct. 1404 (1988).

[618] Private Express Statute, 18 U.S.C. 1693-1699, 39 U.S.C. 601-606 (1988), the law allows private carriers to transport unstamped mail within that organization as long as it involves current business.

[619] Regents of Univ. of Cal. v. Public Employment Relations Bd., 108 S. Ct. 1404, at 1409 (U.S. 1988).

[620] Rosen v. Public Employment Relations Bd., 530 N.Y.S.2d 534 (N.Y. 1988).

[621] AFSCME Council 75 v. Oregon Health Sciences Univ., 755 P.2d 141 (Or. Ct. App. 1988).

phases of the collective bargaining process.[622] For example, it was an unfair labor practice when a university considered its geographically separate north and south units as one bargaining units.[623] The institution had consolidated the two hospitals as one and refused to bargain with the existing separate nurses bargaining group for the one hospital. The court upheld the NLRB ruling that the consolidation of the two university hospitals' administration did not result in the consolidation of the two separate existing collective bargaining units.

These cases point out the complexity of adapting legislation designed originally to control employment relationships in industry to organization types that do not fall into the business model of decision making. Because of basic differences in the way businesses and universities make decisions, litigation proceeded by defining the scope of the bargaining unit in institutions of higher education. These different types of organizations resulted in other issues involving the matters to be negotiated, which received attention in the courts.

Matters to be Negotiated

In both public and private institutions, employee concerns that are subject to negotiations between the bargaining unit and the institution have been at issue. Under the provisions of particular federal or state labor laws, some institutions claimed that certain matters were classified as managerial prerogatives and, therefore, were non-negotiable or outside the authority of union grievance procedures. For example, one institution established that the number of faculty to be hired and the criteria for hiring them were managerial prerogatives not subject to negotiation with the labor union.[624] In a recent Massachusetts case, the court found that it was a management prerogative to determine not only the vacancies in an academic department but also the qualifications

---

[622] *See e.g.*: Connecticut State College AAUP v. State Bd. of Labor Relations, 495 A.2d 1069 (Conn. 1985); Green River Community College Dist. 10 v. Higher Educ. Personnel Bd., 730 P.2d 653 (Wash. 1986), Palm Beach Junior College Bd. of Trustees v. United Faculty of Palm Beach Junior, 475 So.2d 1221 (Fla. 1985), Regents of Univ. of Cal. v. Public Employment Relations Bd., 214 Cal. Rpt. 698 (Cal. Ct. App. 1985), State Employment Relations Bd. v. Ohio State Univ., 520 N.E.2d 597 (Ohio Ct. App. 1987).

[623] Staten Island Univ. Hosp. v. NLRB, 24 F.3d 450 (2d. Cir. 1994).

[624] Board of Regents of Higher Educ. v. Labor Relations Commission, 465 N.E. 2d 1245 (Mass. App. Ct. 1984).

necessary to fill the positions.[625] The bargaining agent unsuccessfully claimed that a faculty member terminated from a program because of financial exigency was qualified for the newly created position. An Illinois court, however, found that it was an unfair labor practice when the institution bargained to impasse to exclude certain matters from the grievance procedures.[626] The institution attempted to exclude the subjects of discharge, demotion, position classification, and discrimination from the grievance procedures.[627] In another case, a court found that the board must consider a "remonstrance" on individual faculty tenure questions, but the actual tenure policy is a management prerogative[628] as are the criteria used to determine promotion, tenure, and the evaluation of faculty.[629] A budgetary decline resulting in a decision to freeze salaries rather than lay off employees[630] or the elimination of a position[631] was a management prerogative. Management prerogatives are outside the negotiation process under collective bargaining laws.

Other issues, however, are subject to the reach of the negotiation process. Examples of issues subject to negotiations are: work load and student contact hours,[632] and methods used to award summer faculty teaching contracts.[633] In Illinois, when a union agreed to limit outside employment, its members waived any privacy rights, which might inhibit the completion of a form reporting outside remuneration.[634] Salary increases negotiated at public institutions usually do not bind the legislature to a certain level of appropriations because language in the contract hinges salary awards on legislative appropriations. Where a state typically uses such language in the collective bargaining agreement but fails to

---

[625] Higher Education Coordinating Council/Roxbury Community College v. Massachusetts Teachers Ass'n, 66 N.E.2d 479 (Mass. 1996).
[626] Board of Trustees of Univ. of Ill. v. Illinois Educ. Labor Relations Bd., 612 N.E.2d 1365 (Ill. App. Ct. 1993).
[627] *Id.* at 206.
[628] Professional Ass'n of College Educators v. El Paso County Community Dist., 678 S.W.2d 94 (Tex. Ct. App. 1984).
[629] University Educ. Ass'n v. Regents of Univ. of Minn., 353 N.W.2d 534 (Minn. 1984).
[630] Schoolcraft College Ass'n of Office Personnel/MESPA v. Schoolcraft Community College, 401 N.W.2d 915 (Mich. Ct. App. 1986).
[631] Guild of Admin. Officers of Suffolk County Community College v. County of Suffolk, 510 N.Y.S.2d 914 (N.Y. App. Div. 1987).
[632] Vermont State College Faculty Fed'n v. Vermont State Colleges, 547 A.2d 1340 (Vt. 1988).
[633] Commonwealth v. Commonwealth, Pa. Labor Relations Bd., 474 A.2d 1213 (Pa. Commw. Ct. 1984).
[634] Cook County College Teachers Union v. Board of Trustees, 481 N.E.2d 688 (Ill. App. Ct. 1985).

include it for one institution, the court may find the legislature obligated to award the increase.[635] As the literature reflects, the scope of the negotiations in higher education has expanded over time to cover a fairly broad range of institutional factors.[636] However, litigation has drawn some boundaries with regard to issues under negotiation.

Grievance Procedures and Binding Arbitration

When the union and the employer are negotiating a collective bargaining agreement, an impasse in the negotiations could result in a move to arbitration if the law provides for such an option. An arbitrator will listen to both sides of the dispute and recommend an equitable solution. Under some labor laws, this could be binding arbitration, in which case the two parties are obligated to accept the arbitrator's resolution.

Most collective bargaining agreements contain a procedure to resolve issues that have developed between the employee(s) and the employer. The procedures used to resolve issues involving an interpretation of the scope of the agreement are called grievance procedures. In some cases, a grievance procedure will proceed through several levels until a resolution is realized. These levels can include binding arbitration, where both parties must accept the final decision of the arbitrator. Litigation in this area included questions whether arbitration is an available remedy, court jurisdiction over an arbitrators' decisions, whether issues raised were grievable, and the appropriateness of the arbitrator award.

Whether arbitration, a mediation device, is available as a remedy in labor disputes depends on both the nature of the state labor laws and the provisions of the collective bargaining contract.

A Massachusetts court ruled that mediation procedures available during the negotiation phase could not be used for issues arising after the ratification of the contract. The issues in questions were not part of the ratified contract.[637] Issues covered by the con-

---

[635] Carlstrom v. Washington, 694 P.2d 1 (Wash. 1985).

[636] T. Fenton, *University Faculty and The Institution of Collective Bargaining*, 69 KY. L.J. 37 (1980); A. Frank, *Two Trends In Academic Collective Bargaining: A Faculty Representative's Perspective*, 13 J. OF L. & EDUC. 651 (1984); B. Lee and J. Begin, *Criteria For Evaluating The Managerial Status of College Faculty: Applications of Yeshiva University by the NLRB*, 10 J. C. & U.L. 515 (1983).

[637] Massachusetts Community College Council MTA/NEA v. Labor Relations Comm'n, 522 N.E.2d 416 (Mass. 1988).

tract would be grieved through the procedures established in the collective bargaining agreement. However, where questions fall under federal laws such as title VII or the Equal Pay Act, the state's collective bargaining act could hold a grievance in abeyance where relief was sought through an outside source.[638] At least in Ohio, however, the university could be required to arbitrate the professor's complaint.

Although a collective bargaining agreement may define the particular grievance and arbitration procedures to be followed, issues that lead to litigation can still arise. A federal court ruled that where a private university entered into a collective bargaining agreement subjecting all disputes to arbitration, it must arbitrate a dispute over the reorganization of a department.[639] A New York court ruled that certain grievance procedures, based on the language of the collective bargaining agreement, were the exclusive available remedy in one case.[640] An Illinois court found, however, that where the collective bargaining agreement gave deference to the state's civil service system and retirement board, it was not an unfair labor practice for the institution to refer a grievance to the State Civil Service Board and refuse to commence arbitration.[641]

Grievance procedures to be followed under collective bargaining agreements depend on the agreement's terms. For example, the presence of a union representative at a disciplinary hearing of a university hospital medical intern was at issue in a New Jersey case.[642] After repeated evaluations of the intern by the medical staff, the staff commenced disciplinary action. The evaluations had found that the safety of patients was compromised because the intern had demonstrated inadequate knowledge and indecisiveness. The court found that under the collective bargaining agreement, when academic and medical matters were at issue in the disciplinary hearing, the right to union representation ended.

A different case showed that a union's failure to pursue arbitration after a terminated employee failed in a grievance procedure

---

[638] Wedding v. University of Toledo, 884 F. Supp. 253 (N.D. Ohio 1995).

[639] Hahnemann Univ. v. District 1199C, National Union of Hosp. and Health Care Employees, 765 F.2d 38 (3d. Cir. 1985).

[640] Post-Adjunct Faculty Ass'n v. Board of Trustees of Long Island Univ., 511 N.Y.S.2d 874 (N.Y. App. Div. 1987).

[641] Board of Governors of State Colleges and Univs. *ex rel.* Northeastern Ill. Univ. v. Illinois Labor Relations Bd., 524 N.E.2d 758 (Ill. App. Ct. 1988).

[642] *In re* University Med. and Dentistry of N.J., 677 A.2d 721(N.J. 1996).

did not violate the collective bargaining agreement.[643] In yet another case, the fact that two arbitrators reached the same conclusion for different reasons did not negate the arbitration decision.[644] A California court, however, found that a collective bargaining agreement does not waive a terminated faculty member's right to procedural due process.[645] Under the provisions in the faculty manual, the terminated faculty member was entitled to pre-termination notification and reasons for termination and a post termination hearing. The union could not bargain away his due process rights.

The existence of a collective bargaining agreement will not result in the waiving of an individual's constitutional rights. However, the grievance procedures as part of the collective bargaining agreement will fulfill the constitutional requirements to protect the employers' due process where a liberty interest or property right are implicated.

Some employment questions are termed nongrievable issues under the agreement. For example, a Connecticut court found that under the terms of the contract in question, the dismissal of an employee during the probationary period was consistent with the provisions of the agreement and was, therefore, a nongrievable question.[646] The court reached this ruling in light of the fact that the supervisor had misinformed the employee that the probationary period had ended. Several cases affirmed the authority of the university to set the criteria used in the evaluation process[647] or for promotion and tenure decisions.[648] While the selection of criteria was nongrievable, the manner in which the criteria were applied to individual employees would be grievable. Finally, a court ruled that the arbitrator could not read into a contract provisions it did not contain.[649] The case involved the dismissal of a faculty member where the arbitrator read into the contract a requirement that the faculty member first be placed on probation before dismissal. From the above cases, it is evident that terms of the of the collective bargaining agreement will determine which issues will be subject to arbitration.

---

[643] Kaplan v. Ruggieri, 547 F. Supp. 707 (E.D. N.Y. 1982).

[644] Rockland Community College Fed'n of Teachers, Local 1871 v. Trustees of Rockland Community College, 531 N.Y.S.2d 117 (N.Y. App. Div. 1988).

[645] Phillips v. California State Personnel Bd., 229 Cal. Rptr. 502 (Cal. Ct. App. 1986).

[646] State v. AFSCME, Council 4, 537 A.2d 517 (Conn. Ct. App. 1988).

[647] Board of Trustees v. Cook County College Teachers, 487 N.E.2d 956 (Ill. App. Ct. 1985).

[648] University of Haw. Professional Assembly v. University of Haw., 659 P.2d 717 (Haw. 1983).

[649] Board of Control of Ferris State College v. Michigan AFSCME, 361 N.W.2d 342 (Mich. Ct. App. 1984).

The authority of an arbitrator in adjudicating labor disputes is an essential issue in collective bargaining. One case in higher education, decided by the First Circuit Court of Appeals, established the premise of the arbitrator's authority to impose a resolution of a labor dispute.[650] Citing *W.R. Grace v. Rubber Workers Local 759*,[651] the court found that the arbitrator's ruling should be given substantial deference in interpreting the provisions of a collective bargaining agreement. In this case, the arbitrator had found inequities in three faculty members' salaries and ordered salary adjustments. Other examples of the scope of the arbitrator's authority have been decided in a number of states. A Hawaii court ruled that where an arbitrator found that the tenure procedures were arbitrary and capricious, he had the authority to award tenure.[652] An arbitrator in Pennsylvania had the authority to order a community college to cease refusing to allow a teacher to teach a credit course.[653]

These examples clarify that courts will defer to the arbitrator's authority to adjudicate the merits of a dispute and order an award to a specific party. This authority will be upheld as long as the arbitration procedures are fundamentally fair and the arbitrator follows sound judicial standards. The terms of the collective bargaining agreement will play a significant role in the ultimate decision.

The First Amendment and Collective Bargaining

First Amendment issues also have been raised in the application of collective bargaining provisions to education. In higher education, several issues have been adjudicated by the courts. One of these issues is the application of the National Labor Relations Act to church-affiliated colleges and universities within the context of separation of church and state. Another is the use of union dues to support causes that violate either the religious freedom or

---

[650] Trustees of Boston Univ. v. Boston Univ. Chapter of AAUP, 746 F.2d 924 (1st Cir. 1984).

[651] 461 U.S. 757 (1983).

[652] University of Haw. Professional Assembly, Daeufer v. University of Haw., 659 P.2d 720 (Haw. 1983).

[653] Community College of Beaver County v. Society of the Faculty, 513 A.2d 1125 (Pa. Commw. Ct. 1986).

free speech rights of employees as members or nonmembers of the bargaining unit. Finally, there is the issue of employee speech rights under the provision of a collective bargaining agreement.

Separation of church and state was at issue in the application of the National Labor Relations Act (NLRA) to church-related schools. The United States Supreme Court, in *NLRB v. Catholic Bishop*,[654] dodged the separation of church and state issue by ruling that the NLRA did not give the NLRB jurisdiction over church-affiliated schools.[655] The same question was before the courts involving higher education. The First Circuit Court of Appeals, citing the *Catholic Bishop* case, ruled that a Catholic university was outside the jurisdiction of the NLRA.[656] It would appear that church-affiliated institutions will continue to be viewed as outside the jurisdiction of the NLRA.

Religious freedom and freedom of speech issues surround the use of union dues. A United States Supreme Court case, *Abood v. Detroit Board of Educ.*,[657] sets the guidelines courts use in adjudicating these issues. The state of Michigan, in establishing collective bargaining laws for public employees, instituted a union shop provision. A union shop provision requires that both member and nonmember employees pay union dues where public employees have chosen to form a union. The Court ruled that the use of union dues for collective bargaining, contract administration, and grievance adjudication does not violate any constitutional protections of employees.[658] The court found, however, that where the union used fees to promote certain political viewpoints or candidates, a First Amendment violation of free speech rights could exist.[659] The court found that the union must be free under the First Amendment to support political causes which fall outside its collective bargaining responsibility, and at the same time, it must ensure that members are not compelled to contribute to causes to which they object or which would be a violation of their First Amendment rights.

---

[654] 440 U.S. 490 (1979).

[655] *Id.* at 504; *See supra* note 3.

[656] Universidad Central De Bayamon v. NLRB, 778 F.2d 383 (1st. Cir. 1985); *See also* Universidad Cent. De Bayamon v. NLRB, 778 F.2d 906 (1st Cir. 1985), *en banc* hearing of full court (*supra*) vacated this decision by three-judge panel of the court.

[657] 431 U.S. 209 (1977).

[658] *Id.* at 222.

[659] *Id.* at 234.

What has evolved from the *Abood* case is the concept that the determination of which parts of the dues assessed to members and nonmembers are used for political advocacy is the responsibility of the union.[660] Those matters that are related to the collective bargaining responsibilities of the union and include funding lobbying efforts with legislative bodies involving employee or labor relations matters are chargeable fees.[661] The use of union dues, however, to support the organization of other employees, or to support an affiliated union's strike, were not chargeable to nonmembers.[662] Thus, while unions are free to use union dues for political purposes outside the immediate responsibilities to conduct collective bargaining for the members, they need to develop a mechanism to ensure that members and nonmembers who object to a particular cause are not being forced to support that cause. The burden lies with the unions to account for the expenditure of membership fees and to not charge the objector for that portion of the fee going to a challenged cause. The objecting member will bear the responsibility to prove that the activity contested is outside the accepted responsibilities of the collective bargaining agency. Contested activities could include some lobbying activities on behalf of the employees.

A recent case indicates that if the objecting union member or nonmember meets his or her burden of showing that the union failed to provide adequate information to determine whether collected fees violated the First Amendment, a preliminary injunction could halt the collection of union fees.[663] When the University of Cincinnati and the service employees union entered into a collective bargaining agreement, it was determined that nonunion employees would pay 90% of union dues as a "fair share fee." It also provided procedures through which members and nonmembers could challenge the fees, but failed to provide details as to how the union spent the dues. The plaintiff, seeking to stop the withholding of union fees from pay based on potential First Amendment violations, was denied a preliminary injunction by a federal district court. On appeal, the Sixth Circuit Court of Appeals reversed and remanded the case. Citing *Chicago Teachers*

---

[660] *See* Chicago Teachers Union v. Hudson, 106 S. Ct. 1066 (1986).

[661] Lehnert v. Ferris Faculty Ass'n, 707 F. Supp. 1473 (W.D. Mich. 1988), *aff'd*, 881 F.2d 1388 (6th Cir. 1989).

[662] *Id.*

[663] Weaver v. University of Cincinnati, 764 F. Supp. 1241 (S.D. Ohio 1991), *rev'd and remanded*, 942 F.2d 1039 (6th Cir. 1991).

Union Local No. 1 v. Hudson,[664] the court applied the criteria necessary to determine whether the plaintiff were eligible to receive a preliminary injunction. The court found that the failure to provide a detailed accounting of not only how union fees were spent but also which organizations the union was affiliated with could result in irreparable injury to the plaintiffs in the form of a First Amendment violation. Furthermore, the court found that the union's plan to put the contested fees in an escrow account until the matter was resolved was a "constitutionally inadequate plan." The courts have required unions to resolve any challenges based on First Amendment protection before they collect the contested portion of the fee.

Other First Amendment freedom of speech issues have also been litigated. A state court found that an institution would be obligated to grant access to space designated for the display of a banner to an organization attempting to organize employees for the purpose of bargaining collectively.[665] Where two bargaining associations were involved, however, an institution could refuse access to the banner space because to allow access would favor one of the bargaining organizations over the other.

Another First Amendment issue was decided by the United States Supreme Court in *Minnesota State Board for Community Colleges v. Knight.*[666] Plaintiffs, nonmembers of the collective bargaining organization, claimed their First Amendment rights were violated when they were denied access to meet and confer provisions of the collective bargaining agreement. These "meet and confer" provisions provided for periodic meetings between union representatives and key administrators within the institution. The court found that the nonmember faculty, as public employees, had no special rights under the constitution for a voice in policy decisions.[667] That is, there is no constitutional obligation for public policymakers to listen. The court stated:

> The academic setting of the policymaking at issue in this
> case does not alter this conclusion. To be sure, there is a
> strong, if not universal or uniform, tradition of faculty
> participation in school governance, and there are numer-
> ous policy arguments to support such participation.... But

---

[664] 475 U.S. 292 (1986).

[665] Regents of Univ. of Cal. v. Public Employee Relations Bd., 223 Cal. Rptr. 127 (Cal. Ct. App. 1986).

[666] 465 U.S. 271 (1984).

[667] *Id.* at 1067.

this Court has never recognized a constitutional right of faculty to participate in policymaking in academic institutions.[668]

No constitutional right of speech or association has been abridged by the recognition by management of the union's "meet and confer" representatives.[669] Nor does the agreement prevent nonmembers from speaking out publicly or privately on policy issues.

Conclusions

The nature of higher education organizations, which differ significantly from industrial organizations, has resulted in a variety of litigation involving labor relations law. Since the labor relation's statutes were designed for business organizations, their application to higher education has been problematic. For example, the courts have had to determine which employees of colleges and universities are "employees" qualified to bargain collectively, as opposed to "managers" not qualified to bargain collectively. Because of the diversity within higher education organizations, different results have been reached: some faculty were found to be managers and other faculty were found to be employees.

Further, the problematic application of labor relation's law to higher education has resulted in litigation as to what is negotiable or nonnegotiable within the context of collective bargaining. Some decisions in higher education such as criteria for promotion and tenure were found to be managerial prerogatives and therefore not grievable. Other decisions such as the application of those criteria to individual faculty were grievable decisions. The terms of the collective bargaining agreement loom large in determining what the grievable issues are in a particular case.

Finally, First Amendment issues surrounding the use of union dues for political activity were adjudicated in the courts. One court case established that faculty input into institutional policy making is not a constitutional right. Institutions, then, are not obligated to provide each faculty member with input on policy questions. Further institutions can recognize a specific organization as the vehicle through which faculty have input on policy without violating First Amendment rights.

---

[668] *Id*. at 1067.
[669]*Id*. at 1068.

CHAPTER VIII

Student — Institutional Relationships

Central to the mission of colleges and universities is the relationship between students and the institution. Hendrickson and Gibbs outlined these multi-situation specific relationships between students and institutions.[670] Historically, the relationship between the institution and students has been one characterized as *in loco parentis*, where the institution stands in place of the parent. *In loco parentis* resulted in a reluctance by the courts to impose themselves on affairs viewed as being within the college's purview. Early case law reflected this bias. A Kentucky court stated:

> College authorities stand *in loco parentis* concerning the physical and moral welfare and mental training of pupils, and we are unable to see why, to that end, they may not make any rules or regulations for the government or betterment of their pupils than a parent could for the same purpose.[671]

The civil rights movement and the quest for equity in society chipped away at this notion and a newer relationship between the institution and students has evolved. Issues of access to higher education brought the courts to the college gate. *Dixon v. Alabama*[672] brought the courts through those gates and caused a change in the way the student—institutional relationship was viewed. New rights emerged after *Dixon* creating the constitutional relationship between the college and the student. Other relationships became more important as the *in loco parentis* relationship waned. These included the fiduciary relationship and the contractual relationship discussed in the chapter on liability issues.

This chapter will focus on the developing constitutional relationship and federal regulations enacted to enforce these constitutional guarantees. A review of the history of civil rights issues will provide the background needed to understand this constitutional relationship. The litigation on access to higher education in areas such as admissions, nonresident tuition, and financial aid

---

[670] R. M. Hendrickson and A. Gibbs, THE COLLEGE, THE CONSTITUTION, AND THE CONSUMER STUDENT: IMPLICATIONS FOR POLICY AND PRACTICE, ASHE-ERIC Higher Education Report No.7, 1, (1986).

[671] Gott v. Berea College, 161 S.W. 204 (Ky. 1931).

[672] Dixon v. Alabama, 294 F.2d 150 (5th Cir. 1961), *cert. denied*, 286 U.S. 930 (1961).

will show how federal legislation on discrimination based on sex, race, and disability has profoundly affected administrative practice. The evolution of other constitutional rights guaranteed to both individual students and groups such as litigation surrounding the First Amendment, privacy, and due process rights, will demonstrate how this constitutional relationship continues to evolve.

The Court Approaches the College Gates

"Separate but equal" facilities based on race met the constitutional provisions of the Fourteenth Amendment during the first half of this century. However, minority students began to challenge their exclusion from all-white professional schools during this period. This was particularly necessary because professional schools for African Americans were not provided in many states in which they were denied admission to the all-white institutions. A later Supreme Court decision, *Missouri ex rel. Gaines v. Canada*,[673] forced many of these states to establish professional programs for African Americans. In this case, a qualified African American applicant who was denied admission to Missouri's all-white state university law school, was offered a course of law, either at the all-black college that would commence operation at his request or at a program in another state at the state of Missouri's expense. The Supreme Court ruled that the state's failure to provide legal education to African Americans, while providing it to whites, violated the Equal Protection Clause of the Fourteenth Amendment. The state could provide a "separate but equal" facility for African Americans in legal education in compliance with constitutional requirements, but it failed to actually establish such a program. Financial provisions for education outside the state did not meet the state's Equal Protection Clause guarantees. This case and others were litigated to force states to provide "equal" facilities for African American students.[674]

With the establishment of separate black professional programs, the question arose as to whether these black programs were equal to or inferior to the all-white professional programs provided by the state. A federal district court found that while the

---

[673] Missouri *ex rel*. Gaines v. Canada, 305 U.S. 337 (1938).
[674] Sipuel v. Board of Regents of the Univ. of Okla., 332 U.S. 631 (1948); Fisher v. Hurst, 333 U.S. 146 (1948); Pearson v. Murray, 182 A. 590 (Md. 1936).

all-white university law program was superior to the all-black college law program, the programs were rendered equal by the advantages of studying in an environment similar to that within which one would practice on graduation. However, on appeal, the court found that the programs were unequal in violation of the Equal Protection Clause.[675] The Supreme Court reached a similar ruling in *Sweatt v. Painter*.[676]

As states were ordered to admit minorities to their all-white professional schools, the question arose of how minorities must be treated in relation to the white students in these programs. The Supreme Court, in *McLaurin v. Oklahoma State Regents for Higher Education*,[677] ruled that a state could not separate an African American student from the rest of the law school class. Rather, the school must treat him equal to or the same as white students in all aspects of education or services provided by the institution. Other cases followed the premise that African American and white students must be treated equally.[678]

These cases logically brought the Supreme Court to its decision in *Brown v. Board of Education of Topeka*.[679] A combination of cases from the states of Kansas, South Carolina, Virginia, and Delaware were brought to the Court. These cases challenged the existence of separate public schools for African American and white residents of the state. African Americans alleged that separation of the races into public schools of one race violated the Equal Protection Clause of the Fourteenth Amendment. The existence of compulsory education laws and the great expenditure on education demonstrated the importance society placed on education. The Supreme Court found that education had become a right that states must make available to all on equal terms. The Court decided that, in the field of public education, the doctrine of separate but equal education had no place. Segregation deprived state citizens of equal protection under the law. This new doctrine of integration and equity was substituted for the antiquated doctrine

---

[675] Epps v. Carmichael, 93 F. Supp. 327 (M.D. N.C. 1950), *rev'd*, McKissick v. Carmichael, 187 F.2d 919 (4th Cir. 1951).
[676] 339 U.S. 629 (1950).
[677] 339 U.S. 637 (1950).
[678] State *ex rel.* Hawkins v. Board of Control, 47 So.2d 608 (Fla. 1950); *enforcing*, 60 So.2d 162 (Fla. 1952); State *ex rel.* Hawkins v. Board of Control, 350 U.S. 413 (1956); Parker v. University of Del., 76 A.2d 225 (Del. Ch. 1950); Wichita Falls Junior College Dist. v. Battle, 101 F. Supp. 82 (N.D. Tex. 1951); *aff'd*, 204 F.2d 632 (5th Cir. 1953); *cert. denied*, 347 U.S. 974 (1954); Holmes v. Danner, 191 F. Supp. 394 (M.D. Ga. 1961); Gray v. University of Tenn., 97 F. Supp. 463 (E.D. Tenn. 1951).
[679] Brown v. Board of Educ. of Topeka, 347 U.S. 483 (1954).

of separate but equal facilities and was affirmed for higher education in a number of cases.[680]

The evolution of higher education admissions case law demonstrates how the court brushed closer to the college gates;
however, it was not yet prepared to pass through those gates. It
was not ready to scrutinize closely institutional procedures or the
rights students possessed in their relationship with institutions.
The closest it came to such scrutiny was in *McLaurin v. Oklahoma
State Regents for Higher Education, supra*, where the Supreme Court
ordered the institution to treat students equally but did not define
the rights students might have within that relationship. The court
certainly opened the gates to equal access for all, but was not yet
willing to impose itself on the specific relationship between the
student and the college or university.

The court stepped through the gate and onto the campus in
Dixon v. Alabama, supra, when it ruled that students at public colleges had a property right to their education that required due
process of law in questions of dismissal. The court was now im-
posing constitutional guarantees on the student-institutional
relationship. The court had arrived on campus, and subsequent
litigation would emanate from this logical next step that established the constitutional student-institutional relationship.

Admission to Higher Education

Dixon, supra, and subsequent civil rights legislation would
expand the court's interest in student-institution relationships.
Access to higher education continued to generate benchmark litigation in a number of areas. Race, gender, and disability
discrimination cases dominated the access issue. The use of standardized tests in admission decisions is an area of more recent
litigation.

Economic access to higher education was also an area of active litigation. For example, the use of higher nonresident tuition
than tuition charged for state residents was an issue brought to

---

[680] Franklin v. Parker, 223 F. Supp. 724, (M.D. Ala. 1963); Booker v. Tennessee Bd. of
Educ., 240 F.2d 689 (6th Cir. 1957); Fair v. Meredith, 202 F. Supp. 224 (S.D. Miss.
1962), *rev'd and remanded*, 305 F.2d 343 (5th Cir. 1962), *cert. denied*, 371 U.S. 828
(1962); Lucy v. Adams, 134 F. Supp. 235 (N.D. Ala. 1955), *injunction aff'd*, 350 U.S. 1
(1955), district court decision *aff'd*, 228 F.2d 619 (5th Cir. 1955), *cert. denied*, 351 U.S.
931 (1956).

the courts as an equal protection claim. Student access to financial aid and institutional eligibility as bona fide institutions where students on financial aid can enroll are issues currently active.

Affirmative Action in Admission

With the passage of title VI of the Civil Rights Act of 1964 and title IX of the Education Amendments of 1972, institutions sought compliance through the development of affirmative action admissions programs. These programs, which had special provisions for the admission of minorities, resulted in a whole series of litigation, characterized as reverse discrimination cases. What resulted was some of the most closely watched and debated cases in the history of the Supreme Court.[681]

The first case, *Defunis v. Odegaard,*[682] involved Marco Defunis, a white male who sued alleging discrimination after he was denied admission to law school. Pending an appeal to the Supreme Court, Justice Douglas stayed the state supreme court opinion reversing a trial court order of admission. Therefore, at the time of the Supreme Court decision, Defunis was in the last quarter of his legal education and the Court ruled the case moot. However, in a dissenting opinion, which pointed to a rationale the court would subsequently pursue, Justice Douglas discussed at length the requirements mandated by the Equal Protection Clause and the use of criteria including race in admissions decisions.

In a subsequent case, *Regents of the University of California— Davis v. Bakke,*[683] Allen Bakke, a white applicant to the University of California—Davis Medical School, sued. He alleged discrimination based on race in the denial of his admission. The institution had implemented a dual admissions process and set aside a number of seats in the medical school for a minority admissions program. All applicants in the regular admissions program were treated in a standard way. Applicants for the minority program, however, were reviewed with separate and modified standards. Minority applicants were members of the African American, Chicano, Asian, and American Indian races. The Supreme Court applied the "strict scrutiny" test, which is used when race, a suspect class, is used to give differential treatment to certain categories

---

[681] A.P. Sindler, BAKKE, DEFUNIS, AND MINORITY ADMISSIONS: THE QUEST FOR EQUAL OPPORTUNITY 2, (1978).
[682] 416 U.S. 312 (1974).
[683] 438 U.S. 265 (1978).

of citizens. Under strict scrutiny a state can show a compelling state interest to use a suspect class—here categorizes based on race—where a judicial, legislative, or administrative finding substantiated past discrimination and a remedy such as preferential treatment was enacted to right the previous wrong. The remedy, however, must be narrowly tailored to cause minimal harm to other citizens. The Court found that the state of California was unable to demonstrate a compelling state interest requiring the use of race and a grant of preferential treatment in its medical school admissions decisions. The Court ruled that the dual admissions practice violated the Equal Protection Clause of the Fourteenth Amendment, but that race could be one of a number of factors used in determining admission as long it was not the sole determinant. The *Bakke* case established the precedent for administrative practice in admissions. While it continues to be the standard institutions follow to avoid questions of discrimination based on race,[684] several cases that are more recent raise serious question about race-based admissions and scholarship programs.

Affirmative action challenges to the stand taken in *Bakke* began to emerge in the 1990s. The issues litigated surrounded the application of strict scrutiny when government used a preferential treatment system based on race. For example, using the doctrine of strict scrutiny in *Wygant v. Jackson Board of Education*,[685] the state established that the need for minority role models in the schools was a compelling state interest based on past societal discrimination. In *Richmond v. J.A. Croson Co.*,[686] the city of Richmond failed to substantiate a compelling state interest that would allow them to set aside 30 percent of their city contracts for minority contractors (the set-asides were race-based). The court departed from the strict scrutiny standard and adopted "intermediate scrutiny" in a federal case about racial preference in *Metro Broadcasting, Inc. v. FCC*.[687] The court allowed preferential treatment based on race in federal programs using the rationale of the Fifth Amendment. However, this rationale would end during the 1994-95 term of the court. In *Adarand Contractors, Inc. v. Pena*,[688] the Court re-

---

[684] *See* Baker v. Board of Regents of State of Kan., 721 F. Supp. 270 (D. Kan. 1989); Phelps v. Washburn Univ., 632 F. Supp. 455 (D. Kan. 1986), Phelps v. Washburn Univ., 634 F. Supp. 556 (D. Kan. 1986), *appeal dismissed*, Phelps v. Washburn Univ. of Topeka, 807 F.2d 153 (10th Cir. 1986).
[685] 476 U.S. 267 (1986).
[686] 488 U.S. 469 (1989).
[687] 497 U.S. 547 (1990).
[688] 515 U.S. 200 (1995).

jected *Metro Broadcasting, Inc.* as error, and again applied the strict scrutiny doctrine to all government situations where a suspect category is used to give preference to one racial group over another.

In the growing controversy over the use of race as a factor in admissions, the *Adarand* case is the most recent decision we have on affirmative action from the Supreme Court. *Adarand* involved federal agency contract rules that gave contractors a financial incentive to award subcontracts to minority-controlled businesses. A white-owned subcontractor, the low bidder, sued when the general contractor for a federal highway project in Colorado awarded the subcontract to a minority-owned business. The Court, in a six to three opinion, applied strict scrutiny requiring the federal government to provide a compelling governmental interest to support the race-based preferential treatment of minority subcontractors. The Court remanded the case to determine if the government could substantiate a compelling governmental interest and a narrowly tailored remedy that would cause the least harm to others. The case is important because the opinion relied on *Bakke* to develop the premises behind the ruling. The *dicta* of the case points to the conclusion that race may be a factor, but not the sole factor, in a preferential treatment program that is based on race.[689]

Two Circuit decisions dealing with admission in higher education are seen as direct challenges to *Bakke* and give the *Adarand* case more importance as a predictor of whether the Court will uphold or reject the *Bakke* standard. The first specific challenge to *Bakke* involved a scholarship program available to African Americans only. The case, *Podberesky v. Kirwan,*[690] resulted from a claim brought by Hispanic students who challenged merit scholarships available solely to African Americans as a violation of both title VI and the Equal Protection Clause of the Fourteenth Amendment. In federal district court, the university successfully argued that under the strict scrutiny doctrine the institution had justified a compelling state interest in the remedy of prior *de jure* discrimination. However, the Fourth Circuit Court reversed, not based on the volume of the University's evidence of past discrimination, but rather on the Office of Civil Rights' insufficient evidence about the present effects of discrimination. On remand, the university provided the court with voluminous evidence of the present ef-

---

[689] *See* R. M. Hendrickson, *The Bell Curve, Affirmative Action, and the Quest for Equity,* in Measured Lies, J. L. Kincheloe, S.R. Steinberg, and A. D. Gresson, III (Eds.).
[690] 764 F. Supp 364 (D. Md. 1991); *rev'd and remanded,* 956 F.2d 52 (4th Cir. 1992).

fects of past discrimination.[691] In citing the effects of past discrimination, the university noted its continuing difficulty in recruiting minority students, the under representation of African-American students in the student body, the high attrition rate of African-American students, and the perceived hostile climate at the university. In each of these areas, the university supported its position with substantial research and data. The court found the remedy of minority scholarships for African-Americans to be a narrowly tailored remedy as required under strict scrutiny.[692] However, on appeal to the Fourth Circuit Court of Appeals, the court again reversed and remanded the case.[693] Applying strict scrutiny, the court found that the university lacked a strong evidentiary basis that past discrimination supported a compelling state interest to provide remedial aid in the form of race-based scholarships. Present effects of past discrimination were not established by the perceived hostile campus climate and the university's poor reputation in the African-American community. The court found that further proof was required to establish a link between the present effects of past discrimination and low graduation rates and retention rates of under represented African-Americans. This case does not weaken *Bakke*, since it is a preferential program based solely on race, a violation under the *Bakke* ruling.

The second and more serious challenge to *Bakke* came in a public law school admissions case, *Hopwood v. Texas*.[694] In a case reminiscent of *Bakke*, the University of Texas law school had developed a dual admissions process, one process for majority applicants and another process for minority applicants.[695] Two subcommittees of the admissions committee were formed, one for general applicants and the other for minority applicants. Different procedures and application evaluation techniques were used by each subcommittee. While no specific quotas were set for admissions, the committee was operating under requirements established by the Board of Regents and the Office of Civil Rights (OCR).[696] The Board mandated that out-of- state admissions not exceed 15 percent of the entering class, and the size of the entering class include at least 500 students. OCR, through the Texas Plan,

---

[691] Podberesky v. Kirwan, 838 F. Supp. 1075 (D. Md. 1993).

[692] *Id.* at 1094.

[693] Podberesky v. Kirwan, 38 F.3d 147 (4th Cir. 1994); *cert. denied*, 115 S. Ct. 2001 (1995).

[694] 861 F. Supp. 551 (W.D. Tex. 1994).

[695] *Id.* at 558-562.

[696] *Id.* at 563.

had set admission goals of 15 percent Hispanic and 5 percent African-Americans. One white female and three white males combined to file suit, claiming discrimination in the denial of their admission to the law school. Using strict scrutiny, the United States District Court for the Western District of Texas, citing *Bakke,* found that the university failed to establish a compelling state interest for its treatment of minority applicants as a separate class.[697] Further, the remedy used to ameliorate past discrimination was not narrowly tailored so as to protect others outside the minority class. However, the court found that the law school had provided legitimate nondiscriminatory reasons for the denial of admission to the plaintiffs. Reversing on appeal, the Fifth Circuit Court, found that the dual admissions process of the Texas law school violated the Equal Protection Clause of the Fourteenth Amendment and, rejecting *Bakke,* ruled that use of race as a criterion in admission is prohibited.[698] The Supreme Court refused to hear the case, because the law school had already changed its admission policies. Whether the Supreme Court will again endorse the position of *Bakke,* that race may be a factor in the decision as long as it is not the sole factor, has yet to be determined. As we await a case to come before the Supreme Court, we know that in the Fifth Circuit, race cannot be a factor in the admissions decisions. It remains to be seen whether other Circuits will follow the Fifth Circuit lead or whether *Bakke* will continue to be the standard to follow. At the heart of this issue are the criteria used in admissions decisions and the use of standardized tests for administrative convenience. There are some who argue that if the number of data points are expanded to include those used in minority admissions programs and the criteria are applied uniformly to all applicants, minority applicants will be competitive and receive a fair share of the available spaces eliminating the need for preferential treatment policies.[699] The use of standardized tests will be discussed in a later section of this chapter.

Gender Discrimination

Discrimination in admissions based on gender is covered under title IX. Title IX exempted historically single-sex institutions from the provisions of the act. However, the exemption was not

---

[697] *Id.* at 584.
[698] Hopwood v. Texas, 78 F.3d 932 (5th Cir. 1996), *cert. denied,* 518 U.S. 1933 (1996).
[699] Hendrickson, *supra* note 20.

absolute. In the seminal case in this area, a male denied access to the nursing program at the Mississippi University for Women sued, claiming violations of Fourteenth Amendment rights to equal protection and the anti-sex discrimination provisions of title IX. The Supreme Court ruled that the test for acceptability of a state's use of gender in awarding services would consist of two parts: the state must show, one, that the classification meets an important governmental objective; and, two, that the discriminatory classification is directly related to the achievement of the objective. The Court found that the existence of single-sex institutions could not be used as a device to compensate for previous discrimination based on gender. The state failed to substantiate a valid state objective in maintaining a single-sex nursing program when it allowed men to audit the nursing classes at the women's school.[700]

The issue of gender discrimination was fully litigated in an Illinois case, *Cannon v. University of Chicago*.[701] The plaintiff, a female, sued, alleging that a private medical school receiving federal financial assistance had denied her access to a medical education because of her gender. The district court dismissed the suit, claiming that title IX does not provide for a private right of action. The Supreme Court reached a determination as to whether Congress intended the Act to allow a private right of action. First, the Court determined that the law was intended to protect a special class of individuals to which the plaintiff belonged. Second, while the specific title is silent on whether a private right of action exists, the Court found other language in the legislative package that implied a private remedy. Third, the Court found that a private right would be consistent with the goals of the statute. Finally, the Court found that discrimination based on sex was a matter of concern to the federal government. Based on these principles, the court found that a private remedy or right of action existed under title IX. Subsequent litigation on the merits found that the medical colleges had not discriminated against the plaintiff in admissions.[702]

Mrs. Cannon and her husband, who was the attorney representing her in the litigation, appealed to the court to have the unsuccessful 1986 decision on the merits changed to a summary judgment in order to have the state claims returned to state court. In denying this request, the court admonished the plaintiff and

---

[700] Mississippi Univ. for Women v. Hogan, 455 U.S. 1014 (1982).
[701] Cannon v. University of Chicago, 441 U.S. 677 (1979).
[702] Cannon v. University of Chicago, 648 F.2d 1104 (7th Cir. 1981); Cannon v. University Health Science/Chicago Med. Sch., 710 F.2d 351 (7th Cir. 1983); Cannon v. Loyola Univ. of Chicago, 609 F. Supp. 1010 (N.D. Ill. 1985).

her counsel to discontinue this stream of litigation that had turned into harassment of the defendant institutions and the court. Further sanctions would be assessed if the plaintiff continued to ignore the court's admonishments.[703] Later, on a motion by the defendants in these cases, the plaintiff and her attorney were found in contempt of court for continuing this litigation after admonishment by the court. They were fined $100 per business day for each day Mrs. Cannon continued to violate the court's January 22, 1987 order. Further, the court ordered that her husband be banned from representing her in any subsequent litigation on this matter.[704]

Sex discrimination was also an issue at some military academies. A district court ordered the Massachusetts Maritime Academy to cease any admission practices that operated to discriminate based on sex. Through an injunction, the court ordered the institution to cease any vestiges of past discriminatory practices. While the institution had officially ceased discrimination based on sex, the court found that residual practices were perpetuating past discriminatory activity. The court found that while the Maritime Academy was exempt under title IX, it was covered by title IV of the Civil Rights Act of 1964.[705] Two more recent cases, filed as Equal Protection Clause claims, have serious implications for state-operated military academies as single-sex institutions.

United States v. Commonwealth of Virginia[706] involved a challenge to the single- sex admissions policy of the Virginia Military Institute (VMI). Since historically single-sex institutions and military academies are exempt under title IX, the government brought this claim against the state under the Equal Protection Clause of the Fourteenth Amendment. Using intermediate scrutiny, the Fourth Circuit Court of Appeals remanded the case back to the district court to allow the state of Virginia to select among several remedies for the equal protection violation of not providing equal educational opportunities to both genders. The options outlined by the court included admitting women to VMI, establishing a comparable parallel program for women, or abandoning VMI as a public institution. The state adopted a plan to establish a parallel military institute for women at Mary Baldwin College, a public women's college. This plan was approved by the District Court and affirmed by the Fourth Circuit Court.[707]

---

[703] Cannon v. Loyola Univ. of Chicago, 116 F.R.D. 244 (N.D. Ill. 1987).
[704] Cannon v. Loyola Univ. of Chicago, 676 F. Supp. 823 (N.D. Ill. 1987).
[705] United States v. Massachusetts Maritime Academy, 762 F.2d 143 (1st Cir. 1985).
[706] 766 F. Supp. 1407, *vacated*, 976 F.2d 890 (4th Cir. 1992), *cert. denied*, 113 S. Ct. 2431 (1993).
[707] United States v. Commonwealth of Va., 44 F.3d 1229 (4th Cir. 1995).

In South Carolina, a military college's admission policy, which denied admission to women, was challenged in *Faulkner v. Jones*.[708] Shannon R. Faulkner applied for admission to The Citadel and was originally accepted but later rejected when it was discovered that she was a woman. The District Court, citing the decision in *VMI*, found that the State of South Carolina violated the plaintiff's right to equal protection under the law when it failed to provide a parallel program for women. It ordered the state to adopt a plan to meet constitutional requirements, but also found that it was too late to establish a parallel program for the plaintiff and issued a preliminary injunction ordering her immediate admission to The Citadel. The Fourth Circuit Court modified the decision. The court ruled that only by the admission of females to The Citadel would the state be in compliance with the Equal Protection Clause.[709] Female students now attend both The Citadel and VMI.

Title IX, as was discussed in the chapter on "The Quest for Equity and Diversity in Faculty Employment in Higher Education," was given new regulatory authority by the Civil Rights Restoration Act of 1988. How these changes will translate into litigation based on gender discrimination in admissions and other areas is still unfolding and will give some indication of the scope of the problem of discrimination based on sex in admission. On the surface, it appears that most institutions have developed admission policies to prevent discrimination based on sex. Much of the unfolding title IX litigation has involved athletic programs. For example, a Louisiana case involved female athletes who brought a class action suit against a state institution for unequal accommodation in scholarships assigned to intercollegiate athletic teams.[710] In order to bring itself into compliance with title IX, LSU decided to elevate both men's and women's soccer, formerly club sports, to varsity status, and also established women's fast pitch softball as a varsity sport. The District Court found that the women's fast pitch softball athletes had standing to litigate because they were eligible to participate in fast pitch softball and the university had yet to complete the process of establishing the sport as a varsity sport. However, the female soccer plaintiffs lacked standing to litigate because their eligibility to participate in collegiate soccer had expired under NCAA rules and the university had provided equal accommodations for men's and women's club soccer during the period of the women's collegiate eligibility. The

---

[708] 858 F. Supp. 552 (D. S.C. 1994).

[709] Faulkner v. Jones, 51 F.3d 440 (4th Cir. 1995), *cert. denied*, 516 U.S. 910 (1995).

[710] Pederson v. Louisiana State Univ., 912 F. Supp. 892 (M.D. La. 1996).

university's only violation of the equal accommodation provisions of title IX was its failure to provide a fast-pitch softball team for women.

Using the shifting burden of proof strategy of title VII, a male nursing student was unable to prove gender discrimination under title IX in his academic dismissal.[711] The plaintiff failed to establish a *prima facie* case of gender discrimination by showing that his academic performance met the legitimate expectations of the program's educators. It appears that the proof strategy utilized to adjudicate the merits of title IX gender discrimination claims will be the same as those used for title VII.

Discrimination Based on Disability

In the area of discrimination based on a disability the key authority is the Rehabilitation Act of 1973. This Act was also given new regulatory authority by the Civil Rights Restoration Act of 1988. The Supreme Court defined the requirements under the Act in *Southeastern Community College v. Davis.*[712] An applicant to a community college nursing program was denied admission. On review by the state nursing board, it was found that her hearing impairment would inhibit her ability to perform the tasks required of a nurse on the job. The board found that her hearing impairment would cause serous delays in her response to emergency situations and surgery because she relied on lip reading. Thus, she would have to rely on visual perception of flashing lights instead of warning buzzers in emergencies on the floor and would not be able to understand doctor's commands when surgical masks were required. The Court ruled that the Rehabilitation Act of 1973, § 504, prohibits discrimination based on a disability when an individual is an "otherwise qualified" applicant. According to the court, the law does not require affirmative action, but rather requires that an "otherwise qualified" disabled individual not be excluded from the program. An "otherwise qualified" individual is one who meets the programs requirements in spite of the disability. The individual must be able to perform the job tasks, and the employer is not required to hire others to assist the employee in the performance of the specific tasks. The court differentiated between an individual's ability to perform job tasks and the modification of physical surroundings to eliminate barriers to task performance as required by the law. In finding that the plaintiff

---

[711] Andriakos v. University of So. Ind., 867 F. Supp. 804 (S.D. Ind. 1992).
[712] Southeastern Community College v. Davis, 442 U.S. 397 (1979).

was not an "otherwise qualified" applicant, the Court noted that an institution should not be required to lower or modify important performance standards to accommodate disabled individuals. Subsequent case law reflects this specific definition of an "otherwise qualified" disabled individual.[713]

Another case further illuminates the issues facing an institution attempting to achieve compliance with the law. A woman with severe emotional problems was denied readmission to medical school after repeated episodes, psychiatric treatments, and examinations resulted in her leaving medical school. After being denied readmission, she sued, charging discrimination based on her disability. In a procedural move, the former student sought to have the case placed on the court's active calendar and to shift the burden of proof to the institution since negotiations with the Department of Health Education and Welfare on this matter had failed. Although the case was placed on the active calendar, the burden did not shift to the institution because the negotiations between the federal agency and the institution were not adjudicatory in nature.[714] In adjudication, the district court threw out the testimony of experts and evaluated the plaintiff's ability to cope with stress during the period of time since leaving the medical school. The court ruled she was an "otherwise qualified" disabled individual. The circuit court reversed the district court and used the shifting burden analysis in cases involving disability discrimination. The court found that the plaintiff met her burden of establishing that she was a disabled person qualified for admission apart from the disability. The institution, in the court's view, met its burden of establishing through expert testimony (erroneously excluded by the lower court) that the risk of recurrence of the emotional instability was an acceptable reason for refusing admission. Finally, the plaintiff failed to meet her burden of showing that she was an "otherwise qualified" disabled individual.[715]

There are examples of the existence of an "otherwise qualified" disabled individual. In Colorado, a federal district court found that an applicant for a program was discriminated against because he was a disabled individual. The applicant for a psychiatric residency program suffered from multiple sclerosis, and as a result, had impaired speech and writing capabilities and was con-

---

[713] Anderson v. University of Wis., 665 F. Supp. 1372 (W.D. Wis. 1987), *aff'd*, Anderson v. University of Wis., 841 F.2d 737 (7th Cir. 1988); Kling v. County of Los Angeles, 769 F.2d 532 (9th Cir. 1985), *cert. denied*, 474 U.S. 1086 (1986); Stephanidis v. Yale Univ., 652 F. Supp. 110 (D. Conn. 1986), *aff'd*, 814 F.2d 654 (2d Cir. 1987).

[714] Doe v. New York Univ., 511 F. Supp. 606 (S.D. N.Y. 1981).

[715] Doe v. New York Univ., 666 F.2d 761 (2d Cir. 1981).

fined to a wheelchair. The university hospital faculty rejected him because they felt his disability would hinder his performance. However, testimony given by doctors from the medical college that had awarded the plaintiff his M.D. degree indicated that he had the requisite performance capabilities. The court found that the university hospital failed to establish that the applicant was not an "otherwise qualified" disabled individual.[716] In a different case, another court found that a disabled student had been evaluated similarly to other students based on his potential academic success. The court noted that sobriety could be a valid factor to consider when evaluating student performance.[717]

AIDS or HIV status has impacted the Rehabilitation Act. A dental student at a private university was disenrolled when he tested positively for HIV. The student sued for damages under the Rehabilitation Act.[718] The dental school faculty determined that the student would not be able to perform invasive procedures, a requirement for the award of the degree, since such procedures clearly would risk a patient's health and safety. The federal district court found that the decision was an academic one and was, therefore, subject to judicial deference. Consequently, in this case, the student was not deemed an "otherwise qualified" disabled individual.

The requirements of these laws are slightly different from some of the other anti-discrimination provisions. The primary issue in these cases is the question of whether the individual is an "otherwise qualified" disabled individual. Further, the courts have differentiated between physical barriers that must be removed and criteria required for job performance. For the job performance criteria, courts have said that valid performance standards set by the institution need not be modified.

Using Standardized Tests

The use of standardized tests in admissions decisions have resulted in several court cases. One such case was based on accusations of cheating. The validity of a student's test results was questioned by the testing service. Eventually the testing service notified the school that the applicant's test results were being cancelled. Based on the cancellation of the scores, the institution

[716] Pushkin v. Regents of the Univ. of Colo., 504 F. Supp. 1292 (D. Colo. 1980), *aff'd*, 658 F.2d 1372 (10th Cir. 1981).
[717] Pushkin v. Regents of the Univ. of Colo., 504 F. Supp. 1292 (D. Colo. 1980), aff'd, 658 F.2d 1372 (10th Cir. 1981).
[718] Doe v. Washington Univ., 780 F. Supp. 628 (E.D. Mo. 1991).

withdrew its offer of admission. The district court ruled that the testing service was not an agent of state government under the concept of state action[719] and, therefore, found no violation of constitutional guarantees by the testing service's action.[720] More recently in New York, a student filed a breach of contract claim against ETS, the service that administers the SAT, when they suspended his scores based on suspicion that an imposter had taken the test.[721] The court found that the testing service had breached a duty of good faith when it refused to consider the student's evidence refuting the imposter claim.

Another issue was the use of a standardized test to screen students enrolling in education courses at a Texas public college. Those who failed to demonstrate competency in basic skills were denied access to education courses. The plaintiffs in this case charged that the test discriminated against African American and Hispanic students. The district court issued a preliminary injunction restraining the state from implementing the test.[722] The court found the testing procedures had the potential of violating both title VI of the Civil Rights Act of 1964 and The Equal Opportunity Act of 1974. On appeal, the circuit court reversed the decision and found that the district court failed to determine whether the skills used to predict teacher performance were valid, nondiscriminatory performance criteria.[723] More recently, in *Groves v. Alabama State Board*,[724] the federal district court ruled that the board's use of minimum scores on the ACT examination as a cutoff for admission to an undergraduate teacher-training program had an adverse racial impact. Further, there was no educational justification to show that the ACT cutoff scores predicted future teaching ability or performance.[725]

The importance of standardized tests in admissions decisions will continue to result in litigation. Notice, however, that to date the courts have not found that private testing corporations are agents of state government subject to enforcement of constitutional guarantees simply because public institutions use these corporations' test results for admission decisions. Further, the court will only approve as nondiscriminatory admissions criteria that can

---

[719] For a discussion of state action, *see* R. M. Hendrickson, *State Action and Private Higher Education*, J. OF LAW & EDUC., 2 (1973): 53-75.

[720] Johnson v. Education Testing Serv., 615 F. Supp. 633 (D. Mass. 1984), *aff'd*, 754 F.2d 20 (1st Cir. 1985), *cert. denied*, 105 S. Ct. 3504 (1985).

[721] Dalton v. Educational Testing Serv., 614 N.Y.S.2d 742 (N.Y. App. Div. 1994).

[722] United States v. Texas, 628 F. Supp. 304 (E.D. Tex. 1985).

[723] United States v. LULAC, 793 F.2d 636 (5th Cir. 1986).

[724] 766 F. Supp. 1518 (M.D. Ala. 1991).

[725] *Id.* at 1531.

be adequately linked to the measurement of future valid job performance standards. Standardized tests as the sole determinant of admissions do not appear to withstand the scrutiny of the courts. The racial performance disparity of standardized tests will result in continued scrutiny of the way these tests are used in admissions decisions.

Economic Access

Nonresident Tuition

The use of a differential tuition rate for nonresidents enrolling in a state college or university is another issue that has been challenged as violating the Equal Protection Clause of the Fourteenth Amendment. At issue is the balancing of the state's right to promote fiscal integrity and the individual's right to equal protection. The Supreme Court affirmed a state's right to charge differential tuition for nonresidents and the use of a one-year waiting period to establish residency in *Starns v. Malkerson*.[726]

Most states use the establishment of a domicile as the criteria to determine residency for tuition purposes. Domicile or the place where one resides legally would typically be established by registering to vote, paying taxes, establishing a mailing address, acquiring a driver's license, licensing a motor vehicle, and paying for local utilities such as water, sewer, garbage pickup, etc. Some states require a one-year waiting period to establish residency.

In *Vlandis v. Kline*,[727] The Supreme Court, considered the issue of residency. Connecticut had established a rule that for tuition purposes residency was determined by the mailing address of the individual at the time of application for admission to a state institution of higher education. An applicant, who was married to a Connecticut resident, but was living out-of-state at the time the admission application was filed, was classified as a nonresident for tuition purposes. Another applicant from Ohio had applied for admission from Ohio but subsequently claimed to be a resident of Connecticut after moving there joined this litigation. She was classified as an out-of-state student for tuition purposes. The Court ruled that the effect of the law was to establish an irrebut-

---

[726] Starns v. Malkerson, 401 U.S. 985 (1971).
[727] Vlandis v. Kline, 412 U.S. 441 (1973).

table presumption of residency in violation of Fourteenth Amendment due process requirements. The Court noted that the purpose of the law was to prevent nonresidents who were not sharing the burden of paying state taxes from getting a low- cost education at the state's expense. However, a law that classified a bona fide state resident (i.e., a person married to a tax-paying citizen of the state) as a nonresident did not achieve the stated objective. This case, then, established the right to due process in a determination of residency. Subsequent litigation involved these due process rights in residency classification cases.[728]

More recently, the state of Utah was able to bypass the one-year waiting period while conforming to due process requirements. The state Board of Regents established a policy that a person must maintain continuous residency in the state in order to qualify as a resident for tuition purposes. The policy specifically required that absence from the state for more than thirty days in any year would result in classification as a nonresident. Failure by the student to rebut the presumption of nonresidencey would mandate the payment of nonresident tuition. The Supreme Court of Utah upheld the policy.[729] The fact that this case was never challenged in federal court indicated that the state of Utah may have found an effective way within constitutional parameters to differentiate tuition based on residential status.

Financial Aid

Due to rising costs of higher education, access to higher education is affected by economic factors. Financial aid became such a politically important issue that the Department of Defense Authorization Act of 1983[730] made those who had failed to register for the draft ineligible for financial aid. The Minnesota Public Interest Research Group sued alleging that the statute was a bill of attainder (establishing guilt without due process) and that it violated Fifth Amendment rights against self-incrimination.[731] The Supreme Court, reversing the lower court decision, ruled that the

---

[728] *See* Baillie v. State Bd. of Higher Educ., 719 P.2d 1330 (Or. Ct. App. 1986); *In re* Bybee, 691 P.2d 37 (Kan. 1984); Molesworth v. University of Vt., 508 A.2d 722 (Vt. 1986); Spielberg v. Board of Regents, Univ. of Mich., 601 F. Supp 994 (E.D. Mich. 1985). Establishing the rights of aliens to equal protection under the law in the determination of residency for tuition purposes, Moreno v. University of Md., 420 F. Supp. 541 (D. Md. 1976), *aff'd*, 645 F.2d 217 (4th Cir. 1981), *aff'd*, Toll v. Moreno, 454 U.S. 815 (1982).
[729] Frame v. Residency Appeals Comm. of Utah State Univ., 675 P.2d 1157 (Utah 1983).
[730] Department of Defense Authorization Act of 1983, 1113(f) (4).
[731] Doe v. Selective Serv. Sys., 557 F. Supp. 937 (D. Minn. 1983).

Act was not a bill of attainder. Since the Act gave the non-registrant thirty days after notice of ineligibility to register and become eligible, it did not violate the Fifth Amendment.[732] Others objected to the same regulations on religious grounds. However, the First Circuit Court, reversing a lower court opinion, found that the provisions allowing a non-registrant to show cause why he might be exempt from the draft registration met constitutional guarantees under the First Amendment.[733]

Student eligibility for veterans' benefits was also before the Supreme Court in *Traynor v. Turnage*.[734] Veterans alleged that they should be exempt from the ten-year limitation on the use of veterans' education benefits because of their disability: alcoholism. The Court found that defining alcoholism as "willful misconduct" for the purpose of tolling the years of the benefits was not a violation of the Rehabilitation Act of 1973. The eligibility period for veterans' benefits was not extended where "willful misconduct" was the cause of a failure to utilize the benefits.

These cases point to the importance of access to financial aid in recent years. The importance of this issue was also demonstrated in questions of institutional eligibility to receive or award financial aid.

Financial aid to private, religious-affiliated institutions has been before the courts on a number of occasions. The issue is whether financial aid to private religious-affiliated institutions or their students violates the Establishment Clause of the First Amendment in that it promotes religion. At the same time, to deny financial aid to students who chose to go to religious-affiliated institutions may violate the Free Exercise clause of the First Amendment.[735] *Tilton v. Richardson*[736] set out a three-part test to establish whether aid to private, church-affiliated colleges and universities violated the First Amendment separation of church and state provisions. First, the statute must have a secular legislative purpose. Second, the primary effect must be to neither inhibit nor advance religion. Third, the act must not result in excessive government entanglement with religion. In *Tilton*, then, the Court ruled that awarding federal construction grants to private religious

---

[732] Selective Service Sys. v. Minnesota Pub. Interest Research Group, 468 U.S. 841 (1984).

[733] Alexander v. Trustees of Boston Univ., 584 F. Supp. 282 (D. Mass. 1984), *rev'd and remanded*, 766 F.2d 630 (1st Cir. 1985).

[734] Traynor v. Turnage, 108 S. Ct. 1372 (U.S. 1988).

[735] *See* Walz v. The Tax Comm'n of N.Y., 397 U.S. 664 (1970).

[736] Tilton v. Richardson, 403 U.S. 672 (1971); *see* Lemon v. Kurtzman, 403 U.S. 602 (1971), companion case dealing with financial aid to private church affiliated elementary and secondary education.

institutions neither establishes or inhibits religion. Other cases yielding similar results dealt with grants to institutions, loans to institutions, bonds to build buildings, and loans and grants to students.[737] In a more recent case, a federal district court ruled that a state's tuition assistance grant awarded to students attending bible colleges that had been accredited by a bible college accrediting association, failed to meet the three-part test outlined in *Tilton, supra*.[738] However, the Supreme Court ruled that the First Amendment did not prohibit the funding of a blind student's educational rehabilitation needs when he chose to go to a bible college.[739] On remand from the Court, the state supreme court ruled that state law prevented the funding of religious education, and the law was not prohibited by First Amendment guarantees.[740]

Institutional eligibility for publicly funded aid is determined through its eligibility as an accredited institution. For example, a federal circuit court upheld a Department of Education interpretation that students at an unaccredited seminary were ineligible for federal financial aid programs.[741] The institution, under Department of Education requirements, must not only show that students' credits were eligible for transfer but also that some students had actually transferred to an accredited institution.

Because of the inclusion of proprietary institutions in the federal student financial aid program and the current default rate on federal student loans, institutional eligibility issues have become more important in recent years. For example, a federal district court ruled that under federal law, if an institution exceeded a 35 percent default rate for the first two of three preceding fiscal years and 30 percent in the most recent year, the Secretary of Education could declare the institution ineligible to participate in the federal student aid program.[742] The court refused to enjoin the Secretary of Education from enforcing the regulations in an action brought by the Association of Accredited Cosmetology Schools and a college. However, in a case involving two proprietary medical schools, the Secretary of Education's decision terminating eligibility when they exceeded the default threshold was ruled arbitrary and capricious.[743] When the Secretary of Education notified the

---

[737] Hunt v. McNair, 413 U.S. 734 (1973); Roemer v. Board of Pub. Works of Md., 426 U.S. 736 (1976).

[738] d'Errico v. Lesmeister, 570 F. Supp. 158 (D.N.D. 1983).

[739] Witters v. Washington Dep't of Serv. for the Blind, 474 U.S. 481 (1986).

[740] Witters v. State Comm'n for the Blind, 771 P.2d 1119 (Wash. 1989).

[741] Beth Rochel Seminary v. Bennett, 624 F. Supp. 911 (D.D.C. 1985), *aff'd*, 825 F.2d 478 (D.C. Cir. 1987).

[742] Association of Accredited Cosmetology Sch. v. Alexander, 774 F. Supp. 655 (D.D.C. 1991).

[743] Atlanta College of Med. and Dental Careers, Inc. v. Alexander, 792 F. Supp. 114 (D.D.C. 1992).

schools that they had exceeded the default threshold and eligibility would be terminated, the schools provided through an audit by a private accounting firm a list of more than 100 errors in the Department's calculation of their default rate. The Secretary of Education, by ignoring most of these errors and maintaining his original decision, forced the Court's adverse ruling in this case.

Institutional eligibility was also at issue in other cases. For example, a court found that an institution had the right to a formal hearing and procedural due process before its eligibility to participate in a federal financial aid program was terminated.[744]

The specific criteria or procedures used to administer student financial aid programs have also been contested in the courts. For example, ten women were unsuccessful in proving that a test used to award state scholarships discriminated against women.[745] Work-study students at a private university failed to establish a private right of action against the university's noncompliance with regulations governing the award of work-study grants.[746] The work-study students unsuccessfully alleged that the definition of need, the amount of earnable income, and the requirement that students endorse checks over to the university to pay tuition were violations of the federal statute and regulation. Work-study students at another private university were unsuccessful in challenging the amount of earnable income and subsequent termination of employment when that income level was reached.[747]

The extensive litigation in the area of access to student financial aid and, therefore, access to higher education continues to reflect the current economic situation. With the federal debt, increasing tuition, and high default rates, we can continue to expect litigation of this type.

Constitutional Rights[748]

With the ruling in *Dixon v. Alabama, supra,* the courts entered the college gates and the evolution of the constitutional student-institutional relationship began. Subsequent litigation covered

---

[744] Continental Training Serv., Inc. v. Cavazos, 709 F. Supp. 1443 (S.D. Ind. 1989); Ross Univ. Sch. of Med. v. Cavazos, 716 F. Supp. 638 (D.D.C. 1989).
[745] Sharif by Salahuddin v. New York State Educ. Dep't, 127 F.R.D. 84 (S.D. N.Y. 1989).
[746] Student Gov't. Assoc. of Wilberforce Univ. v. Wilberforce Univ., 578 F. Supp. 935 (S.D. Ohio 1983).
[747] Murphy v. Villanova Univ., 547 F. Supp. 512 (E.D. Pa. 1982).
[748] Excerpts from this section are updated versions from R. M. Hendrickson and A. Gibbs, THE COLLEGES, THE CONSTITUTION, AND THE CONSUMER STUDENT, IMPLICATIONS FOR POLICY AND PRACTICE, ASHE-ERIC Higher Education Report # 7, (1986).

areas of First Amendment protection such as freedom of speech, association, and religion. The right to privacy also were defined, as well as due process rights in both disciplinary and academic dismissals. Through the 1980s, litigation seemed to move out of the realm of individual rights to the rights of student groups on campus. This section will present First Amendment, privacy, and due process issues, respectively.

First Amendment Litigation

The definition of the constitutional student-institutional relationship is formed in part by how the First Amendment defines the freedoms of press, speech, assembly, association, and religion.

Freedom of Speech

Hendrickson and Gibbs[749] noted that *Tinker v. Des Moines Independent Community School District*[750] applied First Amendment protections to public educational settings. The case established a student's right to speak out on issues in a non-disruptive way. At issue was the wearing of armbands as a form of protest against the war in Vietnam. First Amendment rights, the same as those applied to citizens, were explicitly extended to college students in *Healy v. James*.[751] The court noted that colleges are the "marketplaces of ideas" where "academic freedom" must be promoted.[752] This reasoning is consistent with the line of cases that established that public colleges and universities, among other public institutions and organizations, should be viewed as public forums.[753] However, individuals will lose their First Amendment rights of access to public forums by inhibiting others' speech, by denying others access to facilities or activities,[754] by participating in disruptive activities, or participating in activities that endanger the safety of others.[755]

---

[749] *Supra* note 79 at 14.
[750] Tinker v. Des Moines Indep. Community Sch. Dist., 393 U.S. 503 (1969).
[751] Healy v. James, 408 U.S. 169 (1972).
[752] *Id*. at 180.
[753] *See* Perry Educ. Ass'n v. Perry Local Educators Ass'n, 406 U.S. 37 (1983); Chess v. Widmar, 635 F.2d 1310 (8th Cir. 1980), *aff'd*, Widmar v. Vincent, 454 U.S. 263 (1981); Police Dept. v. Mosley, 408 U.S. 92 (1972).
[754] Buttney v. Smiley, 281 F. Supp. 280 (D. Colo. 1968).
[755] Stacy v. Williams, 306 F. Supp. 963 (N.D. Miss. 1969); Papish v. Board of Curators of the Univ. of Mo., 410 U.S. 667 (1972).

The First Amendment speech question becomes one of defining the circumstances under which speech on campus can be regulated. Regulation of the content of speech is typically prohibited unless, as cited above, it can be substantiated that the speech could endanger the safety of others or prohibit others' access rights. However, the courts have been reluctant to issue a "prior restraint" (attempt to stop speech) [756] as restraints of speech on the campus are frequently viewed as violations of First Amendment rights.[757] More recent attempts to regulate the content of speech, whether in the form of approving speakers[758] or preventing theatrical productions,[759] have been viewed as First Amendment violations unless they involved the issue of obscenity.[760] When speakers who are running for public office are invited to campus, the First Amendment does not impose a requirement that all political candidates seeking that office be invited.[761] Ceasing to support a legal services program for financial reasons does not violate First Amendment speech rights.[762]

Institutions are allowed to control the time, place, and manner of speech on campus.[763] Recent litigation surrounding the use of shanty towns to protest investments in South Africa and the practice of apartheid or other political issues affirm the institution's ability to regulate the manner and location of speech as long as other avenues of communication are available.[764] Other examples are institutions' right to control the solicitation and sales activities of non-student special interest groups on campus[765] or to limit the election activities of student government candidates for office.[766] The key to regulation of time, place, and manner of speech is that other avenues of speech are left open.

---

[756] New York Times v. United States, 402 U.S. 713 (1971); *see* Near v. Minnesota, 283 U.S. 697 (1931).

[757] *See* Healy v. James, *supra*, note 82; Hammond v. South Carolina State College, 272 F. Supp. 947 (D.S.C. 1967).

[758] Harvard Law Sch. Forum v. Schultz, 633 F. Supp. 525 (D. Mass. 1986).

[759] Brown v. Board of Regents of Univ. of Neb., 640 F. Supp. 674 (D. Neb. 1986).

[760] The obscenity issue will be covered under freedom of press.

[761] Martin-Trigona v. University of N.H., 685 F. Supp. 23 (D.N.H. 1988).

[762] Student Gov't Ass'n v. Board of Trustees of Univ. of Mass., 676 F. Supp. 384 (D. Mass. 1987), *aff'd*, 868 F.2d 473 (1st Cir. 1989).

[763] *See* Grayned v. City of Rockford, 408 U.S. 104 (1972); Bayless v. Maritime, 403 F.2d 873 (5th Cir. 1970).

[764] Students Against Apartheid Coalition v. O'Neil, 660 F. Supp. 333 (W.D. Va. 1987), *aff'd*, 838 F.2d 735 (4th Cir. 1988); University of Utah Students Against Apartheid v. Peterson, 649 F. Supp. 1200 (D. Utah 1986); Auburn Alliance for Peace and Justice v. Martin, 684 F. Supp. 1072 (M.D. Ala. 1988), *aff'd*, 853 F.2d 931 (11th Cir. 1988).

[765] Glover v. Cole, 762 F.2d 1197 (4th Cir. 1985).

[766] Alabama Student Party v. Student Gov't Ass'n of Univ. of Ala., 867 F.2d 1344 (11th Cir. 1989).

Hate Speech

The regulation of hate speech is a phenomenon of recent origins. During the late 1980s and the 1990s, institutions began to develop policies that prohibited students from using discriminatory epithets or demeaning language that created hostile educational environments. The hate speech policies were premised on the notion of prohibiting fighting words as outlined in *Chaplinsky v. New Hampshire*.[767] However, the vagueness of the policy's definition of demeaning language and hostile educational environment clashed with the notions of the overbreadth doctrine of *Broadrick v. Oklahoma*,[768] and vagueness doctrine of *New York v. Ferber*[769] and *Houston v. Hill*.[770] *UWM Post, Inc. v. Board of Regents of University of Wisconsin System*[771] ruled that the policy adopted by the University of Wisconsin System was overly broad and vague and failed to meet the requirements of the "fighting words" doctrine. The court reasoned that the creation of a hostile environment could result from both nonviolent and violent responses by those offended by the speech. Speech can only be limited where it can be shown to invoke the violent response of "fighting words."[772] "A statute is unconstitutionally vague when 'men of common intelligence must necessarily guess at its meaning.'"[773] The court agreed with the plaintiffs that the law is vague in part because it does not differentiate between speech that actually demeans the listener or whether the speaker intended to demean. Based on the examples given with the policy, there is no need to determine the effect of the speech on the listener. However, correcting this flaw would not save the policy from the overbreadth doctrine.[774] This case appears to have ended institutional attempts to develop hate speech codes since they seem to violate First Amendment speech. A case decided in the Fourth Circuit Court lends support to the above ruling. In this case, the court found that a fraternity's First Amendment rights were violated when they were sanctioned by the University for sponsoring an "Ugly Women Contest."[775]

---

[767] 315 U.S. 568 (1942). It should be noted that the Supreme Court has not utilized the fighting words doctrine in subsequent rulings.
[768] 413 U.S. 601 (1973).
[769] 458 U.S. 747 (1982).
[770] 482 U.S. 451 (1987).
[771] 774 F. Supp. 1163 (E.D. Wis. 1991).
[772] *Id.* at 1173.
[773] *Id.* at 1178, citing Broadrick.
[774] *Id.* at 1181.
[775] Iota XI Chapter of Sigma Chi Fraternity v. George Mason Univ., 773 F. Supp. 792 (E.D. Va. 1991), *aff'd*, 993 F.2d 386 (1993).

Religious Speech

The clash between the First Amendment speech protections and separation of church and state provisions has resulted in several controversies. In *Cummins v. Campbell*,[776] Oklahoma State University suspended a student group's showing of the controversial film, *The Last Temptation of Christ*. The Board of Regents suspended the scheduled showing of the film until it could get an opinion from legal counsel. The students sued in federal district court, claiming a violation of their First Amendment speech rights, and asked for a preliminary injunction. As a result of the lawsuit and with encouragement from the District Court, the Board, in a special meeting, determined that the showing of the film would not involve excessive entanglement with religion, which would be an Establishment Clause violation, and lifted the suspension. However, the students continued to pursue their claim. The court determined that the Board of Regents enjoyed a qualified immunity that protected it from damages, where the law was not clear that university sponsorship of religious activity would not be viewed as excessive entanglement. The court further stated that the student group would be entitled to attorney's fees only for work done before the lifting of the suspension.

The issue of conducting an invocation and benediction at a university commencement ceremony was raised in *Tanford v. Brand*.[777] Law students and a university law professor brought this claim to the court two days before the 1995 spring commencement. A preliminary injunction was denied based on the court's determination that the plaintiffs had little chance of success on the merits.[778] In a subsequent decision, the court noted that participation in commencement ceremonies was not mandatory and between 15 and 55 percent of the graduating law students participated in the commencement ceremony held *en masse* in the football stadium. There is a smaller ceremony where individual recognition is given to each law graduate and there is no invocation or benediction at that law school ceremony. The court distinguished this case from *Lee v. Weisman*,[779] finding that these are adult students who were not obligated to either attend or participate in the religious activities within the *en masse* commencement ceremony.[780]

---

[776] 44 F.3d 847 (10th Cir. 1994).
[777] 932 F. Supp. 1139 (S.D. Ind. 1996).
[778] Tanford v. Brand, 883 F. Supp. 1231 (S.D. Ind. 1995).
[779] 505 U.S. 577 (1992).
[780] *Id.* at 1144.

The court also noted that the multiple commencement ceremonies gave students reasonable alternatives where no religious activity was present. Using the three-part test set out in *Lemon v. Kurtzman*[781] the court found that: a brief invocation and benediction had a secular purpose of solemnizing the event; the non-sectarian nature of these prayers neither advanced nor disapproved of religion; and these activities do not result in excessive entanglement between church and state.[782] Courts continue to differentiate between students in higher education and elementary/secondary students when the issue in question involves religious activities.

Commercial Speech

Commercial speech, that is, speech involving business activity, comes under less stringent constitutional restrictions.[783] The regulation of commercial speech is acceptable if it advances a significant governmental interest and is not more extensive than necessary to legitimately serve that interest. Most courts will cite the existence of alternate channels for conducting commercial speech.[784]

Commercial speech on campus can be regulated, although several cases have challenged that premise. American Futures System Incorporated challenged several public institutions' right to control solicitation on college campuses or in the public lounges of the residence halls, student rooms, or door to door.[785] The Supreme Court ruled on a commercial speech case involving the holding of sales meetings in dorm rooms where the alleged business also involved counseling, financial planning, and career choice.[786] The Court found that institutions need only show that there is a reasonable fit between the restrictions on commercial

---

[781] 403 U.S. 602 (1971)

[782] *Id*. at 1145, 1146.

[783] Hendrickson and Gibbs, *supra* note 79 at 42.

[784] Central Hudson Gas and Electric Corp. v. Public Serv. Comm'n at N.Y., 447 U.S. 557 (1980); Virginia State Bd. of Pharmacy v. Virginia Citizens Consumer Council, 425 U.S. 748 (1976); Ohralik v. Ohio State Bar Ass'n, 436 U.S. 447 (1978).

[785] American Futures Sys., Inc. v. State Univ. of N.Y. at Cortland, 565 F. Supp. 754 (N.D. N.Y.1983); American Futures Sys., Inc. v. Pennsylvania State Univ., 553 F. Supp. 1268 (M.D. Pa. 1982), *rev'd order of preliminary injunction*, 688 F.2d 907 (3d Cir. 1982), 568 F. Supp. 755 (M.D. Pa. 1983), *rev'd and remanded with instructions*, 753 F.2d 854 (3d Cir. 1985); Chapman v. Thomas, 743 F.2d 1056 (4th Cir. 1984).

[786] Board of Trustees of State Univ. of N.Y. v. Fox, 492 U.S. 469 (1989), *rev'd and remanded*; Fox v. Board of Trustees of State Univ. of N.Y., 649 F. Supp. 1393 (N.D. N.Y. 1986), *rev'd and remanded*, 841 F.2d 1207 (2d Cir. 1988).

speech and the promotion of a governmental interest instead of "the least restrictive means standard" that the company wanted the institution to follow. Further, the Court found that the non-profit job counseling, tutoring, legal advising, and medical consulting conducted by the university were not commercial speech prohibited by the institutional policy regulating solicitation. On remand, the federal district court found that the case was moot because the complaining students had graduated.[787] The Second Circuit Court of Appeals affirmed the finding that the case was moot.[788]

Freedom of Press

Freedom of press issues typically surround the editorial content of a student newspaper. The benchmark case in this area involved the student editor of the school newspaper who was suspended for writing an editorial criticizing the governor of Alabama.[789] The court, finding that the institution was not financially obligated to support the paper, also found that the institution violated First Amendment rights by suspending the editor because of the editorial contents of the paper. Control over the content of the student newspaper by school officials will not be allowed[790] unless very narrow guidelines governing obscenity have been met.[791] The burden of proving that the material is obscene lies with the institution attempting censorship.

The withdrawal of funds from a student newspaper by an institution does not necessarily violate First Amendment provisions. If the institution can prove that the withdrawal of funds was primarily motivated by financial concerns, then First Amendment protections have not been breached.[792] However, if it can be shown that the withdrawal of funds was motivated by concerns over the content of the newspaper, a First Amendment violation exists.[793]

The newspaper itself can set its own editorial policies. For example, a court found that a newspaper could refuse to run ads in which the sexual orientation of the advertiser is described.[794]

---

[787] Fox v. Board of Trustees of State University, 764 F. Supp. 747 (N.D. N.Y. 1991), complaint amended, 148 F.R.D. 474 (N.D. N.Y. 1993).

[788] Fox v. Board of Trustees of State Univ., 42 F.3d 135 (2d Cir. 1994).

[789] Dickey v. Alabama, 273 F. Supp. 613 (M.D. Ala. 1967).

[790] Joyner v. Whiting, 477 F.2d 456 (4th Cir. 1973).

[791] Antonelli v. Hammond, 308 F. Supp. 1329 (D. Mass. 1970).

[792] Olson v. State Bd. for Community Colleges and Occupational Educ., 759 P.2d 829 (Colo. Ct. App. 1988).

[793] Stanley v. McGrath, 719 F.2d 279 (8th Cir. 1983).

[794] Sinn v. The Daily Nebraskan, 638 F. Supp. 143 (D. Neb. 1986), aff'd, 829 F.2d 662 (8th Cir. 1987).

Liability for the content of the paper also has been at issue. A court did not find the paper or the institution libel for a letter to the editor that critiqued the teaching of a professor,[795] nor did it find that a newspaper published as a spoof had defamed a college administration's character.[796]

Finally, an issue regarding the use of student fees to fund a religiously oriented student magazine at the University of Virginia was decided by the Supreme Court. At issue in *Rosenberger v. Rector and Visitors of the University of Virginia*[797] was whether, based on the separation of church and state, a public institution could deny student funding to a publication with a Christian editorial policy. The student group maintained that the denial of funding violated its First Amendment speech and press rights because it was based on the editorial content of the publication. Both the federal district court and Fourth Circuit Court ruled in favor of the university.[798] The United States Supreme Court reversed in favor of the students. The Court found that providing funding to the publication would not violate the Establishment Clause, because the funding program was neutral toward religion. To exclude funding based on the content of the publication's editorial policy violated First Amendment free speech provisions. The Court also noted that the scarcity of student funds did not permit viewpoint discrimination.

Freedom of Association

The rights of Association, while not explicitly spelled out, are implied rights of the First Amendment speech and press freedoms. Freedom of association rights were applied to colleges and universities in *Healy v. James, supra*, where the Court stated:

> While freedom of association is not explicitly set out in the First Amendment, it has long been held to be implicit in the freedoms of speech, assembly, and petition. There can be no doubt that the denial of official recognition without justification, to college organizations burdens or abridges that associational right.[799]

---

[795] Epstein v. Board of Trustees of Dowling College, 543 N.Y.S.2d 691 (N.Y. App. Div. 1989).

[796] Walko v. Kean College of N.J., 561 A.2d 680 (N.J. Super. Ct. Law Div. 1988).

[797] 115 S. Ct. 2510 (1995).

[798] Rosenberger v. Rector and Visitors of Univ. of Va., 795 F. Supp. 176 (W.D. Va. 1992), *aff'd*, 18 F.3d 269 (4th Cir. 1994).

[799] Healy v. James, 408 U.S. 169 (1972), at 169.

Usually associational rights are implicated when the institution denies recognition to some organizations. Gibbs[800] noted that the denial of recognition results in the loss of significant benefits. These benefits are:

1. The privilege of scheduling campus facilities for meetings and activities, usually rent free;
2. The opportunity to lease a campus post office box;
3. The right to request funds from the student activity funds;
4. The privilege of using the school's name as part of the organization's name;
5. The opportunity to use school media;
6. The right to post notices and appropriate signs announcing activities;
7. The privilege of being listed in the student handbook and the yearbook; and
8. The opportunity to qualify for awards and honors given to college student organizations.[801]

The denial of these benefits was not viewed as inconsequential by the Court in *Healy*.[802] The reasoning that an organization "advocated unlawful acts" was the rationale used by some institutions to deny recognition to gay organizations. The courts have held that while a university or college did not have to give recognition to student groups, once it gave recognition to some, it could not withhold it from others based on the issues they advocated.[803] Like other First Amendment issues, recognition could be withheld only where the organization was disruptive, endangered others' safety, committed illegal acts, or failed to conform to legitimate policies regulating organizations. The courts refused to hold that the mere advocacy of the repeal of laws as opposed to the commission of unlawful acts was enough to deny recognition.[804] More recently, a federal circuit court ruled that the student senate vote, which was content-based and denied funding to a gay group, breached First Amendment rights.[805] Although private institutions

---

[800] A. Gibbs, *Colleges and Gay Student Organizations: An Update*, NASPA J., 22 (1984): 535-540.

[801] *Id.* at 538.

[802] Healy v. James, *supra*, note at 181.

[803] Gay Student Org. of the Univ. of N.H. v. Bonner, 367 F. Supp. 1088 (D. N.H. 1974), *aff'd*, 509 F.2d 652 (1st Cir. 1974).

[804] Gay Alliance of Students v. Matthews, 544 F.2d 162 (4th Cir. 1976); Gay Lib v. University of Mo., 588 F.2d 848 (8th Cir. 1977), *cert. denied*, 434 U.S. 1080, *reh'g denied*, 435 U.S. 981 (1978); Gay Student Servs. v. Texas A & M, 737 F. 2d 1317 (5th Cir. 1984), *cert. denied*, 471 U.S. 1120 (1985).

[805] Gay and Lesbian Students Ass'n v. Gohn, 656 F. Supp. 1045 (W.D. Ark. 1987), *rev'd*, 850 F.2d 361 (8th Cir. 1988).

are subject to different requirements than public institutions, a private institution could not escape the provisions of a local statute prohibiting discrimination based on sexual orientation.[806] Georgetown, a Catholic university, was ordered to give recognition to a gay organization because the District of Columbia has an anti-discrimination housing code that included sexual orientation discrimination.

Group membership has also brought allegations of violations of associational rights. A court found that it was not a constitutional violation for a federal agency to threaten to remove federal funds if an institution continued to recognize an organization that discriminates against women.[807] The court found that the Iron Arrow Society, a male honorary association, infected the entire academic mission of the institution when it discriminated against women who were excluded from membership. The institution withdrew recognition when the group refused to changes its membership rules. The institution had not violated the rights of group members by withdrawing recognition in order to achieve compliance with federal statutes. Here, the court balanced associational rights against laws that promote the constitutional concept of equity. In this case, the institution had given equity rights precedence. Similarly, group composition was before the court when an institution attempted to regulate the composition of student government. The university established membership rules that required student government legislative and judicial bodies to reflect the racial composition of the student population. The court ruled that such provisions violated the Equal Protection Clause of the Fourteenth Amendment.[808]

Recognition of religious groups has also been an issue before the courts. The issues surround not only recognition but also some state provisions that prohibit the use of public facilities for religious purposes. In *Widmar v. Vincent*,[809] the court established that absent a compelling state interest a public institution could not prohibit speech that had religious content. At issue was whether religious organizations could conduct meetings and use university facilities. The court stated:

> Having created a forum generally opened to student groups, a state university may not practice content-based

---

[806] Gay Rights Coalition v. Georgetown Univ., 496 A.2d 567 (D.C. Cir. 1985). The Georgetown University Charter required it to uphold the District of Columbia Charter and would lose the use of tax free bonds if it failed to comply with D.C. ordinances.
[807] Iron Arrow Soc'y v. Heckler, 702 F.2d 549 (5th Cir. 1983).
[808] Uzzell v. Friday, 592 F. Supp. 1502 (M.D. N.C. 1984).
[809] Widmar v. Vincent, 454 U.S. 263 (1981).

exclusion of religious speech when that exclusion is not narrowly drawn to achieve a state interest in the separation of church and state.[810]

Freedom of Speech and Religion and Student Fees

The issue of whether the use of student fees violates the freedom of speech or religion rights of students has been before the courts. The cases involved several uses of student fees. One is the use of student fee money to fund Public Interest Research Groups (PIRGs). PIRGs are lobby groups that advocate particular political positions. Some students with political views opposite to PIRG claimed their freedom of speech rights were infringed when their student fees went to a PIRG. Another is the use of student fees to fund abortions at the student health center in violation of some students' beliefs. Both of these issues have seen significant litigation.

The legal theories applying First Amendment protections in the use of student fees emanate from a Supreme Court case, *Abood v. Detroit Board of Education*,[811] which illuminated a controversy on the use of union dues. The Court ruled that dues assessed to nonmembers could include only those charges for the negotiation and administration of the collective bargaining agreement. The union could not extract fees for political purposes from anyone who objected to those purposes. The Court reasoned that forcing people to contribute to political activities about which they disagreed was to compel them to speak, a corollary to the suppression of speech, a free speech violation.[812]

One of the most prominent case alleging compelled speech was *Galda v. Bloustein*.[813] The university had set up a system of funding for a New Jersey PIRG if 25 percent of the students voted for it and the student government approved. The amount given to the PIRG became part of the student fees automatically collected from all students, but refundable on request. The district court found that the refund policy sufficiently protected students' First

---

[810] *Id*. at 264.
[811] Abood v. Detroit Board of Educ., 431 U.S. 209 (1977).
[812] *Id*. at 210.
[813] 516 F. Supp. 1142 (D. N.J. 1981), *rev'd*, 680 F.2d 159 (3d Cir. 1982); Galda v. Rutgers, 589 F. Supp. 479 (D. N.J. 1984), vacated and remanded, 772 F.2d 1060 (3d Cir. 1985), *cert. denied*, 475 U.S. 1065 (1986).

Amendment rights. On appeal, the opinion was reversed and remanded to determine whether First Amendment rights had been
violated.[814] The district court, on remand, found that the PIRG
was funded in the interest of providing an important educational
component of the university. On appeal, the court found the district court opinion erroneous. The Third Circuit Court found that
the PIRG was an external organization whose purpose was not
educational but rather political. Therefore, the assessment of a
mandatory fee was a violation of students' First Amendment
rights.[815] The court rejected the refund system and seemed to be
endorsing a system where the students could decide in advance
of payment whether they wanted to support such a group.

In a state case, students challenged the constitutionality of
mandatory student fees at the University of California at Berke-
ley.[816] The mandatory fees collected at matriculation could be used
to fund student activities and funding requests from recognized
student organizations. Use of student funds was administered by
the university's student government. The funding policy prohibited using the funds for support of specific positions on public
issues or particular causes.[817] The court found that the collection
of these mandatory student fees violated neither state nor federal
constitutional provisions. On appeal, the state's Appellate Court
affirmed in part and reversed in part.[818] The court affirmed that
the university had the right to collect mandatory student fees;
however, partial refunds were due to students who objected to
particular uses on political or ideological grounds. Further evidentiary proceedings were necessary to determine whether student
fees were expended in the student senate passage and publication
of a political resolution.

Another student who disagreed with the editorial policy of
his school's newspaper, was unsuccessful in challenging the use
of student fees to fund that newspaper.[819] The court found that
the institution had established that the paper was a vital part of its
educational mission and the paper could set its own editorial policy
based on freedom of press provisions.

Students objected on religious grounds to the use of mandatory student fees to fund abortion counseling, abortion referral,
and actual abortions.[820] Students alleged that the use of fees for
abortion purposes violated the First Amendment free exercise of

---

[814] *Id.*, Galda v. Bloustein.
[815] *Id.*, Galda v. Rutgers.
[816] Smith v. Regents of Univ. of Cal., 248 Cal. Rptr. 263 (Cal. Ct. App. 1988).
[817] *Id.* at 265.
[818] Smith v. Regents of Univ. of Cal., 844 P.2d 500 (Cal. 1993).
[819] Kania v. Fordham, 702 F.2d 475 (4th Cir. 1983).
[820] Erzinger v. Regents of the Univ. Cal., 185 Cal. Rpt. 791 (Cal. Ct. App. 1982).

religion clause. The court found that to use student fees in this way was not prohibited by the First Amendment. Making an analogy, the court noted that citizens do not have the constitutional right to refuse to pay income tax simply because they disagree with certain governmental actions. Providing medical services including abortion services was a legitimate governmental function, the court said, and the university could use mandatory student fees to fund those functions.[821]

The use of public funds to support groups that promote alternative lifestyles was before the court in *Gay Lesbian and Bisexual Alliance v. Sessions*.[822] The state of Alabama passed a law making it illegal to use public funds to support groups promoting lifestyles or actions prohibited by sodomy and sexual misconduct laws. The Federal District Court for the Middle District of Alabama found that the statute prohibiting speech based on particular viewpoints violated the First Amendment. The court noted that the law failed to make a distinction between mere advocacy, a protected right, and lawless behavior not protected by the First Amendment. In a subsequent action, the court refused to stay its opinion since the Attorney General had failed to demonstrate the merits of an appeal.[823]

In all of these cases, if institutions showed a compelling interest in funding programs that are in concert with their educational missions, the courts allowed the assessment of mandatory student fees. Another guideline appears to be that functions internal to the community organization that are chosen by the community to promote the public good will withstand scrutiny. Abortion services meet these criteria, but political activities apparently do not.

Privacy

The Bill of Rights does not expressly enumerate a right to privacy; however, privacy has come to be thought of as an implied right through *Griswold v. Connecticut*.[824] The Supreme Court found that the First, Third, Fourth, and Fifth Amendments were guarantees that imply the right to privacy. These amendments create a zone of privacy, or "penumbras, formed by emanation that help

---

[821] *Id.* at 794.

[822] 917 F. Supp. 1548 (M.D. Ala. 1996).

[823] Gay Lesbian and Bisexual Alliance v. Sessions, 917 F. Supp. 1558 (M.D. Ala. 1996); attorneys fees awarded to students, 930 F. Supp. 1492 (M.D. Ala. 1996).

[824] Griswold v. Connecticut, 381 U.S. 479 (1965).

give them life and substance,"[825] guaranteed to all citizens. The Court subsequently ruled that students do not abdicate this privacy right when they choose to live in residence halls.[826] Searches of student rooms by law enforcement officers cannot be conducted without reason to believe that the rooms are being used for illegal activity or in ways that threaten the educational atmosphere. However, this does not infringe on an institution's right to inspect the premises in the maintenance of the facility, or to enter in times of emergency or when there is a threat to the educational atmosphere.[827] Contraband or other evidence found in plain view during a legal entry of a room is admissible in court.[828] As Hendrickson and Gibbs noted:

> The case law in this area indicates that the level of privacy established by the courts is less than that guaranteed to a citizen in the community. Students are protected from warrantless searches by law enforcement officers but must allow institutional authorities access to their rooms for purposes of inspection and when the "educational atmosphere" of the residence hall is seriously threatened....[829]

Congress has extended privacy rights protecting certain papers and records through the Family Educational Rights and Privacy Act (FERPA).[830] However, press challenges to gain access to crime reports filed by campus police have been successful.[831] A student newspaper successfully sought a preliminary injunction of the Department of Education FERPA enforcement decision prohibiting university release to the media of the names of individuals involved in campus police criminal reports. The court found that the plaintiffs were likely to be successful on the merits that the enforcement policy violated First Amendment Rights. In another FERPA case, students were successful in acquiring a preliminary injunction against the university practice of distributing class rosters containing students' social security numbers.[832]

---

[825] *Id.* at 481.

[826] Moore v. Student Affairs Comm. of Troy State Univ., 284 F. Supp. 725 (M.D. Ala. 1968).

[827] Piazzola v. Watkins, 442 F. Supp. 284 (5th Cir. 1971); *see* State v. Dalton, 716 P.2d 940 (Wash. Ct. App. 1986).

[828] Speakes v. Grantham, 317 F. Supp. 1253 (S.D. Miss. 1970).

[829] R.M. Hendrickson & A. Gibbs, *supra* note 79, at 12.

[830] 88 Stat. 571 (1974); regulations at 20 U.S.C.A. § 1232.

[831] Student Press Law Center v. Alexander, 778 F. Supp. 1227 (D. D.C. 1991).

[832] Krebs v. Rutgers, 797 F. Supp. 1246 (D. N.J. 1992).

Voting Rights

Since the voting age was lowered to 18, the right of college students to register and vote in the college community have also been at issue. At issue was whether, for voting purposes, students had established a domicile in the college community. There are two competing constitutional rights in voting rights cases. One is the right of the individual to vote and have voter registration laws that meet the standards of the Equal Protection Clause of the Fourteenth Amendment. The other competing right is the state's right to insure that bona fide state residents vote, thus preventing voter fraud. The Supreme Court has established two constitutional standards in voting cases. One is that state voter regulations must advance a compelling state interest by the least drastic means.[833] The Court also has ruled that voter registration laws cannot treat classes of individuals differently by doing such things as placing additional requirements on student registrants.[834] Recent case law continues to follow these precedents. A federal district court struck down a New York election commission's use of a questionnaire to determine if students were eligible to register to vote in the county.[835] The court found that using the questionnaire exclusively for students was unconstitutional and could not be justified simply as a means of preventing voter fraud. Another New York county election board ruled that students living in the college dormitories were not eligible to vote because a dormitory was not a fixed and permanent residence. The court ruled that a blanket rejection of students because they resided in dormitories was a violation of their constitutional right to vote.[836] Voter registration laws typically require that the individual be domiciled in the community for 30 days. These residency requirements are independent of those used for non-resident tuition. The election board can look at intent to remain in the county to prevent vote fraud but must treat all registrants equally.[837]

---

[833] Dunn v. Blumstein, 405 U.S. 330 (1972); *See* Pheonix v. Kolodzieski, 399 U.S. 204 (1970); Evans v. Corman, 398 U.S. 419 (1970); Cipriano v. City of Houma, 395 U.S. 701 (1969); Carrington v. Rash, 380 U.S. 89 (1965).

[834] *See e.g.*, United States v. Texas, 445 F. Supp. 1245 (S.D. Tex. 1978), *aff'd mem. non sub.*, Symm v. United States, 439 U.S. 1105 (1979); Frazier v. Callicutt, 383 F. Supp. 15 (N.D. Miss. 1974); Sloane v. Smith, 351 F. Supp. 1299 (M.D. Pa. 1972); Newburg v. Petterson, 344 F. Supp. 559 (D.N.H. 1972); Johnson v. Darrall, 337 F. Supp. 138 (D. Ohio 1971); Ownsby v. Dies, 337 F. Supp. 38 (E.D. Tex. 1971); Shivelhood v. Davis, 336 F. Supp. 1111 (D. Vt. 1971); Bright v. Beasler, 336 F. Supp. 527 (E.D. Ky. 1971).

[835] Auerbach v. Kinley, 594 F. Supp. 1503 (N.D.N.Y. 1984).

[836] Williams v. Salerno, 622 F. Supp. 1271 (S.D.N.Y. 1985), *aff'd*, 792 F.2d 323 (2d Cir. 1986); *see* Levy v. Scranton, 780 F. Supp. 897 (N.D. N.Y. 1991).

[837] *Id.*, Auerbach.

Due Process Rights

The application of constitutional rights in due process emanates from the concepts of having a property right or liberty interest. Property cannot be taken from an individual without due process of law under the Fourteenth Amendment. Property is anything that one possesses. A contract is property, for example, and gives one rights to its provisions. Due process would be available for a breach of the terms of the contract. States giving benefits to citizens cannot deny those benefits to a citizen without providing due process. While private institutions are governed by the terms of the contracts they hold with their students, public institutions must provide due process to any student they attempt to dismiss for disciplinary reasons based on the court's ruling in *Dixon v. Alabama*.[838] The court noted that "the state cannot condition the granting of even a privilege on the renunciation of the constitutional right to due process."[839] The court described the nature of procedural due process requirements in public colleges and universities and listed four due process provisions:

1. The notice should contain a statement of the specific charges and grounds justifying expulsion under board regulations;
2. The nature of the hearing would vary according to the circumstances of the case but should be more than an informal interview with an administrator;
3. The rudiments of an adversarial proceeding which might include the names of the witnesses testifying against the student and an oral or written statement of the facts testified; and
4. The accused should be given the opportunity to present a defense and witnesses on his behalf.[840]

The court stated:

...This is not to imply that a full dressed judicial hearing with the right to cross examine witnesses is required. Such a hearing with the attendant publicity and disturbance of college activity might be detrimental to the college's educational atmosphere and impractical to carry out....[841]

Subsequent case law in the decade of the seventies seemed to

---

[838] Dixon v. Alabama, 294 F.2d 150 (5th Cir. 1961).
[839] *Id.* at 156.
[840] *Id.* at 158.
[841] *Id.* at 159.

prescribe very specific requirements for due process.[842] Such requirements were turning the disciplinary hearing into a procedure that followed more closely the adversarial procedures used in court. By the late 1970s, the literature was outlining rules of evidence and cross examination of witnesses along with recommending representation by legal council at the hearing. However, case law that is more recent indicates less rigidity in the procedures to be followed.[843] A recent case in Virginia supports the notion of flexibility in meeting due process requirements.[844] Thus, due process requirements are open for interpretation and case law continues to define their parameters.

A case involving a secondary school, *Goss v. Lopez*,[845] established an institution's right to suspend a student prior to the due process hearing in cases where continued attendance posed a threat to persons or property and/or would be disruptive to the academic process. In addition, hearing procedures must be conducted consistent with concepts of fairness. Fairness involves questions surrounding the makeup of the hearing committee. The hearing committee was not biased in the case where the student senate advisors sat on a hearing committee that dismissed the plaintiff, a student senator.[846] The plaintiff alleged that the advisors were biased because they had disagreed with the plaintiff on other issues before the student governance body.

Bias could also be at issue in procedures used during the hearing and could, therefore, violate due process. For example, the First Circuit Court ruled that the use of transcripts from the plaintiff's previous conviction on rape in the current hearing was pertinent to the misconduct charge and did not, in turn, bias the hearing.[847] The student was charged with peeking under women's dresses in the university library. Another federal court ruled that the use of the transcript of the original hearing did not bias the appeals process.[848]

The specific requirements for hearing procedures have also been before the courts. The Eleventh Circuit Court ruled that the lack of advance notice of accusing witnesses testimony and the failure to allow the student to cross-examine witnesses did not violate the student's due process rights in a hearing that resulted

---

[842] Esteban v. Central Mo. State College, 277 F. Supp. 649 (W.D. Mo. 1967).

[843] *See* R. M. Hendrickson and A. Gibbs, (1986) at 9; F. R. Kremer and K. L. Deutsch, CONSTITUTIONAL RIGHTS AND STUDENT LIFE 351, (1979).

[844] Henson v. Honor Comm. of Univ. of Va., 719 F.2d 69 (4th Cir. 1983).

[845] Goss v. Lopez, 419 U.S. 565 (1975).

[846] Gorman v. University of R.I., 837 F.2d 7 (1st Cir. 1988).

[847] Cloud v. Trustees of Boston Univ., 720 F.2d 721 (1st Cir. 1983).

[848] Nash v. Auburn Univ., 621 F. Supp. 948 (M.D. Ala. 1985), *aff'd*, 812 F.2d 655 (11th Cir. 1987).

in dismissal.[849] The right to counsel does exist at least in limited circumstances. For example, in instances where institutions use legal counsel, the student must be given the same option.[850] However, a more recent state case may indicate that due process rights are not violated when an accused's counsel is not allowed to speak during a hearing.[851] Further, a case in the Sixth Circuit Court rejected the plaintiff's appeal where the school had good cause to expel, and the expulsion was not caused by the denial of assistance from legal counsel.[852] The court found there was no need to remand the case. Based on the above cases, the question of access to legal counsel remains open to further determination.

The actual disciplinary decision must be consistent with the evidence. If the decision appears to be arbitrary or capricious, it will not be upheld in the courts. For example, the Ninth Circuit Court found the institution had not established that the students charged with disruptive acts had individually committed those disruptive acts while participating in a student protest.[853]

One of the more interesting disciplinary cases, *Steffan v. Aspin*,[854] involved sexual orientation and the Naval Academy. The Department of Defense regulations prohibit homosexual persons from serving in the Navy or attending the Naval Academy. The Clinton administration successfully campaigned to change the enforcement of the policy to a "don't ask–don't-tell" policy. When a midshipman at the Naval Academy admitted to being a homosexual, the Navy forced him to resign. The United States Court of Appeals for the District of Columbia ruled that discharge for admitting to a homosexual orientation, rather than for actual homosexual conduct, was a violation of the midshipman's equal protection under the Fifth Amendment[855] due process clause.

When a liberty interest (one's good name or reputation) is involved, due process procedures consistent with those used in other disciplinary dismissal cases must be followed. While charges of plagiarism or cheating are clearly academic matters, they impli-

---

[849] *Id.* at 663.

[850] Barker v. Hardway, 283 F. Supp. 228 (S.D. W.Va. 1968); French v. Bashful, 303 F. Supp. 1333 (E.D. La. 1969).

[851] University of Houston v. Sabeti, 676 S.W.2d 685 (Tex. Ct. App. 1984).

[852] Hall v. Medical College of Ohio at Toledo, 742 F.2d 299 (6th Cir. 1984).

[853] Jackson v. Hayakawa, 761 F.2d 525 (9th Cir. 1985).

[854] 8 F.3d 57 (D.C. Cir. 1993); *see also* Steffan v. Perry, 41 F.3d 677 (D.C. Cir. 1994).

[855] Since the Naval Academy, a federal institution, is involved, the Fifth Amendment due process, rather than the Fourteenth Amendment's due process, applies in this case.

cate a liberty interest requiring due process.[856] In a unique academic case, a university revoked a master's degree from an alumnus after it was discovered that he had falsified data in his master's thesis. After notification and a hearing, the degree was revoked. The Sixth Circuit Court vacated a lower court decision and found that the university possessed the authority to revoke the degree and that due process had been adequate.[857] In another case, the court found that a hearing yielded a finding of fraud, allowing an institution to revoke the degrees of several alumni.[858] The case involved academic charges of misconduct that implicated a liberty interest. However, academic dismissal questions involving questions of performance in course work or the fulfillment of degree requirements do not implicate a liberty interest.

State Action

Private institutions have been differentiated from public institutions when it comes to constitutional guarantees. Their responsibilities are not as onerous in the enforcement of guarantees as those placed on the public sector. However, a doctrine called state action attempts to establish when private institutions, through a significant interdependent relationship, become agents of state government. State action can be found when the private organization is acting under color of state law,[859] or when a significant interdependent relationship exists.[860] The doctrine is elusive and a finding of state action is not the typical result.[861] However, the Second Circuit Court of Appeals found that a private institution's dismissal of students involved in a protest without a hearing was state action because it was conducted under color of state law.[862] The state of New York had passed a law requiring public and private institutions to get tough on civil disobedience.

---

[856] Beilis v. Albany Med. College of Union Univ., 525 N.Y.S.2d 932 (N.Y. App. Div. 1988); Clayton v. Trustees of Princeton Univ., 608 F. Supp. 414 (D.N.J. 1985); Corso v. Creighton Univ., 731 F.2d 529 (8th Cir. 1984); Easley v. University of Mich. Bd. of Regents, 627 F. Supp. 580 (E.D. Mich. 1986) *motion denied*, 632 F. Supp. 1539 (E.D. Mich. 1986), *aff'd in part and remanded*, 853 F.2d 1351 (6th Cir. 1988); Hall v. Medical College of Ohio at Toledo, 742 F.2d 299 (6th Cir. 1984); Jaksa v. Regents of Univ. of Mich., 597 F. Supp. 1245 (E.D. Mich. 1984).

[857] Crook v. Baker, 584 F. Supp. 1531 (E.D. Mich. 1984), *vacated*, 813 F.2d 88 (6th Cir. 1987).

[858] Waliga v. Board of Trustees of Kent State Univ., 488 N.E.2d 850 (Ohio 1986).

[859] Cf. Adickes v. S.H. Kress and Co., 398 U.S. 144 (1970).

[860] Moose Lodge No. 107 v. Irvis, 407 U.S. 163 (1972).

[861] *See* Brown v. Mitchell, 409 F.2d 593 (10th Cir. 1969); Powe v. Miles, 294 F. Supp. 1269 (W.D. N.Y. 1968), *modified*, 407 F.2d 73 (2d Cir. 1968); Grossner v. Trustees of Columbia Univ., 287 F. Supp. 535 (S.D. N.Y. 1968).

[862] Albert v. Carovano, 824 F.2d 1333 (2d Cir. 1987).

However, in a subsequent ruling en banc, the same court found that no state action was involved and the private school's actions would be governed by the terms of the contract with the student.[863] This ruling is consistent with most of the litigation on private institutions that typically involve a breach of the contract that guaranteed due process procedures. For example, a business school breached a contract when it failed to prove that a student's statements to a newspaper about the fiscal management of the college were disruptive as defined in the conduct code.[864] It was a contract breach when a church-affiliated institution withheld a degree from a student who, in confidence, revealed his homosexuality to a school counselor.[865] However, denying legal counsel full participation in the hearing was not a breach of contract.[866] The key in private institution breach of contract questions is the language of the contract and whether the procedures meet the intended provisions of the contract.

Academic Dismissal and Due Process

The concept of academic deference provided the guiding principle in cases involving academic dismissal.[867] The benchmark case is *Board of Curators of the University of Missouri v. Horowitz*,[868] in which a medical student was dismissed for failing to meet clinical requirements for the medical doctor's degree. After several oral and written notifications of deficiencies in clinical practice, the student was dismissed. The Court stated:

Academic evaluation of a student, in contrast to disciplinary determinations, bears little resemblance to the judicial and administrative fact-finding proceedings to which we have traditionally attached full-hearing requirements....The decision to dismiss respondent, by comparison rested on academic judgment of school officials that she did not have the necessary clinical ability to perform adequately as a medical doctor and was not making sufficient progress toward that goal. Such a judgment is by its nature more subjective and evaluative than the typical factual questions presented in the average disciplinary decision. Like the decision of an individual professor as to the proper grade

---

[863] Albert v. Carovano, 851 F.2d 561 (2d Cir. 1988).

[864] Fussell v. Louisiana Business College of Monroe, 519 So.2d 384 (La. Ct. App. 1988).

[865] Johnson v. Lincoln Christian College, 501 N.E.2d 1380 (Ill. App. Ct. 1986).

[866] Turof v. Kibbee, 527 F. Supp. 880 (E.D. N.Y. 1981).

[867] *See* R.M. Hendrickson and A. Gibbs, 11, (1986).

[868] Board of Curators of the Univ. of Mo. v. Horowitz, 435 U.S. 78 (1978).

for a student in his course, the determination whether to dismiss a student for academic reasons requires an expert evaluation of cumulative information and is not readily adapted to the procedural tools of judicial or administrative decision making.[869]

The position of academic deference set out in the *Horowitz* case was strengthened by the court's ruling in *Regents of the University of Michigan v. Ewing.*[870] A university elected not to allow a student to retake an examination after he failed and was dismissed from the graduate program. A retake of the exam had been allowed in other instances where failure had occurred. The court ruled that the university had the right to evaluate academic performance. The court citing *Horowitz* and the quotation (*supra*) stated:

> This narrow avenue of judicial review precludes any conclusion that the decision to dismiss Ewing from the Interflex program was a substantial departure from accepted academic norms as to demonstrate that the faculty did not exercise professional judgment.[871]

The vast majority of subsequent decisions are consistent with the rulings in *Horowitz* and *Ewing* (*supra*).[872] However, some cases that challenged the validity of a university's academic reasons for dismissal were litigated on the merits. For example, one case chal-

---

[869] *Id.* at 90-91.

[870] Regents of the Univ. of Mich. v. Ewing, 474 U.S. 214 (1985); *see* Ewing v. Board of Regents of Univ. of Mich., 552 F. Supp. 881 (E.D. Mich. 1982), *rev'd*, 742 F.2d 913 (6th Cir. 1984).

[871] *Id.* at 514.

[872] *See* Akins v. Board of Governors of State Colleges and Univs., 867 F.2d 972 (7th Cir. 1988); Amelunxen v. University of P.R., 637 F. Supp. 426 (D.P.R. 1986), *aff'd*, 815 F.2d 691 (1st Cir. 1987); Assaad-Faltas v. University of Ark. for Med. Sciences, 708 F. Supp. 1026 (E.D. Ark. 1989); Davis v. Louisiana State Univ., 876 F.2d 412 (5th Cir. 1989); Davis v. Mann, 882 F.2d 967 (5th Cir. 1989); Easley v. University of Mich. Bd. of Regents, 627 F. Supp. 580 (E.D. Mich. 1986); Espenshade v. Pennsylvania State Univ., 563 F. Supp. 1172 (M.D. Pa. 1983); Haberle v. University of Ala. in Birmingham, 803 F.2d 1536 (11th Cir. 1986); Hankins v. Temple Univ., 829 F.2d 437 (3d Cir. 1987); Harris v. Blake, 798 F.2d 419 (10th Cir. 1986), *cert. denied*, 479 U.S. 1033 (1986); Hines v. Rinker, 667 F.2d 699 (8th Cir. 1981); Kashani v. Purdue Univ., 813 F.2d 843 (7th Cir. 1987), *cert. denied*, 484 U.S. 846 (1987); Lewis v. Russe, 713 F. Supp. 1227 (N.D. Ill. 1989); Maduakolam v. Columbia Univ., 866 F.2d 53 (2d Cir. 1989); Martin v. Delaware School of Law of Wiedener Univ., 625 F. Supp. 1288 (D. Del. 1985), *aff'd*, 884 F.2d 1384 (3rd Cir. 1989); Mauriello v. University of Med. and Dentistry of N.J., 781 F.2d 46 (3d Cir. 1986), *cert. denied*, 479 U.S. 846 (1986); Mohammed v. Mathog, 635 F. Supp. 748 (E.D. Mich. 1986); Moire v. Temple Univ. School of Med., 613 F. Supp. 1360 (E.D. Pa. 1985); Paisey v. Vitale, 807 F.2d 889 (11th Cir. 1986); Petock v. Thomas Jefferson Univ., 630 F. Supp. 187 (E.D. Pa. 1986); Radcliff v. Landau, 883 F.2d 1481 (9th Cir. 1989); Schuler v. University of Minn., 788 F.2d 510 (8th Cir. 1986), *cert. denied*, 497 U. S. 1056 (1987); Smith v. Duquesne Univ., 612 F. Supp. 73 (W.D. Pa. 1985); Stoller v. College of Med., 562 F. Supp. 403 (M.D. Pa. 1983); Wilkenfield v. Powell, 577 F. Supp. 579 (W.D. Tex. 1983).

lenged the use of obesity as a bar to completion of a nursing program.[873] Another involved whether there was a previous agreement to count a foreign educational experience,[874] and finally, one case involved a determination of the validity of a charge of sexual harassment.[875] To date, a final determination on these issues has not been published. The lack of final disposition may mean that they have been settled out of court. However, the court's deference to academicians who have exhibited sound professional judgment continues to be the unbending principle in academic dismissal cases.

Conclusions for Administrative Practice

The issue of access to all-white professional programs at public institutions brought the courts to the college gates. The civil rights movement and the evolution of the concept of integration brought the courts through the gates and on to the campus in the *Dixon* decision. This would begin the process of the courts' scrutiny over several institutionals' practices that influence the student-institutional relationship.

Issues of access to higher education continue to be litigated. Much of this litigation centers on the issue of discrimination in admission. In particular, discrimination based on race, gender and disability receives considerable attention.

Discrimination based on race evolved through the development of federal statutes to the point where our public policy was one of affirmative action in the admission of minorities. This resulted in the evolution of the issue that came to be called "reverse discrimination." Suits by whites who claimed discrimination based on race resulted in the Courts' ruling that race could be a factor, but not the sole factor, in the admissions decision.

Gender discrimination, after the passage of title IX, evolved mainly around procedural issues involving the scope of the legislation. With the passage of the Civil Rights Restoration Act of 1988, title IX has been given new vigor. The nature of the forthcoming litigation will give some indication whether adherence to the prohibition of gender discrimination has been achieved within the higher education community.

---

[873] Russell v. Salve Regina College, 649 F. Supp. 391 (D. R.I. 1986).
[874] Banerjee v. Roberts, 641 F. Supp. 1093 (D. Conn. 1986).
[875] Lipsett v. University of P.R., 864 F.2d 881 (1st Cir. 1988).

Discrimination in admission based on disability is slightly different from other forms of discrimination. The law does not require affirmative action, but instead that an "otherwise qualified" disabled individual be granted admission to an institution. The institution need not change its admission criteria that go to job performance, nor is it required to compromise academic standards. "Otherwise qualified" disabled applicants are defined as individuals who despite their disability meet the appropriate criteria. However, physical barriers to job performance or to meeting academic criteria must be removed.

The use of standardized tests in the admissions process is an area of more recent litigation. If the standardized test is measuring valid performance criteria, it will most likely withstand charges that it has a discriminatory effect on a particular class of individuals. Further, the private testing agency is not an agent of state government requiring the guarantee of constitutional rights simply because a public institution uses the test in its admissions decisions.

Economic access to higher education was also actively litigated. Two issues arose: one involved the assessment of nonresident tuition, and the other was concerned with the award and use of student financial aid.

Charging nonresident tuition is not a violation of the Equal Protection Clause of the Fourteenth Amendment. States can use criteria such as whether an individual has established legal residence or domicile within the state in order to determine residency status. A one-year waiting period is valid to establish state residency; however, states cannot irrebuttably presume that an individual is a nonresident. The Utah law requiring the maintenance of continuous domicile within the state may prove to be a very effective way for states to maintain fiscal integrity.

Constitutional rights established in student-institutional relationships include First Amendment, privacy, voter, and due process rights. Each of these areas saw extensive litigation that served to define further the parameters of these guarantees to students.

First Amendment rights include freedom of speech, press, association, and religion. Institutions cannot regulate speech based on the content of the speech. However, an institution can establish regulations that control the time, place, and manner of speech, while maintaining opportunities to speak. The courts are reluctant to issue prior restraints, but will prohibit speech if it can be shown that the speech endangers the safety or property of others or inhibits others' rights to speech. Freedom of press rights are similar in that an institution cannot regulate the editorial content of a student newspaper unless the institution can establish that the content in question is obscene. Institutions are not obligated to provide financial support to the student newspaper. Where financial support is provided, however, its withdrawal must be for reasons other than those that demonstrate an attempt to regulate the editorial content of the publication.

Commercial speech, on the other hand, can be restricted on the campus as long as there is a reasonable fit with the restriction and the promotion of governmental policies. However, other avenues of commercial speech must be available. Nonprofit career counseling, tutoring, or medical consultation are not types of commercial speech.

Freedom of association rights affects the recognition of student groups. As long as an institution chooses to recognize one group, it must treat all groups equally. As with free speech, an institution cannot deny recognition based on objections to the particular advocacy of the group or that the group advocates the repeal of laws. It can, however, deny recognition to groups that break the law or that have endangered the property and safety of others. The free exercise and establishment clauses also affect student rights on campus. Religious groups cannot be denied access to university facilities unless the regulation is carefully drawn to achieve the separation of church and state.

The use of student fees to fund particular activities was another issue brought before the courts. An institution must be careful that it is using funds to achieve some educational purpose. The funding of external political action groups with student fees can be done only where the institution provides a payment scheme that does not force student speech. Students who do not wish to support the political activities of this type of group need to be given the opportunity to elect not to pay for such activities. A refund policy appears to be in violation of the students' speech rights. However, objections to abortion funding on religious grounds were not upheld. Providing abortion services is viewed like other community services. Just as taxpayers cannot withhold taxes because they disagree with governmental action, student fees cannot be withheld because students object to services designed to promote the community welfare.

Privacy is another constitutional right granted to students. The privacy of student rooms must be protected from warrantless searches. However, an institution can inspect the facility for maintenance purposes or when activities within the room endanger the educational atmosphere. Student voting rights are also clearly provided. To balance the states' rights to prevent voter fraud and the individual's equal protection rights, the courts have established the premise that all must be treated equally in voter registration processes. Irrebuttable presumptions that students are not eligible to vote because they live in residence halls will be struck down. Requiring only students to complete a questionnaire about intent to reside in the community violates the Equal Protection Clause.

Due process rights must be guaranteed to students enrolled at public institutions. Dismissal for disciplinary reasons requires a notice of the charges, a hearing, the opportunity to hear witnesses testifying against the charged student, and the opportunity to present testimony and witnesses on the accused's behalf. Students at private institutions would have a property right to due process based on the terms of the contract between the student and the institution. If, at a public institution, a liberty interest (damage to one's name, reputation, or pursuit of happiness) is involved then due process must be guaranteed. Cheating and plagiarism, while involving academic performance, involve a liberty interest and require due process. Dismissal based on poor academic performance does not require the same level of due process as disciplinary dismissal. Courts have given deference to the professional's judgment.

The review of the case law since *Dixon* indicates the courts' willingness to scrutinize a number of areas of the student institutional-relationship, which has had a profound effect on institutional practice.

CHAPTER IX

Liability Issues Surrounding the Student-Institutional Relationship

Student-institutional relationships, prior to the advent of the constitutional relationships discussed in the previous chapter, were thought of as fiduciary or contractual relationships. *In loco parentis*, the traditional view of an institution's relationship with students, is, in legal terms, a fiduciary relationship. A fiduciary relationship exists where there is special confidence reposed in one who in equity and good conscience is bound to act in good faith with due regard to the interests of the one reposing the confidence.[876]

This "trust theory"[877] describes relationships like those of a patient to a doctor or a student to an institution. The doctor or the institution possesses the knowledge of what the most effective plan of action will be for the patient or the student. The patient or the student must place trust in the integrity of the institution or the doctor to provide for his or her best interests in the relationship. Because the student-institutional relationship places students, having less power (as clients), at a disadvantage, the state attempts to protect them from fraudulent programs through licensing procedures.[878] This safeguard is similar to licensing procedures in other professions such as medicine and law in which fiduciary relationships exist. The fiduciary relationship is important to understanding the concept of educational malpractice and contract theory. The law imposes standards of care in various student-institutional relationships. The standards of care required of colleges and universities under a contract, within the fiduciary relationship or surrounding the offer of programs or services, will be reviewed in this chapter.

---

[876]   H. Black, Black's Law Dictionary 753, (5th ed., 1979).

[877]   K. Alexander & E. Solomon, College and University Law 413, (1972).

[878]   These matters were discussed in chapter III on state relations.

The Contractual Relationship

One of the typical relationships between students and institutions has been the contractual relationship. A contract is a promise or a set of promises obligating both parties to perform or behave in certain ways. Failure to perform as set out in the contract will be viewed as a breach of duty to which a court will award a remedy.[879] There are a multitude of contractual relationships between institutions and students.

Contracts may be written or oral, express or implied. The written or oral expression of the terms of an agreement is called an express contract. An implied contract is one in which certain terms have not been stated or written but are, instead, implied from the conduct of the parties. An example of an implied contract would be the performance of a service absent an agreement on compensation, however, with an implied obligation to pay for the reasonable value of the services performed.[880] A contract, expressed or implied, is binding when six elements are present:

1. The parties involved have the capacity to enter into a contract; i.e., mental capacity and requisite age or the authority to obligate the institution (usually found in the charter and by-laws).
2. The contract must be based on an offer (expressed through the institution's documents or implied by statements made within those documents which, for example, may imply the receipt of the degree based on completion of course work).
3. The offer must be accepted (acceptance by a written or oral promise-expressed acceptance, or by performance of the task in question-implied acceptance).
4. The offer and acceptance must be mutual. The key here is proof of a "meeting of the minds" on the terms and nature of the promise.
5. There must be performance in order for one or both parties to be bound by the mutually agreed terms of the contract. (An institution would not be obligated to pay until the contractor performed the services agreed upon.)

---

[879] R. Aiken, *Legal Liability in Higher Education: Their Scope and Management*, 6 J.C. & U.L. 127, 234, (1976).
[880] 17 Am. Jur. 2d Contracts 1-4.

6. The contract must be for a legal purpose or it will not be binding in a court of law.[881]

Authority to enter into a contract is also an important concept to understand. An institution's board of trustees has the ultimate authority to enter into a contract; however, it may delegate such authority to others. The recipients of the delegated authority can in turn bind the institution to a contractual relationship. Those who have "apparent authority" may also bind the institution to a contract.[882] Apparent authority deals with whether there is a reasonable appearance that the person has contracting authority. The court makes the distinction between public and private corporations here. In private corporations, where access to documents is not present and access is barred to knowledge about contracting authority, apparent authority (the appearance of authority) will bind the institution to an agreement. The concept of apparent authority will not be applied; however, at public institutions where access to public documents will define who has contracting authority in the institution. The adage "ignorance of the law is not a defense" is applied to public institutions. The officer of a public institution who acted in good faith where statutory authority is not clear will not be held individually liable when he or she enters into a contract without actual authority. Individual liability will be applied, however, when the officer knew or should have known he entered into a contract without authority.[883]

The granting of admission to students brings with it certain contractual obligations. Student-institutional contracts, however, are viewed as consummated when a student enrolls or registers and pays tuition at the institution. The student may be purchasing a variety of services and obligations from the institution. Many of these will not be listed on the registration form, but rather are contained in a number of documents published by the institution, i.e., the course catalogue, the schedule of course offerings, the student handbook, and admissions and recruitment documents. The application of contract theory to these relationships is reflected in case law.[884] Contract litigation usually centers on allegations of a breach of contract terms, or the existence of a contract based on the six elements of a contract as noted above.

---

[881] R. Hendrickson and R. Mangum, GOVERNING BOARD AND ADMINISTRATOR LIABILITY 13, (1977).

[882] *Id.* at 15.

[883] *Id.*

[884] *See* Carr v. St. Johns Univ., 231 N.Y.S.2d 403 (N.Y. App. Div. 1962), *aff'd*, 235 N.Y.S.2d 834 (N.Y. 1962); Healy v. Larsson, 323 N.Y.S.2d 625 (N.Y. Sup. Ct. 1971), *aff'd*, 360 N.Y.S.2d 419 (N.Y. 1974), extended contract enforcement to a public university.

The Elements of the Contract

The six elements of the contract have been at issue in some of the higher education litigation. A North Carolina case involved questions of contracting authority and the existence of a mutual agreement.[885] An admissions director who lacked authority to admit the student to the regular program described the procedures to be followed to convert from a special student status to regular student status with eligibility to pursue a bachelor's degree. The student alleged that advice to enroll in core course work required for the degree was part of an agreement by the admissions officer to grant the student regular admission. The court ruled that the director of admissions did not have authority under the by-laws of the institution to grant admission. Further, the court found that the advice on how to become a regular degree student was not an offer nor was enrollment in core courses an acceptance of an offer. A contract was not established where there was no meeting of the minds.

A Montana court found that the award of a degree hinged on enrollment in certain courses.[886] When a student neglected to remove an incomplete grade and failed to meet education course requirements, he failed to perform implied duties under the contract. Nonperformance rendered the contract void and removed the institution's obligation even when it reneged on its agreement to transfer courses from another university. These cases illustrate that the absence of any of the six contract elements mentioned earlier renders the contract non-binding in the eyes of the courts.

Breach of Contract

Suits alleging breach of contract are numerous. In one case, a student dismissed for disruptive conduct sued the institution for breach of contract. The student's disruptive activity, as described by the institution, included comments in a newspaper article alleging that the institution had misappropriated funds. The student had a contract with the institution to enroll in a training program to which the institution had denied him access. Further, the institution failed to define specifically disruptive conduct in the student handbook and failed to prove that the plaintiff had been disruptive. The contract to provide training, therefore, had been breached by the institution.[887]

---

[885] Elliott v. Duke Univ., 311 S.E.2d 632 (N.C. Ct. App. 1984).
[886] Bindrim v. University of Mont., 766 P.2d 861 (Mont. 1988).
[887] Fussell v. Louisiana Business College, 478 So.2d 652 (La. Ct. App. 1985).

However, an institution that clearly awarded admission to a master's degree program did not breach its contract with the student by not awarding him that degree.[888] The student failed in his allegation that the institution was obligated to award him the proposed combined degree, which had not been approved at the time of his admission. Another institution did not breach a contract with students when it stated the current tuition rate in a letter of admission and then, in a subsequent year, raised tuition.[889] In another case, an institution's lease with a fraternity's alumni corporation for a facility on campus was not breached when the university terminated the lease after the fraternity ceased to exist on the campus.[890] Finally, five students sued their technical college for violating the state's Consumer Protection Act (CPA) with respect to a real estate appraisal course.[891] The students argued unsuccessfully that the instructor's representation of the course content did not create a contract between the students and the college, and the court dismissed the suit for failure to state a claim upon which relief could be granted.[892]

A unique breach of contract case involved the rescinding of a graduate's degree.[893] The university became aware of fraudulent data used in the student's thesis after a professional association refused to publish an article based on the thesis. The university notified the student that his degree was in jeopardy, and after a hearing, rescinded the degree. Subsequently, professors of the department that awarded the original degree were compelled by the need to clear the record and protect the reputation of the institution and published an article discrediting the results of the student's thesis. The student sued the professional association, which refused to publish an article based on his thesis but ultimately published a professor's article discrediting the thesis. The court found that the professional association had not breached the contract and that the professors had not defamed the student.[894]

Several breach of contract cases involved athletic scholarships. In one case, the court found that the institution had not breached

---

[888] Voight v. Teachers College, Columbia Univ., 511 N.Y.S.2d 880 (N.Y. App. Div. 1987).

[889] Prusack v. State, 498 N.Y.S.2d 455 (N.Y. App. Div. 1986).

[890] Chi Realty Corporation v. Colby College, 513 A.2d 866 (Me. 1986).

[891] Ottgen v. Clover Park Technical College, 928 P.2d 1119 (Wash. App. Ct. 1996).

[892] Further, the court said that the college was exempt from the CPA because the political division in which it was considered to be was not subject to the Act's provisions. *Id.*

[893] Crook v. Peacor, 579 F. Supp. 853 (E.D. Mich. 1984).

[894] *See* Crook v. Baker, 584 F. Supp. 1531 (E.D. Mich. 1984), *vacated*, 813 F.2d 88 (6th Cir. 1987). The case challenged the institution's guarantee of due process.

an injured student's contract when it offered him nine semesters of scholarship aid when eight were required by the contract before terminating aid.[895] In a case involving the deteriorating performance of a player and his relationship with his coach, the court found that the player's contract was not breached.[896] The player alleged that his contract was breached when the coaches interfered with his contractual scholarship relationship with the university. Further, he alleged that the board breached its duty by allowing such interference to continue to the point that the player was forced to forfeit his scholarship.

Deceptive Practices

Practices of an institution that are fraudulent or attempt to misrepresent services are called deceptive practices. Much of the litigation in higher education surrounds an institution's attempts to recruit students or allegations that the degree awarded is not as valuable as it was said to be by the institution. In one case, a student alleged that a proprietary school was involved in deceptive practices in advertising a nonexistent degree program and in awarding students financial aid in the form of loans without conforming to the truth-in-lending laws.[897] Further, the student alleged that the institution reneged on a promise of not charging tuition to the student during a leave of absence resulting from injury in an auto accident. The court found that the institution had exaggerated material facts, intentionally concealed material facts, offered services without intent to sell them, and failed to state the limitations of what was being offered.

In another deceptive practice case, a student relied on the recruitment brochures of a Caribbean medical school regarding information on the institution's faculty, laboratory, library facilities, and hospital affiliation.[898] The court found that the institution's brochures had misrepresented these facilities. In another case, however, a student sued alleging that the institution had misrepresented her ability to become a certified English teacher upon completion of the program.[899] The court found that the institution's

---

[895] Waters v. University of S.C., 313 S.E.2d 346 (S.C. Ct. App. 1984).

[896] Rutledge v. Arizona Bd. of Regents, 711 P.2d 1207 (Ariz. Ct. App. 1985).

[897] Manley v. Wichita Business College, 701 P.2d 893 (Kan. 1985).

[898] Idress v. American Univ. of the Caribbean, 546 F. Supp. 1342 (S.D.N.Y. 1982).

[899] Hershman v. University of Toledo, 519 N.E.2d 871 (Ohio Ct. Cl. 1987).

documents clearly spelled out requirements for the various degrees in addition to requirements for certification. The student's failure to read this documentation carefully was not misrepresentation even if a counselor had implied otherwise.

A proprietary school was involved in two cases of deceptive practices in the way it advertised two different degree programs. In one of the cases, the institution misrepresented developments in the profession to enhance the degree program.[900] The institution was found to have misrepresented another program by leading a student to believe that it would result in a two-year associate degree transferable to a four-year institution.[901]

Institutions of higher education need to take extra care in accurately stating the facilities available and the nature of the programs offered. Language that implies or guarantees employment upon completion of a program of study may obligate the institution to deliver on these promises. A careful review of all written documents and oral communication to ensure that deception or the appearance of deception are eliminated is not only ethically appropriate but could also help to avoid expensive litigation and the damage to reputations such charges bring.

Conclusion on Contract Liability

Contract liability is dependent on two factors. One factor is whether the six elements of a contract are present. The other factor has to do with the terms of the specific contract and whether those terms have been breached. Care in wording the terms of a contract will avoid headaches in the form of litigation later. Finally, an institution should ensure that it adequately represents its programs and the qualifications attached to their completion.

The Fiduciary Relationship

The fiduciary relationship requires that a professional treat a client with an appropriate standard of care. The standard of care in a fiduciary relationship places a greater burden on the professional than the standard of care applied in other tort or liability cases. A novel line of cases addresses the fiduciary relationship and the standard of care through the issue of educational malpractice. According to Hendrickson and Gibbs:

---

[900] Delta Sch. of Commerce, Inc. v. Wood, 766 So.2d 424 (Ark. 1989).
[901] Till v. Delta Sch. of Commerce, 487 So.2d 180 (La. Ct. App. 1986).

A cause of action under malpractice theory has three legal bases: (1) contract theory, where the practitioner breaches an expressed obligation to use adequate skills and care; (2) fraud theory, where the practitioner attempts to deceive the patient with the proposed treatment; (3) tort theory, where the practitioner must use acceptable standards of care in the treatment of patients.[902]

Tort theory is the clear choice in both psychological and educational malpractice litigation.[903] The elements of tort theory are: (1) a legal duty of the practitioner to operate within a standard of care; (2) a breach of the standard of care by the practitioner; and (3) the injury caused by the practitioner as the proximate cause of the damages.[904] All three of these elements are difficult to define in psychological and educational malpractice cases. Part of the problem is inherent in the fact that both professions use verbal treatment. Since there is little consensus within either profession as to which treatment might be more effective, it is difficult to establish a standard of care.[905] Further, it is difficult to show the proximate cause between an injury and the verbal treatment used.

The foundations of malpractice in education have been before the courts in cases involving elementary and secondary schools.[906] The first malpractice case presented here, *Peter W. v. San Francisco Unified School District*,[907] involved a high school student who sued the school district alleging negligence and misrepresentation. His complaint was based on the fact that he was deficient in both math and reading and, in fact, possessed the reading skills of an eighth grade student. He charged that these deficiencies in basic academic skills left him unable to gain employment and rendered him permanently disabled. Negligence was charged because the teachers failed to provide adequate training in basic academic skills; misrepresentation was alleged because the school district awarded a high school diploma to an individual who could read at an eighth grade level. Peter W. contended that the district's

---

[902] R. Hendrickson & A. Gibbs, THE COLLEGE, THE CONSTITUTION, AND THE CONSUMER STUDENT: IMPLICATIONS FOR POLICY AND PRACTICE 49, (1986), *citing* L. Hampton, *Malpractice in Psychotherapy: Is There a Relevant Standard of Care?* 35 CASE W. RES. L. REV. 251 (1984).

[903] *See* R. Funston, *Educational Malpractice: Cause of Action in Search of a Theory*, 18 SAN DIEGO L. REV. 743 (1981); D. Tracy, *Educational Negligence: A Student's Cause of Action for Incompetent Academic Instruction*, 58 N.C. L. REV. 561 (1980).

[904] P. Hampton, *Malpractice in Psychotherapy: Is There a Relevant Standard of Care?* 35 CASE W. L. REV. 251, 256 (1984).

[905] *See* Funston, *supra*; Tracy, *supra* note 25.

[906] The discussion on educational malpractice has been taken from a previous work cited as: R. Hendrickson and A. Gibbs, *supra* note 24.

[907] 131 Cal. Rptr. 854 (Cal. Ct. App. 1976).

alleged negligence in failing to provide him with adequate skills was the proximate cause of his inability to gain employment—the alleged injury. He based the charge of negligence on the assumption that the district's teachers are in a professional relationship with their students; therefore, teachers are obligated under a legal duty to provide services equal to those used by a reasonably prudent professional.

The California court linked the finding of a legal duty toward the student to public policy and, in rejecting the existence of a professional duty or standard of care for teachers, stated:

> Unlike the activity of the highway or marketplace, classroom methodology affords no readily acceptable standard of care, or cause, or injury. The science of pedagogy itself is fraught with different and conflicting theories of how or what a child should be taught, and any layman might—and commonly does—have his own emphatic view on the subject. The injury claimed here is plaintiff's inability to read or write. Substantial professional authority attests that the achievement of literacy in the schools, or failure, are [sic] influenced by a host of factors [that] affect the pupil subjectively, from outside the formal teaching process and beyond the control of its ministers. They may be physical, neurological, emotional, cultural, environmental: they may be present but not perceived, recognized but not identified.[908]

The court questioned not only the necessity of the establishment of a standard of care for teachers but also the ability of the plaintiff to establish a proximate causal relationship between the negligence and the alleged injury. Finally, the court expressed a concern that the establishment of a standard of care for teachers would result in a substantial amount of litigation and create a detrimental burden on the public school system.

In a New York case, *Donahue v. Copiaque Free School District*,[909] the court reached a similar verdict. The plaintiff, a high school graduate who was unable to read or write, alleged that the school had a duty to teach him, to evaluate his learning abilities, and to prescribe effective measures to remediate any deficiencies. Based on this duty, the school was negligent in the supervision of his

---

[908] *Id.* at 860.
[909] 408 N.Y.S.2d 584 (N.Y. Sup. Ct. 1977), *aff'd*, 407 N.Y.S.2d 874 (N.Y. App. Div. 1978), *aff'd*, 418 N.Y.S.2d 375 (N.Y. 1979).

academic training. Donohue, therefore, sued for $5 million in damages. The New York appellate court affirmed the lower court's decision citing the decision in *Peter W., supra,* but took a much stronger turn toward the public policy ban on litigation. The court stated that recognition of a cause of action under educational malpractice would result in the courts' overseeing the management of the public school system, a power clearly reserved by the state's constitution to another branch of government.[910] One member of the three-judge panel dissented.[911] In his opinion, this case was no different from medical malpractice cases. The plaintiff's failing grade represented a condition, like an illness, that the teachers as professionals failed to attempt to diagnose and treat. Thus, arguments exist for an alternative ruling.

A third case, *Hoffman v. Board of Education of the City of N.Y.,*[912] brings an even more interesting result. At the age of four, the plaintiff was evaluated as being of normal intelligence even though immediately after his father's death, the child suffered speech abnormalities. After kindergarten, the child was given another intelligence test by a school psychologist and was diagnosed as possessing borderline intelligence. He was placed in a class with mentally disabled students. The examining psychologist, while not requesting a history on the child before making his diagnosis, recommended that the child be retested within two years. The child's mother was never informed of his low intelligence score or her right to request a reexamination. After the student attended classes for mentally disabled individuals for twelve years, retesting established him as having normal intelligence. Further, the test indicated that his learning capabilities had always been above average. At trial in a suit against the Board of Education, the jury awarded $750,000 in damages to the plaintiff.

The New York Court of Appeals reversed the lower court's decision. Citing *Donohue, supra,* the court, in a four to three decision, ruled that a cause of action under the concept of educational malpractice could not be considered because it involved public policy beyond the court's purview. The court's ruling in this case is consistent with the position of judicial deference to academicians in academic decision making. This deference is similar to the deference given in academic dismissal and faculty promotion and tenure cases referred to in previous chapters.

---

[910]*Id.* at 879.
[911]*Id.* at 882.
[912] 410 N.Y.S.2d 99 (N.Y. App. Div. 1978), *rev'd*, 424 N.Y.S.2d 376 (N.Y. 1979).

Malpractice in Higher Education

A number of higher education cases reached similar results. In a case involving the birth of a child with brain damage, the parents not only sued for medical malpractice but also sued under educational malpractice.[913] They alleged as proximate causes of the injury under educational malpractice: that the intern was not adequately supervised as a physician in training and had not been adequately educated. The court, citing *Peter W., Donohue,* and *Hoffman, supra,* dismissed the educational malpractice argument based on the public policy rationale.

In an Iowa case, a patient who suffered a stroke during a chiropractic procedure sued, alleging educational malpractice among other claims.[914] The plaintiff alleged that the college that trained the chiropractor provided an inadequate education. The state supreme court used the public policy argument to dismiss the complaint.

Another Iowa case involved "athletic malpractice."[915] A university lost a crucial basketball game after a controversial call by the referee. A storeowner printed and sold T-shirts that criticized the referee's knowledge of the game and the fairness of the decision. The referee brought defamation of character charges against the storeowner based on the printed statements on the T-shirts.

Two students were unsuccessful in their suit against a university regarding the misrepresentation of the preparation needed for, and the overall nature of, a graduate-level computer programming course.[916] Although originally presented by plaintiffs as a case involving breach of contract, breach of fiduciary duty, and deceptive practices, the appellate court reversed the trial court's ruling in favor of the students, reclassifying the case as educational malpractice, and ruling that the issues involved were not actionable.[917] The court, reluctant to tread on matters that lay in the education community's domain, ultimately declined to review the educational, pedagogical, and administrative issues involved in the dispute.

Former students sued a proprietary college under RICO, arguing that they did not receive the education promised and were,

---

[913] Swidryk v. St. Michael's Med. Ctr., 493 A.2d 641 (N.J. Super. Ct. App. 1985).
[914] Moore v. Vanderloo, 386 N.W.2d 108 (Iowa 1986).
[915] Bain v. Gillespie, 357 N.W.2d 47 (Iowa Ct. App. 1984).
[916] Andre v. Pace Univ., 655 N.Y.S.2d 777 (N.Y. App. Term 1996).
[917]*See also* Sirohi v. Lee, 634 N.Y.S.2d 119 (N.Y. App. Div. 1995).

therefore, forced to repay loans for educational services that had not been rendered.[918] The trial court granted the college's motion to dismiss, since the students failed to describe the alleged fraud with sufficient particularity. The court, however, granted the students 30 days to file an amended complaint.

While there is literature that supports the premises of educational malpractice as a remedy, courts have refused to give credence to the remedy using the public policy argument. That is not to say that court opinion on this argument will not change. The current lack of litigation may indicate that educational malpractice may be viewed as a difficult, if not impossible, argument for plaintiffs to win. Institutions should ensure, however, if for nothing more than ethical reasons, that their practices are of a quality that will not raise malpractice questions.

Other Liabilities and the Standard of Care

Potential liability exists as soon as an organization opens its doors and commences public service. It must take what the court views as reasonable steps to protect the public on its premises, in the operation of its academic programs, in the extracurricular activities it sponsors, in activities where it allows its name to be used, and in activities where the sponsored group is recognized by the institution. Some of these cases involve claims of negligence against the institution and its employees.[919] A review of case law in this area will give an idea of the standard of care required under a variety of circumstances.

Strict Liability

Strict liability means that the institution will be held liable for injury while the person is participating in the activity defined as inherently dangerous regardless of the standard of care taken. Experimentation involving volatile materials in a laboratory is an example of high-risk activity. A student whose head and face were burned when ether caught fire during a lab experiment was awarded damages.[920] The court found that the institution had not issued proper warnings before the experiments were conducted.

---

[918] Schaeffer v. Ascension College, 964 F. Supp. 1067 (M.D. La. 1997).

[919] Negligence: The omission to do something which a reasonable man, guided by those ordinary considerations which ordinarily regulate human affairs, would do, or the doing of something which a reasonable and prudent man would not do…. Failure to use such care…. BLACK'S LAW DICTIONARY 1032 (6th ed. 1990).

[920] Lavoi v. State, 435 N.Y.S.2d 227 (N.Y. App. Div. 1982).

The plaintiff, who had little knowledge of ether, was found to be not guilty of willful misconduct. However, willful misconduct was an issue when a student was electrocuted after he ignored signs and entered railroad property adjacent to the campus.[921] The court found that the university had no duty to the student off its property and that the railroad had posted adequate warnings.

A Louisiana nursing student sued her school to recover for back and neck injuries she sustained when the classroom chair that she was sitting in broke.[922] An appellate court affirmed the trial court's judgment that the school was 60 percent at fault and the company that provided building maintenance was 40 percent at fault, adding that the state was strictly liable.

In another case, a court reversed on appeal, finding the university not liable for injuries a student sustained when he tripped and fell because of a depression on a campus sidewalk.[923] The Supreme Court of Louisiana said that the university was not strictly liable for the student's injuries because the small depression in the sidewalk was not an unreasonable danger. The court added that it was beyond reasonable expectation for the university to monitor and keep in perfect repair twenty-two miles of sidewalk.

Liability in Academic Programs

Academic programs involve three kinds of activity: participation in research sponsored by the institution, field trips as part of course work, and classroom activity. Research activities conducted by the institution require the researcher to inform participants of the risk involved and have them sign an informed consent. An Illinois case involved a 23-year-old medical student who participated in an experiment requiring him to run two miles.[924] After the experiment, the student's physiological system shut down due to the exertion, and he was hospitalized for one month. The court applied a standard of care evaluating whether the experimenters should have foreseen the consequences of the experiment. The court found nothing to indicate that the defendants should have viewed the plaintiff as anything other than a normal, healthy 23-year-old male able to perform the exercise in the experiment.[925]

---

[921] Heller v. Consolidated Rail Corp., 576 F. Supp. 6 (E.D. Pa. 1982), *aff'd*, 720 F.2d 662 (3d. Cir. 1984).

[922] Davis v. Louisiana *ex rel.* Charity-Delgado Sch. of Nursing, 675 So.2d 1227 (La. Ct. App. 1996).

[923] Boyle v. Board of Supervisors, La. State Univ., 685 So.2d 1080 (La. 1997).

[924] Turner v. Rush Med. College, 537 N.E.2d 890 (Ill. Ct. App. 1989).

[925]*Id.* at 563.

The plaintiff in a North Carolina case alleged neurological injury after an experimental underwater dive to extreme depths.[926] The court, refusing to apply strict liability, found that the plaintiff had been informed of the hazardous nature of the experiment. Since the experimenters had disclosed certain dangers, the plaintiff, by electing to participate, assumed the risk.

Field trips sponsored by the institution also carry a duty of care. These trips are usually conducted as part of course work for credit. A Louisiana court held the institution liable for the injuries a woman received in an automobile accident while on a field trip.[927] The court found that while a student driver was negligent when driving the school van, the school had failed to provide a qualified driver for the trip.

In Utah, a court found that the university did not have a duty to protect students against intoxication or the consequences of an individual student's drinking.[928] The intoxicated student fell off a cliff during a field trip. The court, analyzing the relationship between the institution and students, found that the university had no duty to enforce the university code and state policy making the consumption of alcohol by minors illegal. The court found that the college does not assume a custodial relationship with students making it liable for student decisions to consume alcohol illegally.[929]

Classroom activities have also come under the scrutiny of the court. A New York Court found that a physical education teacher's use of plastic garbage bags for a sack race on the gym floor was negligent.[930] However, damages awarded to a plaintiff injured during the sack race were reduced by 25 percent because of the plaintiff's contributory negligence.[931] In California, a court found that a release signed by a student enrolled in a scuba diving class did not release the institution from negligence claims.[932] A Texas court found that the state's tort claim act did not shield the professor and director of a play from a claim of negligence when a student actor majoring in drama was injured on stage.[933] The selection of

---

[926] Whitlock v. Duke Univ., 637 F. Supp. 1463 (M.D. N.C. 1986), *aff'd*, 829 F.2d 1340 (4th Cir. 1987).

[927] Whittington v. Sowela Technical Inst., 438 So.2d 236 (La. Ct. App. 1983).

[928] Beach v. University of Utah, 726 P.2d 413 (Utah 1986).

[929] *Id*. at 419.

[930] Yarborough v. City Univ. of N.Y., 520 N.Y.S.2d 518 (Ct. Cl. 1987).

[931] *See also* Liberty v. Geneva College, 690 A.2d 1243, (Pa. Super. Ct. 1997), in which a student who sustained an injury in a bowling class was found to be 49% at fault, while the institution was determined to be 51% at fault. An appellate tribunal affirmed that the trial court did not err in computing damages in this case.

[932] Scroggs v. Coast Community College Dist., 239 Cal. Rptr. 916 (Cal. Ct. App. 1987).

[933] Christilles v. Southwest Texas State Univ., 639 S.W.2d 38 (Tex. Ct. App. 1982).

the appropriate prop for use by the actor was not a policy question shielded from liability under the act.

Other courts, however, failed to find negligence on the part of instructors or institutions.[934] In Nebraska, the court reviewed whether the technique in teaching a golf class indoors was the proximate cause of the injury when a female student was struck in the eye.[935] The court found the reasons for holding the class indoors valid and the formation and equipment used to be within the standards of care required in these situations. The institution was not negligent in this case. In Florida, a court applied the "doctrine of expressed assumption of risk," finding the institution free of liability when a police officer was injured while trying to disarm another trainee during a training exercise.[936] In Utah, a court granted sovereign immunity to a professor in a claim of damages from a student who asserted he was forced to read profanity in the course reading assignments.[937] In addition, a university was not held vicariously liable for a students' injuries sustained in an automobile accident while participating in a foreign volunteer internship.[938] In Colorado, a board was found to be entitled to statutory immunity, because a student who had injured her thumb while cleaning a printing press in a graphic arts class failed to prove that her injuries were caused by a "physical or structural defect in the building."[939] In perhaps one of the most extreme cases illustrating assumption of risk, a student was killed during a rock climbing class.[940] A California court found that a university owed no duty to this student under the doctrine of "primary assumption of risk."

These cases indicate that the mere fact that the student is enrolled at the institution or in a course will not result in liability when injuries occur during the conduct of the class. However,

---

[934] *See e.g.*, Niles v. Board of Regents of the Univ. Sys. of Ga., 473 S.E.2d 173 (Ga. Ct. App. 1996), in which a doctoral student who suffered injuries in a laboratory experiment was unsuccessful in his attempts to recover for those injuries. The court said that, because of his education and training, the student should have known the consequences of mixing hazardous materials, and, therefore, neither the university nor the supervising professor had the duty to warn the plaintiff.

[935] Catania v. University of Neb., 329 N.W.2d 354 (Neb. 1983).

[936] Black v. District Bd. of Trustees of Broward Community College, 491 So.2d 303 (Fla. Dist. Ct. App. 1986).

[937] White v. University of Idaho, 768 P.2d 827 (Idaho Ct. App. 1989).

[938] Chen v. Georgetown Univ., 685 F. Supp. 83 (S.D. N.Y. 1988), *aff'd*, 862 F.2d 45 (2d Cir. 1988). *See* Forester v. State of N.Y., 645 N.Y.S.2d 971 (N.Y. Ct. Cl. 1996), for another example of a case in which a university was not held vicariously liable.

[939] Reynolds v. State Bd. for Community Colleges & Occupational Educ., 937 P.2d 774 (Colo. Ct. App. 1996).

[940] Regents of the Univ. of Cal. v. Superior Ct., 48 Cal. Rptr. 2d 922 (Cal. Ct. App. 1996). This wrongful death suit was filed by a survivor.

liability can result if it can be shown that the institution or its staff is negligent in actions or procedures or by failing to provide adequately trained personnel.

Liability in University Activities

An institution becomes accessible to claims of liability when it sponsors extracurricular activities. The liability may be alleged because an injury takes place during a university-sponsored event or while the individual is involved in an activity sponsored by a university-recognized group. Sometimes the injury results from the commission of a crime such as rape or the illegal use of alcohol. Other cases involve negligence in either the organization or supervision of university events. The essential question in each of these areas surrounds where the institution's duty lies in protecting students or non-students from harm. Some may argue that such duties mark the return of the existence of *in loco parentis*. The extent of the duty will determine whether *in loco parentis* returns. Liability issues in several of these areas will be covered in this section.

Rape as a crime on campus has been on the increase. This may be due in part to many campuses acknowledging date or friendship rape as a problem to be openly discussed in the last few years. Several liability cases involving rape have recently been reported in the courts. The most notorious case involved the murder and rape of a coed and the stabbing of a non-student by a conditionally released prisoner-student of the institution.[941] The state failed to inform the institution of the prisoner-student's history of drug abuse and psychiatric disorders. The court found the state's failure to inform the college of the prison record did not absolve the college from negligence. The institution had failed to establish adequate criteria to screen prisoner applicants, to take measures to minimize any risk participation in the prisoner release program involved, and to protect other students from the zone of danger it created. This zone of danger did not apply to the non-student but it did apply to the student. The rape and murder of the student was foreseeable and precautions should have been taken to prevent such incidents.

However, another institution was not found negligent in the abduction, rape, and murder of a coed cheerleader after a basket-

---

[941] Eiseman v. State, 489 N.Y.S.2d 957 (N.Y. App. Div. 1985).

ball game.[942] The court found that the criminal act was not fore-seeable after a review of criminal activity on the campus and surrounding area indicated that there had been only one attempted rape in a ten-year period. Based on criminal activity in the area of another case, however, a California court found an institution neg-ligent for failing to warn students, to patrol the area where repeated assaults had occurred, and to trim the foliage adjacent to a stair-way, the scene of several assaults.[943] The court found that the student raped in the parking lot was an "invitee" to whom the institution owed a duty of due care.[944] The key in all of these cases was whether the crime was foreseeable, requiring the institution to take reasonable precautions to protect its students.

Liability for Student Risk Taking

Injury to students or non-students resulting from the consump-tion of alcohol on or off the campus has been actively litigated in the past few years. The institutional duty may vary according to who serves the alcohol, the age of the consumers, and the courts' interpretation of the student-institutional relationship. The bench-mark case, *Bradshaw v. Rawlings*,[945] involved students injured in an automobile accident after attending a class picnic where alco-hol was consumed. The institution sponsored the class picnic. At issue was whether the institution's prohibition of alcoholic bever-ages and the relationship with its students imposed a special duty on the institution. The Third Circuit Court of Appeals discussed the changing relationship between students and the institution and stated:

> Our beginning point is a recognition that the modern American college is not an insurer of the safety of its stu-dents. Whatever may have been its responsibility in an earlier era [*in loco parentis*], the authoritarian role of today's college administrator has been notably diluted in recent decades. Trustees, administrators, and faculties have been required to yield to the expanding rights and privileges of their students. By constitutional amendment, written and unwritten laws, and through the evolution of new cus-toms, rights formerly possessed by college administrations have been transferred to students. College students are

---

[942] Brown v. North Carolina Wesleyan College, 309 S.E. 2d 701 (N.C. Ct. App. 1983).
[943] Peterson v. San Francisco Community College Dist., 685 P.2d 1193 (Cal. 1984).
[944] *Id*. at 1198.
[945] 612 F.2d 135 (3d Cir. 1979).

no longer minors; they are now regarded as adults in al-
most every phase of community life.[946]

The court found the school's alcohol policy conformed to state
law, and did not establish a special relationship requiring the imposition of procedures to protect the students from their own
actions.

Other cases have followed the *Bradshaw* decision.[947] For example, in *Beach v. University of Utah*,[948] the court based its decision
in part on the premise that the existence of the institution's policy
on alcohol consumption did not create a duty for the institution to
protect students from their own behavior. In an Indiana case, the
court ruled that the institution would not be held liable for the
injuries a non-student sustained while a passenger in a student's
automobile.[949] The student and a non-student had been drinking
in the student's fraternity room that was located in space leased
in a college residence hall. The court found that the location where
the drinking took place without the college's or the fraternity's
knowledge did not establish a special institutional duty to protect
the student or non-student from risky behavior.

A case that initially appeared to turn away from the *Bradshaw*
precedent was decided in Colorado.[950] On appeal, the court affirmed a jury's finding that the university had a duty to protect
students from injury during the use of a trampoline located on
university property leased by a fraternity. The court reasoned that
there was a growing knowledge of the dangers of trampolines including limitations on their use in local public schools. However,
the Colorado Supreme Court reversed that decision.[951] Citing
Bradshaw, the court ruled that nothing in the student handbook or
in the student institutional relationship imposed a duty "to control the [personal] risk taking decisions of its students."[952] Nor
was there anything in the lease that obligated the university to
control the use of trampolines. The court affirmed the position
that in matters of personal decision making that involves some
risk, such as the consumption of alcohol or the use of a trampoline

---

[946]*Id.* at 138 (footnote omitted).

[947] G. Stewart, *Social Host Liability on Campus: Taking the "High" out of Higher Education*, 92 DICK. L. REV. 665, 676 (1988).

[948] 726 P.2d 413 (Utah 1986).

[949] Campbell v. Board of Trustees of Wabash College, 495 N.E.2d 227 (Ind. Ct. App. 1986).

[950] Whitlock v. University of Denver, 712 P 2d 1072 (Colo. Ct. App. 1986).

[951] University of Denver v. Whitlock, 744 P.2d 54 (Colo. 1987).

[952] *Id.* at 60.

after using alcohol, the institution has no duty to control or directly supervise students.[953]

A New Jersey case affirms this position.[954] In this case, the court found that the institution's law prohibiting the consumption of alcohol in the football stadium did not impose on the institution a special duty to those attending football games. The suit involved injuries sustained by an intoxicated student who fled from campus security personnel in the stadium, leaped over a wall, and fell thirty feet to a sidewalk below.

Several other cases involved the serving of alcohol on the campus. For example, a New York court found that the institution had no responsibility for an individual's injuries sustained in a fall on campus after consuming alcohol in a campus pub.[955] Another New York court held that the institution was not liable for the rape of a female student in a campus restroom by an assailant who had consumed alcohol at a campus pub.[956] Even where the institution is serving alcohol to those of legal age, the courts seem unwilling to establish a special duty for the institution to control the personal risky decisions of consumers. However, social host liability may be applied to those serving alcohol when alcohol is the proximate cause of subsequent injury.

Social host liability for those serving alcoholic beverages, however, implicates a special duty. Serving alcohol to minors will bring the courts to impose liability. The organization does not have to physically serve the beverages but rather only provide substantial assistance to others who actually serve the minors. This was true in several Pennsylvania cases.[957] Similarly, Pennsylvania also brought criminal prosecution against fraternities that served alcohol to minors.[958] It should be noted that this court also found that the use of undercover police officers at fraternity parties open to the public did not violate the fraternity's expectation of privacy.

---

[953] A case involving risk-taking but neither alcohol nor fraternities, Pitre v. Louisiana Tech Univ., 673 So.2d 585 (La. 1996), also did not result in institutional liability. Here, a student hit a light pole on campus after sledding down a hill, and, as a result, became quadriplegic. His suit against the university was ultimately unsuccessful because the Supreme Court of Louisiana determined that the university owed him no duty of care. In its reasoning, the court said that the light pole was of great social utility, the likelihood of harm from it was minimal because it was obvious, risks of colliding with it were well known, and the condition was not unreasonably dangerous.

[954] Allen v. Rutgers, State Univ. of N.J., 523 A.2d 262 (N.J. Super. Ct. App. Div. 1987).

[955] Allen v. County of Westchester, 492 N.Y.S.2d 772 (N.Y. App. Div. 1985).

[956] Humiston v. Rochester Inst. of Tech., 510 N.Y.S.2d 351 (N.Y. App. Div. 1986).

[957] Fassett v. Poch, 625 F. Supp. 324 (E.D. Pa. 1985); *rev'd*, Fassett v. Delta Kappa Epsilon (N.Y.), 807 F.2d 1150 (3d Cir. 1986); Jefferis v. Commonwealth, 537 A.2d 355 (Pa. Super. Ct. 1988).

[958] Commonwealth v. Tau Kappa Epsilon, 560 A.2d 786 (Pa. Super. Ct. 1989).

Alcohol consumption involving fraternities is another variation on the alcohol consumption litigation. For example, a court found that a fraternity breached a duty when it forced pledges to participate in heavy drinking as part of initiation.[959] On the contrary, in a related case, an Air Force Reserve Officer Training Corps was not held liable for the death of a new officer trainee during a hazing incident.[960] Since the Air Force Reserve Officer Training Corp did not recognize this group, they had no control over the student organization. ROTC student involvement in the group was a discretionary function and not covered under the Federal Tort Claims Act.[961] Further, a fraternity and its National Affiliate Organization were not held to have a duty to protect a member from death caused by acute alcohol intoxication. A member not of legal drinking age had consumed liquor from his own supply both before and after a fraternity mixer. Other cases involving the personal decisions of students produced similar results.[962] These cases all fit into the *Bradshaw* rationale. Where the risky activity is forced by the organization, liability is more likely. However, where the activity is a matter of a personal decision by the student, the courts refuse to obligate the institution or a student organization with a special duty.[963]

Liability in Athletic Activities

Liability standards and issues are applied both to athletic activities that involve intercollegiate competition and recreational sports. In institution-funded and institution-sponsored intercollegiate sports, injuries or deaths have resulted in a number of claims. It should be noted that athletes are not employees merely because the institution awards scholarships or simply because the sport is considered big business.[964] Had the court found that athletes were employees, additional standards of care or duties on the institution would apply.

An institution was found negligent in its maintenance of a softball field, and damages were awarded to an injured player.[965]

---

[959] Quinn v. Sigma Rho Chapter of Beta Theta Pi Fraternity, 507 N.E.2d 1193 (Ill. App. Ct. 1987).

[960] Mercado Del Valle v. United States, 856 F.2d 406 (1st Cir. 1988).

[961] *Id.* at 408; Federal Tort Claims Act, 28 U.S.C. 2671-2680 (1982).

[962] Alpha Zeta Chapter of Pi Kappa Alpha Fraternity v. Sullivan, 740 S.W.2d 127 (Ark. 1987); Rabel v. Illinois Wesleyan Univ., 514 N.E.2d 553 (Ill. App. Ct. 1987).

[963] *See e.g.*, Kappa Sigma Int'l Fraternity v. Tootle, 473 S.E.2d 213 (Ga. Ct. App. 1996).

[964] Townsend v. State, 237 Cal. Rptr. 146 (Cal. Ct. App. 1987); *see also* Hanson v. Kynast, 494 N.E.2d 1091 (Ohio 1986).

[965] Lamphear v. New York, 458 N.Y.S.2d 71 (N.Y. App. Div. 1983).

Another institution failed to warn cheerleaders that the practice of a maneuver on artificial turf, as opposed to regular turf, increased the risk of injury.[966] The institution paid partial damages to the injured cheerleader. Finally, an institution and its coach, who should have appreciated the severity and potential problems of an eye injury that a player sustained after being hit by a softball, were found negligent.[967] The coach's failure to seek immediate medical attention for the player exacerbated the extent and reparability of the injury. A university was held liable for injuries a pole-vaulter sustained because the accident in which he was involved was foreseeable.[968] The court said that the coaches knew that certain pole-vaulters had been injured before and also had failed to place supplemental padding around the pit, even though it was available.

Many courts find that athletes assume the risk when participating in sports and therefore do not hold the universities liable for injuries that these student-athletes sustain. For example, a member of a rugby club who broke his neck during practice sued the university for negligent supervision.[969] The court found that the university was not liable to the student because the student had assumed the risk of injury: he was an experienced rugby player who had previously suffered injuries in the sport, a sport in which the risk of harm is apparent.

Several courts found that sovereign immunity protects institutions and their team staff members from claims in the deaths of football players resulting from exertion at practice.[970] No negligence was found in the treatment of a sprain[971] or in the failure to replace wire reinforced glass with safety glass in an indoor football practice facility.[972] Finally, a player whose actions during competitive play resulted in the injury of an opponent was not found to be involved in an intentional tort.[973] Earlier, the Ohio Supreme Court ruled that there was no negligence when the institution failed to have an ambulance at the field during a competition.[974]

---

[966] Kirk v. Washington State Univ., 746 P.2d 285 (Wash. 1987).

[967] Stineman v. Fontbonne College, 664 F.2d 1083 (8th Cir. 1982).

[968] Moose v. Massachusetts Inst. of Tech., 683 N.E.2d 706 (Mass. App. Ct. 1997).

[969] Regan v. State, 654 N.Y.S.2d 488 (N.Y. App. Div. 1997).

[970] Sorey v. Kellett, 673 F. Supp. 817 (S.D. Miss. 1987), *rev'd*, 849 F.2d 960 (5th Cir. 1988); Greenhill v. Carpenter, 718 S.W.2d 268 (Tenn. Ct. App. 1986).

[971] Gillespie v. Southern Utah State College, 669 P.2d 861 (Utah 1983).

[972] Curtis v. State, 504 N.E.2d 1222 (Ohio Ct. App. 1986).

[973] Hanson v. Kynast, 526 N.E.2d 327 (Ohio Ct. App. 1987).

[974] Hanson v. Kynast, 494 N.E.2d 1091 (Ohio 1986).

The key difference between these cases is the definition of what is perceived by the court as behavior that falls below accepted standards of practice and is, therefore, negligence. Further, courts acknowledge that there is a certain level of the assumption of risk on the part of the athlete.

The assumption of risk also affects the courts' ruling in injuries resulting from recreational sports. For example, a player, not the referee or the institution, was found to be negligent when he was injured while executing an illegal maneuver under the rules of the game.[975] A federal court found that a medical student in poor health assumed the risk of possible death when he voluntarily entered a road race sponsored by the medical school.[976] Another court found that the institution did not have a duty to supervise student organized recreational games.[977] Finally, a court found there was no breach of duty when a knee injury occurred on a properly maintained field during a touch football game played as part of freshmen orientation activities.[978] The assumption of individual risk by participants will be overcome, yielding an award of damages only where it can be shown that the institution was in some way negligent or breached a duty.

Liability on University Premises

When an institution opens its facilities to the public, it has a duty to maintain the premises adequately. This duty may include a duty to warn about unsafe areas. For example, when the institution lowered the height of protective glass at the hockey arena, it had a duty to warn spectators of the increased risk.[979] However, an institution did not have a duty to warn a bicyclist about a low support beam or mark the beam with a different color.[980] The bicyclist sued for injuries received when he left a sidewalk and rode under the bleachers at an athletic field and struck the beam. Another institution was not required to warn a student of the hazards of sledding using a cafeteria tray.[981]

The maintenance of a safe environment is a duty the institution must observe. For example, a court found that an institution must properly light the exterior of its buildings.[982] A student was

---

[975] Pape v. New York, 456 N.Y.S.2d 863 (N.Y. App. Div. 1983).
[976] Gehling v. St. George's Univ. School of Med., 705 F. Supp. 761 (E.D. N.Y. 1989).
[977] Swanson v. Wabash College, 504 N.E.2d 327 (Ind. Ct. App. 1987).
[978] Drew v. State, 536 N.Y.S.2d 252 (N.Y. App. Div. 1989).
[979] Sawyer v. State, 485 N.Y.S.2d 695 (N.Y. Cl. Ct. 1985).
[980] Poerio v. State, 534 N.Y.S.2d 459 (N.Y. App. Div. 1988).
[981] Boaldin v. University of Kan., 747 P.2d 811 (Kan. 1987); see Pizzola v. State, 515 N.Y.S.2d 129 (N.Y. App. Div. 1987).
[982] Donnell v. California W. School of Law, 246 Cal. Rptr. 199 (Cal. Ct. App. 1988).

assaulted on a dark city street adjacent to the school building. In another case, a court found that the institution was negligent in the way it piled snow in the parking lot, creating a perpetually icy condition.[983] The key in this case and others cited is that the potential danger was foreseeable, just as the danger of allowing water to stand on a locker room floor creates a foreseeable dangerous condition.[984]

A university was found responsible for the hanging death of an arrestee in its security detention facility.[985] The court found that it was foreseeable that the physical makeup of the detention facility was such that an attempt at hanging would be successful. Further, the court found negligence in the security officer's failure to monitor adequately the behavior of an arrested intoxicated student.

An Indiana court, however, found that an institution's responsibility for a student ended once she safely stepped onto a grass boulevard from a campus bus.[986] The responsibility for the student's actions was her own and not the institution's. Unfortunately, she stepped off the curb and into the path of an oncoming car. Nor could an institution be held liable for the criminal actions of a student who shot several individuals.[987] If the institution had reason to believe a student may commit a criminal act, however, it would have a duty to warn others about its belief.[988]

The duty of the university acting as landlord brings several issues forward. For example, if an architect's design flaw results in injury as in one case, the architect will be found liable.[989] In that case, the student fell from the third floor of a residence hall through an open door. In another case, an institution was found negligent when there was evidence of other accidents in the same location resulting from a muddy, wet floor.[990] The dangerous condition developed every time it rained. A rape victim was successful in showing that the institution had failed to adequately maintain a secure residence hall.[991] A North Carolina court affirmed a finding that it was not reasonably prudent for the university to replace a screen door with a glass panel in a married student-housing unit,

---

[983] Russell v. Board of Regents of Univ. of Neb., 423 N.W.2d 126 (Neb. 1988).

[984] Van Stry v. State, 479 N.Y.S.2d 258 (N.Y. App. Div. 1984).

[985] Hickey v. Zezulka, 443 N.W.2d 180 (Mich. Ct. App. 1989).

[986] Heger v. Trustees of Ind. Univ., 526 N.E.2d 180 (Tex. Ct. App. 1988).

[987] Smith v. University of Tex., 664 S.W.2d 180 (Tex. Ct. App. 1984).

[988] Tarazoff v. Regents of the Univ. of Cal., 551 P.2d 334 (Cal. 1976).

[989] Leeper v. Hillier Group, Architects Planners, P.A., 543 A.2d 258 (R.I. 1988).

[990] Goldstein v. C.W. Post Ctr., 504 N.Y.S.2d 734 (N.Y. App. Div. 1986).

[991] Miller v. State, 478 N.Y.S.2d 829 (N.Y. 1984).

and the resulting injury was foreseeable.[992] The glass panel was put in because young children in the unit kept pushing the screen out of the door. A Kansas university was found negligent in failing to light adequately a stairwell.[993]

Another court, however, found a student negligent in the way the student proceeded down a flight of stairs in the residence hall. No hazard on the stairs existed and the student's negligence was the cause of the injury.[994] Similarly, a university was not found negligent when a visitor fell after stepping off the sidewalk onto a dirt path.[995]

A car hit one student as she crossed a publicly owned street on a university campus.[996] She filed suit, claiming that the university had negligently failed to install crosswalks in the area where the accident occurred. The trial court granted the university's motion for summary judgment, reasoning that the college had no duty to the student with respect to the public street. The court found that the university had neither authority nor control over the public road even though the street was located on the university campus.

While standing in line at a campus cafeteria, one student was struck by a traffic cone that had been thrown by another student.[997] The student sued the community college and others, charging that they failed to provide proper security. An appellate tribunal affirmed the ruling of summary judgment in favor of the defendants, saying that no duty existed on the part of the defendants to protect the student and that the act of the student who threw the cone was not foreseeable. In a more violent matter, a university was found to be vicariously liable where a student sustained a gunshot wound during an altercation with a resident assistant because the incident took place in a dormitory while the resident assistant was on duty.[998] The court found that since the resident assistant was on duty the university was vicariously liable.[999]

In sum, liability will be found where the institution should have foreseen the danger in allowing a particular condition to ex-

---

[992] Bolkhir v. North Carolina State Univ., 365 S.E.2d 898 (N.C. 1988).

[993] Burch v. University of Kan., 756 P.2d 431 (Kan. 1988).

[994] Cotrona v. Johnson and Wales College, 501 A.2d 728 (R.I. 1985).

[995] Thompson v. Kent State Univ., 521 N.E.2d 526 (Ohio Ct. Cl. 1987).

[996] Rothbard v. Colgate Univ., 652 N.Y.S.2d 146 (N.Y. App. Div. 1997).

[997] Ruchalski v. Schenectady County Community College, 656 N.Y.S.2d 784 (N.Y. App. Div. 1997).

[998] Emoakemeh v. Southern Univ., 654 So.2d 474 (La. Ct. App. 1995).

[999] Vicarious liability: the imposition of liability on one person for the actionable conduct of another based solely on a relationship between two persons. BLACK'S LAW DICTIONARY 1566 (6th ed. 1990).

ist. Institutional responsibility will also be involved where a duty exists to warn people of a foreseen risk or where it has reason to believe that a student will follow through with dangerous threats. However, the institution will not be held responsible for the injured individual's negligent behavior.

Conclusions on Liability and the Standard of Care

A valid contractual relationship between a student and an institution must contain at the minimum the six elements of a contract set out at the beginning of this chapter. Absent any of these elements, the contract will not be binding in the eyes of the court. Failure to perform the terms of the contract will be considered a breach of contract, with the court awarding damages to the nonbreaching party. Using deceptive practices to enter into a contract will not only result in litigation, but will also result in significant harm to an institution's reputation.

Traditionally the fiduciary relationship sets up a trust relationship between a patient and a physician or, as here, an institution and a student. Since the relationship is tipped in favor of the one with the expertise (i.e., the institution), the court places more stringent standards of care on the institution. Educational malpractice litigation emanates from fiduciary theory. Courts, however, have used public policy arguments to fail to reach findings under the educational malpractice rationale.

Other tort liability is applied to a variety of student/institutional relationships. The key in many of these areas is the standard of care. In inherently dangerous activities, strict liability has been applied. However, in questions of academic activities, the court will review whether informed consent puts the risk on participants in research activities, or whether the institution was negligent in staffing or operating the program when the injury occurred. The court also will review the level of risk attributed to the student.

In university activities, the court will determine whether the injury was foreseeable and whether a duty to warn or prevent the foreseen injury should be applied. However, the courts have not defined the student/institutional relationship as obligating the institution to protect students from their own decision to participate in risky behavior. Athletes are not employees and need to be protected from negligence, but they also assume some risk by virtue of their participation in sports. Reasonable care must be taken to foresee potential dangers and remove them from residence halls or university property. Failure to do so will result in institutional negligence. However, institutions do not have a duty to protect the public from their own negligent behavior when they enter its grounds.

Table of Cases

Index